Financing Our Future

Stefan Brunnhuber

Financing Our Future

Unveiling a Parallel Digital Currency System
to Fund the SDGs and the Common Good

Stefan Brunnhuber
Dresden, Germany

ISBN 978-3-030-64825-1   ISBN 978-3-030-64826-8   (eBook)
https://doi.org/10.1007/978-3-030-64826-8

This Palgrave Macmillan imprint is published by the registered company Springer Nature Switzerland AG.
The registered company address is: Gewerbestrasse 11, 6330 Cham, Switzerland

The original version of this book was revised. The correction to this book can be found at https://doi.org/10.1007/978-3-030-64826-8_7

Isaac Newton once famously said: "If I have seen further, it is by standing on the shoulders of giants." Each generation plants the seeds that will be harvested by the next one.

This book is dedicated to Bernard Lietaer (February 7, 1942–February 4, 2019), whose shoulders we are now standing on as we look at the future of money and sustainability, and whose knowledge is now bearing fruit.

Preface

This book seeks to initiate a debate that has not taken place in monetary economics thus far. We have traditionally relied on a monetary monoculture to finance and regulate global commons. Despite all the intellectual and mathematical scrutiny devoted to the topic, the debate ultimately boils down to austerity on the one hand versus stimulus, regulation and redistributive efforts on the other hand. None of the official academic positions really tackle the nature of the monetary system itself and its negative impact upon sustainability. We thus have failed to provide an answer to how we can really finance common goods and our future. This is exemplified by the current debate on the 2015 UN Sustainable Development Goals (SDGs).

The present text argues for the introduction of new financial engineering to achieve the SDGs and our commons, using a stepped approach that integrates new forms of monetary incentives into the conventional system: a parallel, optional, complementary form of additional liquidity that does not compete with the existing system. The arguments go beyond regulatory efforts and co-financed redistribution.

There is a subtle but substantial difference to other suggested theories: while acknowledging that there are multiple lock-ins and constraints, which we are going to explain in this text, what we are proposing is not an "ideal-typical" solution for the financial system (such solutions are doomed to remain mere theoretical propositions). We are rather advocating for the best single practical next step in the development of our monetary system that will maximize our ability to finance our common future over the next 15 years. The advantages of implementing this or a similar mechanism are manifold: firstly, it could be implemented relatively inexpensively in a fast and targeted manner. Then, it would have an anti-cyclical, anti-inflationary and resilient impact on our trading and payment system. Moreover, it builds upon findings in systems theory, thus bypassing the discussions between the different schools of economics. Further, it addresses findings in the life sciences of neurobiology, clinical and social psychology in order to match real human behavior beyond the "homo economicus". And finally, it can address the magnitude, volume and significance of the global challenges ahead. In short: The Future Wealth of Nations is based on a new kind of thinking related to redesigning and creating a monetary ecosystem to make the world a better place.

Dresden, Germany   Stefan Brunnhuber

The TAO of Finance Team

The World Academy of Art and Science (WAAS) has organized several dozens of conferences, meetings, hearings and panels over the last years on "How we can finance our future?". The following members have substantially contributed, modified, improved and criticized the main argument explained in this text. Though I take the full responsibility, the results would not have been possible without the contribution and support from the entire "TAO Team", which includes:

Zbigniew Bochniarz
Katalin Botos
Marianna Bozesan
Tomas Björkman
Alexander N. Chumakov
Emil Constantinescu
Wouter van Dieren
Frank Dixon
Dragan Djuricin
Michael Dorsey
Ian Dunlop
Rodolfo Fiorini
Garry Jacobs
Hazel Henderson
Erich Hödl
Charly Kleissner
Jan Kregel;
Ketan Patel
Mila Popovich
Stefan Schepers
Walter Stachel
Stephanie Tache
Tibor Todt

A Report to the World Academy of Art and Science

Impressum:
Author: Brunnhuber Stefan & TAO of Finance Team
Design: Wolf & Team (FFHD)—Alistair Bell
Language: Margaret Hiley
Literature/References: Sarah Heincke & Susanne Haase

Contents

List of Figures

List of Graphs

List of Boxes

List of Tables

What This Book Is All About: Finance—Future—Balance and the Rest

Exploring the world and reflecting upon ourselves, we realize that we never know enough and often need to rely on the insights of past generations and different practices from other parts of the world. In this sense, we can see that no-one is ever 100% wrong. Consequently, we begin to defend and fight for the opinions of others, even though we do not support them. This engenders the reciprocal tolerance required in times when democracy, our society, the planet and our future are at stake—as they are now.

There have been times in the relation between the scientific community and society as a whole in which individual disciplines made significant contributions to the progress of mankind. The discoveries of the periodic system—Mendel's law, vitamins, and the structure of DNA—are some examples. In the field of social sciences, these achievements include the Keynes multiplier and negative income tax, and in the fields of behavioral science and neuroscience, they include Pavlov's conditioned reflex and Maslow's motivational hierarchy.

There have also been times when different disciplines, working concurrently but independently of one another, have generated insights, discovered laws of nature or similar patterns in our social world. The physicist Werner Heisenberg famously said that the most fruitful and creative developments in human thought occurred at points in history when two different lines of thinking met. These lines may have their roots in quite different disciplines, cultures, points in history or religious beliefs. Once they encounter and interact with one another, the result is a deeper understanding, a new development or a transformation benefiting mankind. We are currently living at such a point in time.

For the first time in history, humans are fundamentally changing the course of the planet through the use of land, global warming, biodiversity degradation, and nuclear armament among other factors. Humans are now in the driver's seat, as it were, determining the fate of the planet. Hence the name of the new geological era we find ourselves in: the "Anthropocene" (P. Crutzen).[1] In the previous era, the "Holocene", we did not really experience limits or boundaries of this kind, and thus were able to think and act in an exponential way. This way of thinking has reached its end point and we now find ourselves confronted with both relative and absolute limits. Environmental science has identified at least nine planetary boundaries. However, this is just half of the story. In addition to these external limits, we also face internal limits—limits to the way we think and act under conditions of uncertainty. These include a tendency towards risk aversion, the limitations of our mental frames, a focus on short-termism, as well as a distorted perception of correlations and causalities. We therefore need a new mindset if we are to solve the problems of the Anthropocene, a new mindset that also will enable us to question our supposedly sacrosanct monetary system.

Financing Our Future is not a book about a new monetary theory. It explores the parallels between Eastern philosophies and ideas in Western economic thinking. It is kind of a TAO of Finance. This promises to provide both a better understanding of the economic process in general as well as links to a more sustainable future. Following the disappointment of the Western thought process and Western economic modeling in the 2008 financial crisis, we need to look at economic and monetary processes from a completely different perspective. Eastern thinking and Taoism in particular provide a promising approach with which to frame economic activities in the era of the Anthropocene.

The purpose of this book is to explore the interaction between two fields, finance and sustainability, using the information now available to us from different fields and practices. As well as being a psychiatrist and the Chief Medical Officer of a psychiatric hospital, I have engaged as an academic teacher in research on economics and finance and been involved in corporate and institutional consulting for over two decades. After spending time in China and Egypt, I became interested in the Eastern counterparts of the perennial mystical traditions in the West. This book argues that the concepts and philosophy of Taoism provide us with a deeper understanding of how finance can truly benefit humanity and the planet. Eastern ways of thinking reveal a more holistic view of the economic process and the impact of the monetary/financial system. This TAO of Finance attempts to provide an example of this interplay that touches upon some fields currently presenting humanity with its greatest challenges: money, sustainability and our common future.

This book is intended for a general readership with a dual interest in Eastern thinking, more specifically Taoism, and finance. However, no previous knowledge of finance is required to understand this book. The main concepts and theories are presented in non-technical language without mathematical equations. My hope nonetheless is that the book's readers will include some individuals with an expertise in finance and monetary theory or in politics who have not yet been exposed to the religious philosophy of the East. Some elements of Taoism are gaining momentum already, for example through a more cyclical understanding of our real economy. We are now focusing on cascade economics, where resources are reused over and over again; we are considering cyclical and recycling processes, which allow a steadier state with regard to resource depletion; and we are starting to reach out towards a more integral perspective that takes into account the entire value chain and its associated costs. And there is more to come, as is explained in this book.

The main text is written to be accessible to anyone who has a bank account, has ever made a financial transaction or simply has gone shopping. But it also addresses professional players in the field. You could be the CEO of a global player, an investment or commercial banker, a day trader, work at an insurance company, or in the field of financial engineering or derivatives; you could be a lawyer, in the consulting business, work as a lobbyist, or hold a position in monetary regulation, accounting, philanthropy or the public finance sector. Even if you are a macro trader, are active in long/short equity, are a high-frequency trader, are a hostile activist, are an event driver, or manage a hedge fund, venture capital or a private equity fund, you may benefit from the TAO of Finance. Even if you have an MBA in economics or finance, or are pursuing an academic career in macroeconomics, you may find this book contains an additional perspective on the field. We all operate within the financial system but have different incentives, conflicting interests and opposing ideas about economics, finance and the future, and thus this book can offer all of us exciting and hitherto overlooked insights into the way we need to finance our future.

Note

1. Crutzen (2016) and Stoermer (2000).

Chapter 1
A New Narrative for the Anthropocene Era: On Boundaries, Interconnectedness and the Global Commons

1.1 A Bold Statement to Begin With

Imagine a mechanism, a thought process, a collective behavior or a social invention with the potential to overcome absolute poverty within 18 months. One that leads to the protection of biodiversity, halts global warming, reduces water depletion, and mitigates fraud and illicit financial transactions, while simultaneously expanding school education, increasing access to health care and fostering global peace—all in one. Imagine this process being expedited through democratic channels more quickly and easily than through a lengthy global governance approval process; imagine it starting in less than six months with fewer than 250 staff. Imagine a mechanism that enables billions and billions of human beings on this planet to sustain themselves and their neighborhoods and take better care of the environment—all at once and all the time.

And imagine this being achieved using new technologies, with a simultaneous change in our mindset. Suddenly, the insurmountable problems of ongoing ecological degradation and endless human suffering turn into goals and challenges that we as humans are capable of overcoming. Just imagine.

1.2 A New Mindset

The precondition for introducing such a revolutionary mechanism is a major change in mindset. It is not left or right, Keynesian or Austrian, Marxist, institutional or behavioral economics that will determine how to properly finance our future. Rather, it is the way we think, perceive, and evaluate the world that will make the difference. And it is easy to get lost in the false frames, which tell us the wrong stories, backed up by poor interdisciplinary evidence, leading political decisions astray.[1]

© The Author(s), under exclusive license to Springer Nature
Switzerland AG 2021
S. Brunnhuber, *Financing Our Future*,
https://doi.org/10.1007/978-3-030-64826-8_1

It is only when we start taking into account empirical evidence from systems theory, neurobiology, and both clinical and social psychology that we can begin to envision a completely different monetary system. Rather than following the paradigm of economic growth first and partial redistribution of revenue through taxation, fees or philanthropy to finance commons second, we advocate designing a parallel optional monetary system that is more compatible with the nature of the global commons and our common future. Our thinking will need to be bold, deep and far-reaching if we are to achieve a balance to the given financial system in order to safeguard our common future.

1.3 Living in the Anthropocene: Interconnectedness Within Boundaries

1.3.1 Major Characteristics of the Anthropocene

We now are living in the era of the Anthropocene, a period in which human activity has become the dominant influence on the climate and the environment.[2] Five factors in particular define this era. First, as long as we do not successfully adapt, we now are living within quantifiable and measurable planetary boundaries that have various geo-ecological tipping points. Once these boundaries have been transgressed, there can be no return to the previous state. Second, we are living in a state of ongoing interconnectedness of everything, everywhere.[3] Third, the increasing complexity of our world is forcing us to operate with greater uncertainty and ambiguity. Fourth, the growth of our economy at the expense of the ecosystem is causing non-linear, complex feedback loops.[4] We need to learn to abandon single cause–effect relations and replace them with circular, multi-looped processes that amplify, delay or curb each other. And lastly, since 1950, most—if not all—human activities and their impact on the geophysical components of our planet have become exponential in a so-called "great acceleration". To be more precise here, right at the beginning of our study: it is not humanity, but the "wealthy few that stress the planet" (Raworth, 2012). And we are dealing with a situation in which 99% of all changes on the planet are triggered and caused by just 1% of events.[5]

However, living in the Anthropocene does not mean that the developments and adjustments ahead are insurmountable or a natural law. They are not a mystery. On the contrary, for the first time in history, humans are sitting in the driver's seat, determining both their own future and that of the planet. Our fate is not inescapable, but it is we who must decide which future we wish to live in. In short: everything could be different (Fig. 1.1).[6]

The five factors that characterize the Anthropocene have their origin in 1750 with the invention of the steam engine, followed by the Haber-Bosch procedure, then antibiotics. Since 1950, most human activities with negative spillovers and their ensuing geophysical impact have developed exponentially. From the 1990s onwards,

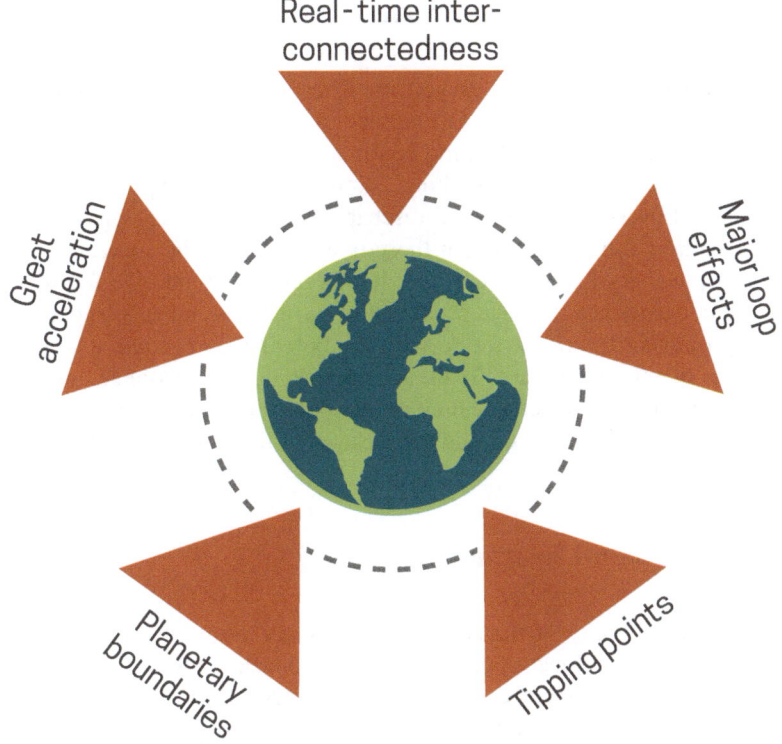

Fig. 1.1 Living in the Anthropocene—tipping points—planetary boundaries—interconnectedness—kickbacks and feedback loops

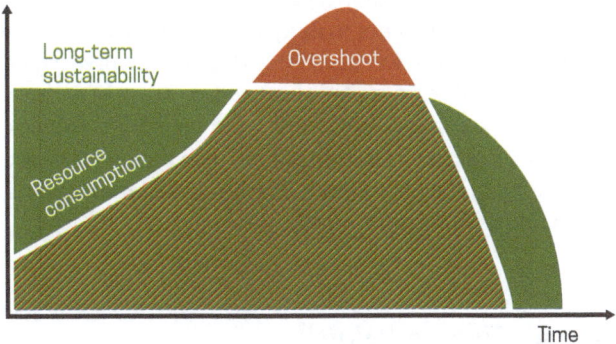

Fig. 1.2 Overshoot and collapse (the Seneca effect)

the damage caused by negative social and ecological externalities such as the loss of biodiversity, melting ice caps, forced migration, unprecedented income and wealth disparities, and increasing asymmetric wars has become a financial liability that we have to pay for and include in our budgets (Fig. 1.2).[7]

1.3.2   A Five-Second Time Frame

Yet the amount of destruction caused by these negative externalities has only occurred in what is the equivalent of five seconds within the five-billion-year time-frame of our planet's history. As time continues to pass, the costs of "business as usual", "wait and see" or "doing nothing" strategies increase exponentially. In fact, these costs will oversteer any other foreseeable scenario unless significant change occurs in the near future. Looking at these five seconds in the context of our five-billion-year planetary history opens up a longer-term view into the future. We see that we are currently at a leverage point where earlier eras and epochs could culminate in a promising future—a future with the potential to become a second axial time or form of enlightenment.[8] To attain to this second Renaissance, we will need to change our mindset and achieve a more integral form of consciousness. One way this can be achieved is by integrating the wisdom of the East (Fig. 1.3).

1.3.3   Living with Uncertainty

Under the new dynamics of the Anthropocene, even those who have done everything "right" become subject to the non-linear feedback loops, asymmetric shocks, unforeseen contingent disruptive changes and irreversible social and ecological tipping points of this era.[9] Instead of clear causal links, we now find ourselves confronted with multiple correlations, breaking points and probabilities.[10] While humans have the sensory capacity to smell, taste, hear, touch and see, they are able neither to sense exponential developments nor to act upon them. Accordingly, these various phenomena produce a greater level of uncertainty. Because uncertainty is unavoidable, the best approach is not to deny it, but to find an effective way of coping with it.[11] The reflex response to uncertainty does not involve a mental process— it is either a flight/fight reflex or a play-dead reflex. If we want to appreciate the value of uncertainty in a constructive way, we must first step back and become mindful. There will be no perfect solution and no plan that is 100% secure. If we are to value uncertainty, we first need to learn to tolerate and even embrace it; we need to become comfortable with losing control.

1.3.4   Numerous Tipping Points[12]

Living in the Anthropocene thus entails non-linear pathways that are much less foreseeable or predictable than anything previously experienced. In this era of increasing tipping points, small events can trigger disproportionately large changes.

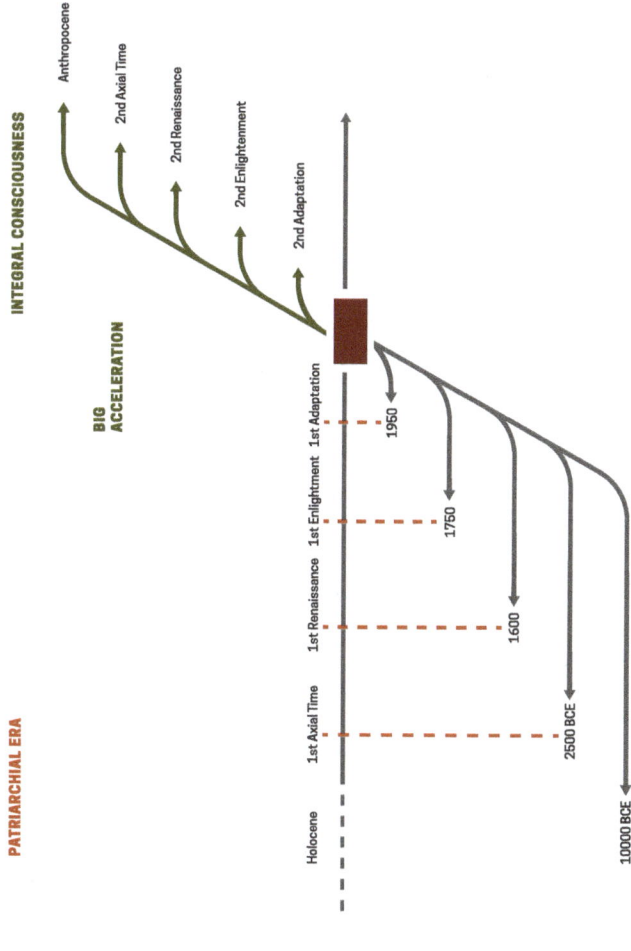

Fig. 1.3 The last five seconds within a very long perspective

Table 1.1 Major negative ecological and some (negative and positive) social tipping points

Ecological tipping points	Negative social tipping points	Positive social tipping points
Boreal forests	Migration	Value changes
Coral reefs	Corruption	Access to objective information
El Niño, Southern Oscillation	Asymmetric wars	Increased education
West and East Antarctic ice sheet	Relative inequality	De-investment strategies
Amazon rainforest	Unemployment	Human settlements and citizen involvement
Greenland ice sheet	Lack of social mobility	Disruptive renewable technologies
Jet stream	Financial crisis	New social security systems
Permafrost	Lack of access to resources to cover basic needs	Fading out fossil subsidies
Indian summer monsoon	Lack of security and trust	Climate policy enforcement
Alpine glaciers	Total transparency, control and lack of privacy	Lifestyle changes
Arctic winter sea ice	Sense of loss of self-efficacy	Population control

Like the single drop of water that makes a bucket pivot and overflow, tipping points are critical thresholds where small changes can alter the state of a whole system.[13] Examples include small groups of committed people changing a political system, or small changes in global temperature causing significant shifts in the environment. On a large scale they become particularly relevant because of the magnitude, the timing, the speed and the very nature of the new state such domino effects can trigger.[14] The following table summarizes major ecological and social tipping points (Table 1.1).

Social and ecological tipping points are intertwined and can re-enforce one another. More than a dozen such Seneca cliffs have been scientifically recognized.[15] If we as humans are not able to come up with clever forms of adaptations, once a tipping point is reached, the ensuing sequence of events appears to become unpredictable and happen more or less on autopilot, with humans having little to no control over the subsequent process. The political and economic costs of adapting to a post-tipping point situation are unpredictable (Fig. 1.4).[16]

Taken together, the realities of the Anthropocene change our brains, our minds and our way of making decisions and interacting with one another.[17] The Anthropocene also changes the way we conduct governance, politics and economics. Basically, it changes everything.

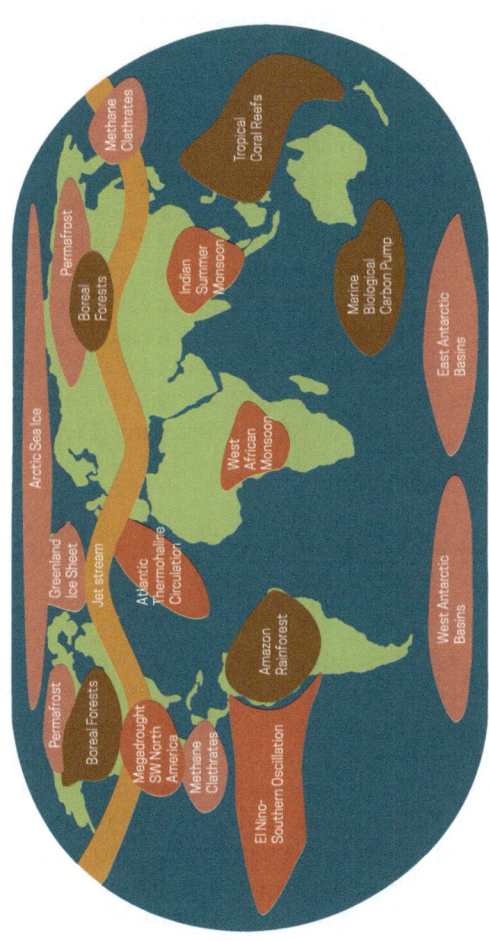

Fig. 1.4 Ecological tipping points that reinforce each other

1.3.5 The Fork in the Road

As systems become increasingly unstable in the Anthropocene, we are reaching a critical fork in the history of humanity. There are many possibilities—the only one that is no longer an option is turning back. While a small critical mass can lead the change, a dual strategy is required, which involves discerning the correct pathways within faulty structures. Traditional stories no longer hold and the common forms of self-efficacy and linear thinking within a given path lose their impact (Fig. 1.5).

If we take a long-term view and look at parameters such as longevity or wealth in a very general sense, humans were caught in so-called Malthusian cycles for centuries, if not millennia. Each time the population and birth rate increased, a decline in food supply, harvest defaults and wars decreased the overall population again. There was no real development. What happened around 1750–1850 to change this? It was not increased resource efficiency or capital accumulation, but a fundamental shift in our mindset. This was the era of the Enlightenment, when humans started to apply critical and rational thinking, where new forms of government and regulation emerged in the form of liberal democracies and law and order, when fundamental human rights began to emerge and modern science and technology took off. All these developments came prior to capital accumulation and resource allocation. In fact, it was this shift in our personal and collective consciousness that enabled us to think, act, perceive and behave differently (Fig. 1.6).

1.4 The Anatomy of Western Narratives: Conflicting Stories—The Good and the Ugly

What makes the human species so successful has less to do with individual competitiveness, sophisticated tool use, walking upright and forms of abstract intelligence than with humans' capacity to tell credible stories. In most cases, these stories do not refer to the objective natural world around us, but to an interactional, self-made type of second cultural reality. The stories we tell one another require some form of abstraction to transcend the immediate facts that we sense and perceive around us. These narratives are mainly about God, Death, Technology, Laws of Nature, Money, Power and Politics. It is precisely the reciprocal belief in these fictional stories that provides the mental frames that allow humans to coordinate and to collaborate in large numbers. This coordinated form of anonymous cooperation has represented a selection advantage. However, it obliges humans to do more than simply adapt passively to their given environment; instead, they need to strive constantly for a better world. Humans do not simply reproduce themselves, but are constantly driven to maximize and optimize what they are doing. Curiosity and discovery, science and technology, the organization of large social cohorts, greater labor specialization in combination with the drive to improve is what distinguishes us from bee and monkey populations.[18]

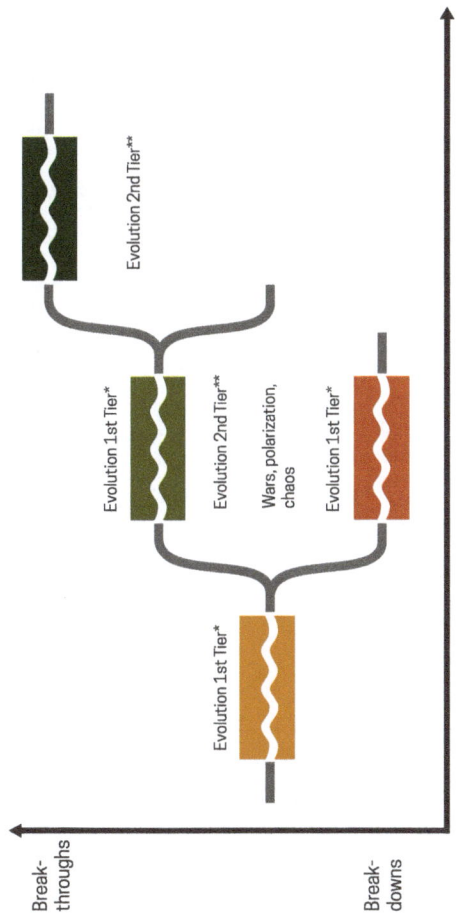

Fig. 1.5 The fork—bifurcations explain the shift and change required better than linear processes

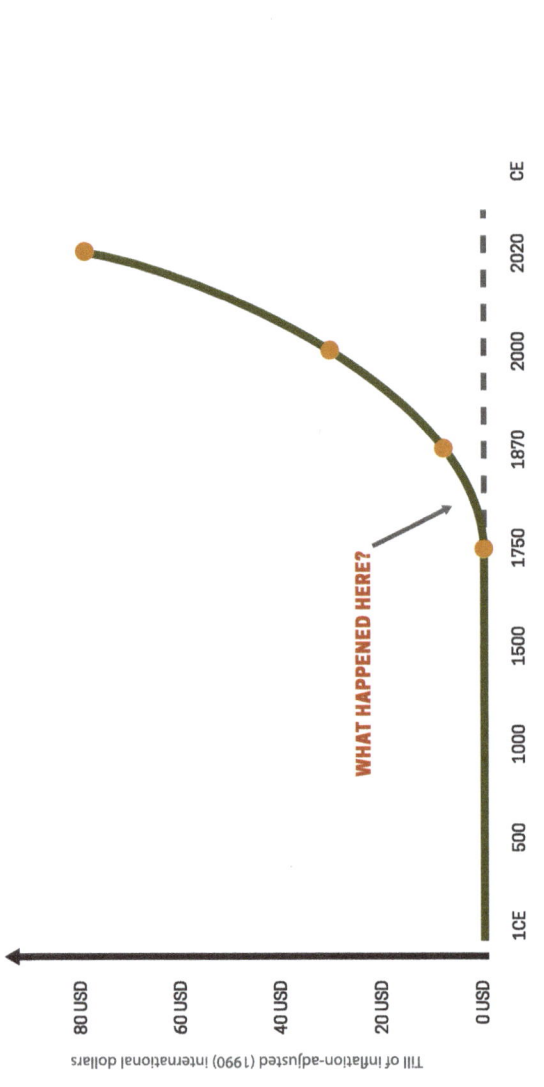

Fig. 1.6 What happened here? It was not capital accumulation or resource efficiency, but a shift in mindset that triggered human wealth and welfare

The more costly and expensive the narrative becomes over time, the more powerful it is. Although this sounds paradoxical, it derives from the fact that until an alternative story is found, we are forced to give the victims and the losses incurred as a result of this initial narrative a final sense of purpose. Another powerful narrative in monetary economics is "endless growth first and redistribute wealth second". Most aspects of these fictitious narratives are either wrong or at least incomplete.[19]

History has shown that it is better to have a wrong story than no story at all. Narratives, even when they are false, serve to stabilize both the individual and the societal psyche. Only time will tell whether the fictional story about the future confirms current human activities, whether it is self-fulfilling, or whether it is self-destructive.[20]

As long as we do not have an alternative story to tell ourselves, or a different mental frame to explain the world around us, any threat to our sense of coherence will override scientific facts. In short, frames prevail over facts. In this sense, the story in this book is not about alternative facts, but about an alternative mental frame that allows us to gain a different view on economic facts and political decision-making.[21]

So what is the meta-narrative for the twenty-first century that will allow us to regain a selection advantage? This narrative will need to honor the human condition with all its uncertainties, multiple timelines, and ignorance as well as the transitory character of each existing solution. It also will need to highlight the potential rather than the problems we have as humans—the chances rather than the setbacks.[22]

The challenge, as illustrated by the two sets of graphs below, is that good and bad stories occur simultaneously. In the first graphs, exponential trends lead to a negative impact on the planet and future generations. The second graphs illustrate a positive story, where the human species has achieved cultural progress (Figs. 1.7 and 1.8).

How can we reconcile the two? Both narratives, the good and the ugly, are true. We have robust empirical evidence to support both narratives' agendas. In order to reconcile these two opposing stories, we have to take into account a substantial shift in our awareness and perception of ourselves and the world around us. Our average collective consciousness has shifted faster towards higher expectations and standards than the objective change happening in the real world. We have simply become more sensitive towards and intolerant of ailments, grievances and disasters. This is true for the objective development of poverty and crime rates, child labor and female education rates, the development of our social capital, longevity, happiness and our health status. This is also true for the relative and absolute decline in crime rates and terrorist attacks, suicide rates as well as the improvement of our water and air quality and democratic indexes over time. Only because we are living in the best world humans have ever lived in are we now able to develop higher sensitivity and greater empathy and access more data and objective information that leads us to see a hunger and poverty rate of 10% globally as unacceptable while knowing that 200 years ago 90% of the world population lived at in poverty. This is also true for the over 90% decline in crime rates and air pollution in one century, or the over 80% increase of immunization and enrollment rates in half a century.[23] Both narratives remain true, but we can only evaluate and continue the success of any social intervention if we are able to objectively appreciate the real impact of such interventions in the real

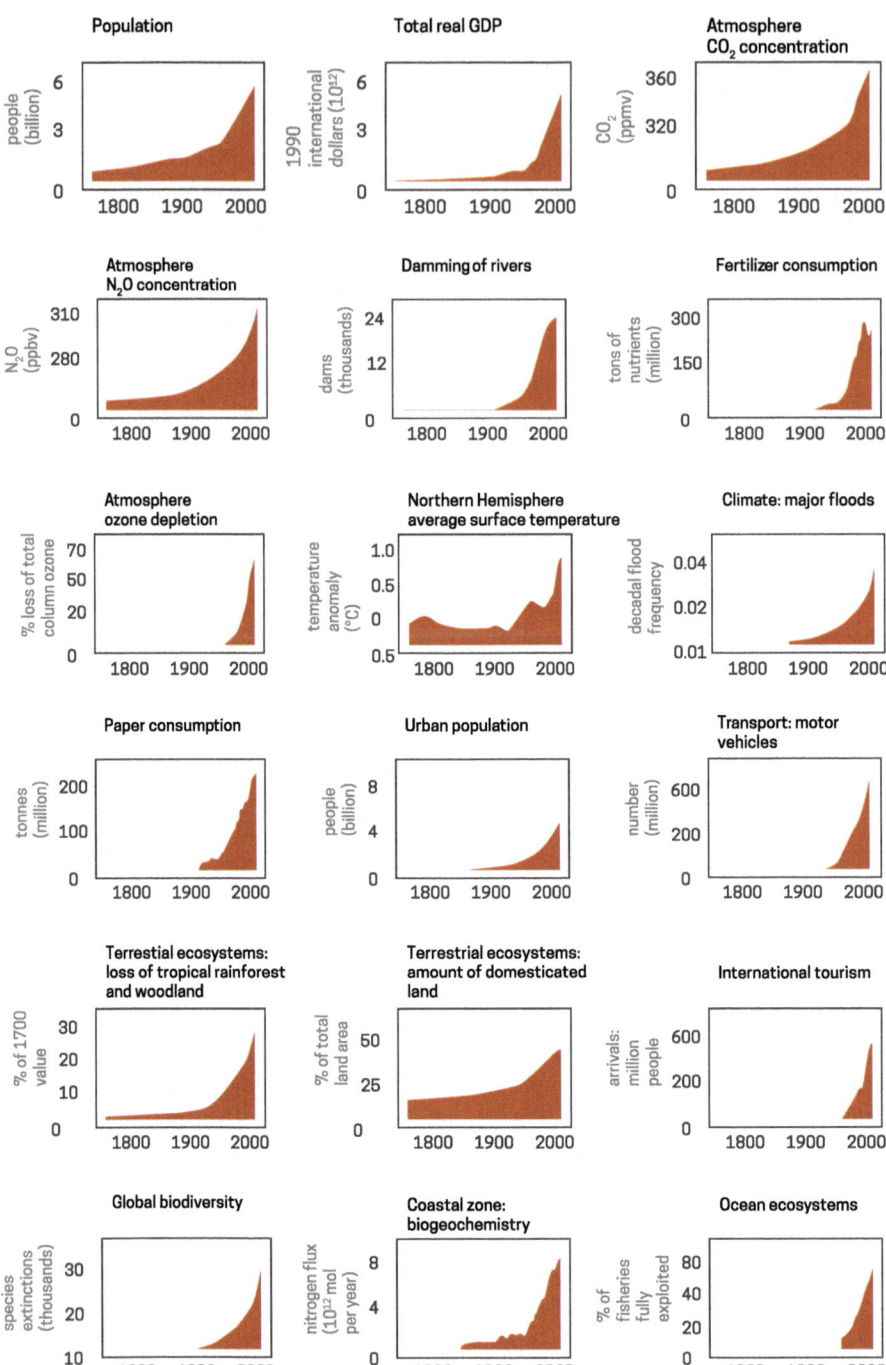

Fig. 1.7 The bad story: kickbacks and big loops. (See also update: Steffen, Broadgate, Deutsch, Gaffney, & Ludwig, 2015)

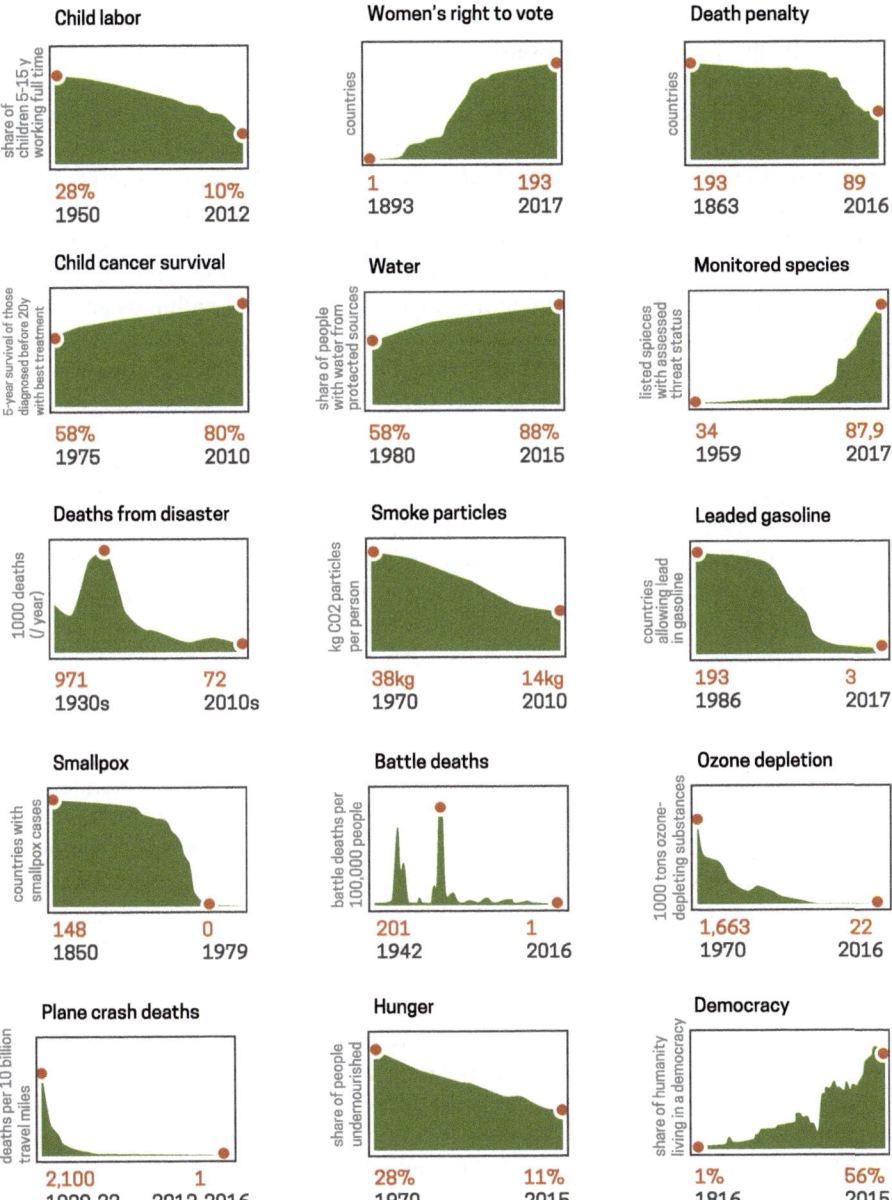

Fig. 1.8 The good story: improvements and gains. (See also: Rosling, Rosling Rönnlund, and Rosling (2018), Gapminder (2020), The world in data (2020))

world. Only then are we able to do the right thing and continue with that which has helped in the past, moving towards a more human-centered approach. And this should also hold for financial sector.

We need a new narrative to usher in this art of transformation. Something that does not describe a final state or ideal-typical scenario, something that is not fully transparent and that cannot control what lies ahead. Rather, this narrative should describe a transitory period from the perspective of a place where and a time when the given narratives no longer hold and the full picture is unknown. This future is open, multi-optional, non-determined, and includes many hybrids and uncertainties, failures and setbacks. This might at first increase the anxiety within us all and particularly in those in executive decision-making positions in the corporate and public arenas. But this transition period is also full of options, potential and empowerment. If we have the right narrative, this period can become a kind of second Enlightenment or a second Renaissance.[24]

If we agree that the narrative closest to reality is the one that provides us with the highest selection advantage, we need to be critical about the story we tell ourselves in order to live in this new complex and uncertain world. How do we do this? We need to psychologically anchor our reference point in a past perspective of hardship and difficulty. This is because in the absence of knowledge, humans tend first to focus on negative current events, and because truly momentous challenges lie ahead. For example, as mentioned above, in the early nineteenth century, the poverty rate worldwide was 90%; at the beginning of the twenty-first century, it has dropped to less than 10%. Life expectancy 125 years ago was less than 40 years; now it is 80. Smallpox, which caused over 300 million deaths in the twentieth century, has now been eradicated. And 50 years ago, 80% of the world population was illiterate, while now the global illiteracy rate is 20%.[25] This new mindset does not ignore the bad stories, but puts them into their proper historical perspective. In this sense, we do not need even more empirical data to prevent future shock scenarios; rather, the existing data needs to be interpreted differently.

If the negative narrative prevails over our consciousness and consequently our decision-making, we risk becoming pessimistic and disruptive, not honoring past achievements to the extent that they deserve. Conversely, if we allow the positive narrative to dominate, we risk a degree of naiveté towards the challenges and unforeseen events ahead. Which of the two future narratives prevails depends on the psycho-social narrative in place. In order to be able to sustain both narratives, a significant amount of what psychologists call tolerance for ambiguity is necessary. Tolerance for ambiguity allows us to hold in our minds a combination of push factors, such as risk, adverse events and disruptive technology, and pull factors, such as positive stories, potential and possibilities.

Although these narratives have their positives and negatives, both are embedded in a Western perspective. Human activities in general and economic activities in particular make decisions based on assumptions stemming from materialistic or naturalistic world views. Western thinking is advantageous in that it advocates the freedom of science, generates verifiable and reproducible results, seeks improvement, favors a thinking that is emancipated from religious beliefs and/or political convictions, and relies on an analytical approach that prefers data to theory. However, this is an out-ward-facing approach reflecting only one type of rationality: an analytical, linear, causal, materialistic and reductionist way of thinking. In the West, we are trapped in the belief that more of the same thinking will help us to better understand the world and make better decisions to improve it.

In the field of the social sciences, variables such as unemployment figures, inflation or the gross domestic product (GDP) are used as a proxy for the more intangible assets of wellbeing or happiness. Although this analytical and reductionist approach is true, it remains incomplete. For example, it is false to conclude that GDP is the major driver of life expectancy, wealth, health and happiness. In most cases, especially after basic needs have been met, the game changers are education, basic hygiene measures and social contacts.

Thus, the psychological capacity to embrace conflicting and opposing stories of ourselves, the world and the future will determine whether we are capable of living together on this planet. The mindset of Taoism, as we will see next, favors balanced narratives and seeks out opposites. But how do we get there? The parable of the elephant and the blind experts illustrates some of the preconditions required to change our mindset.

1.5   The Elephant and the Blind Experts

A dozen wise but blind experts and an elephant are sitting in a room. The experts are trying to answer the following question: what does the elephant look like and how does it affect each person in the room? No-one with an overview of the situation, such as a king or ruler, is available for advice.[26] Each expert touches and describes different parts of the elephant, such as its tail, trunk, or ears. And accordingly each expert fundamentally disagrees with the findings of the other wise, blind experts. So, not only do the parts not represent the whole, but the partial views provided by the experts are able to synthesize neither the impact of the whole on the parts, nor its effect upon those in the room. This slightly modified ancient parable tells us a story of silo thinking, where the whole is never understood, and the full impact of the elephant in the room cannot be grasped.

It appears that we are living in a world of wise, blind experts exploring different aspects of the elephant in the room. No-one wishes to discuss and consider its overall impact on our life, our planet and our future. Each expert is right in her or his individual conclusions, but each perspective is limited to the area they have mastered. This is true for the economist, who measures GDP and the Consumer Price Index (CPI), or models unemployment rates and the debt burden; this is true for the demographer, who looks at the changes in birth and fertility rates; it is also true for the statistician who explores Big Data correlations.[27] Because no-one is 100% wrong in their assessment, their findings all carry some truth, albeit a partial truth.

The precondition for a shift in mindset would be for each expert to adopt a mental state of humility. Humility would allow them to accept the limits of their own viewpoints, to consider the perspective or rationale of others, and to acknowledge that the entire elephant and its impact on those in the room can never fully be understood. This requires not only a horizontal shift in our mindset, but a transformation of our gravity of consciousness as a world community. This transformation will enable our thinking to become more integral than fragmented, more holistic than siloed, more truthful than refutational, and more significant than irrelevant. This is the thought process we need when it comes to understanding the impact of the elephant in the room.[28] This newfound humility will make it possible to create a new narrative for living in the era of the Anthropocene.

In fact, we know what is required to solve this complex situation: we need to reduce CO_2 emissions by more than 50% by 2050 in order to remain within the planetary geo-ecological boundaries[29] while attending to the basic global social needs of all humans (shelter, food, education, health care, employment and living in safety).[30] This means that global warming and basic human needs come top of the priority list.[31] And they both complement each other somewhat.[32] However, these two imperatives constitute a non-trivial dilemma: expansive economic growth, which would enable us to meet the basic social needs, finds itself confronted with the planetary boundaries; and degrowth scenarios, which would allow us to reduce carbon emissions, risk destabilizing the political and economic system, preventing us from solving social challenges like poverty or hunger.[33]

What if the elephant in the living room were the monetary and financial system? A system that is constantly overlooked in terms of its impact on our life, our planet and our future? In order to create a new narrative and overcome the existing biases in our Western thought process, we will now look at Taoism.

1.6   TAO (道): A First Glimpse

The Chinese term 道 or TAO (pronounced "DOW") is well known but little understood—and used even less. Originally deriving from Confucianism, TAO means the "right path" or "lead principle". It refers to knowing what to do and the correct path to follow. In this sense, TAO is more of a practice than a theory, a practice that is perfectly balanced and in harmony from one moment to the next, integrating complete mindfulness and contrasting opposites. It excludes nothing and nothing is left behind; everything is considered and has its proper place. In its purest form, it resembles a practice without effort and force. Whenever there is an imbalance or overshoot, TAO offers the complementary values required to overcome this lopsidedness: weakness where there is power, symmetry where there is asymmetry, fragility where there is force, smallness where there is bigness, female where there is male, slowness where there is speed. It reveals a glimpse of this cosmic pattern of stillness and activity, emergence and decay, subtlety and grandiosity, invention and discovery, causality and complementarity, understanding and changing. Yin and Yang are the inseparable and contradictory components that form an ultimate unity, the TAO. This is true even in the subtlest forms in which emptiness manifests, like the empty space between the lines, or when form dominates content.

Accordingly, this Eastern tradition of looking at the world is one of interrelatedness and interconnectedness at both a societal and an individual level.34 When everything is connected with everything everywhere and at all times, we learn that this interconnectedness is not random or chaotic. It does not happen by chance, but pursues complementarities, where chaos and creation, rules and randomness, silence and sound, fullness and emptiness, humility and mastery are intertwined with one another. A new mindset is required to identify and fully grasp the power and beauty of proportionality, where harmony and balance prevail. The fundamental components of this mindset are respect and humility, grace and grit. TAO is in fact ever present and is something we can always discover—and indeed need to discover, especially in Western culture, society and economics. It resembles a property to be cultivated and realized anew in a unique way in each era, each society and each generation.[35] From this process, forms of self-regulation and self-healing, equilibrium and modesty, renunciation and omitting will emerge that in part are unknown to Western thought. In this sense, The TAO of Finance is a manifesto for the twenty-first century. It requires an institutional framework that makes proportion, beauty and the good possible at the same time. Indeed, every living being always has a relationship to the whole. At its core, TAO transcends dualism, generates oneness, and reflects a path that is balanced, proportional and sound. It reflects the place where the world falls into one.[36]

By contrast, the Western worldview tends to divide up an otherwise connected reality. At a societal level, we thus see entities such as states, communities, corporations and societies; on an individual level, we see isolated egos with singular utility-maximizing behaviors. From an Eastern perspective, this divided view is seen as a form of Avidiya, or ignorance. Immanuel Kant (1784) introduced the Western intellectual movement of the Enlightenment as the individual capacity to critically reason and assume the moral imperative of being responsible for one's own autonomous attitude and behavior.[37] The Western Enlightenment is completely different to the concept of enlightenment found in the East. Eastern enlightenment identifies motion and change as intrinsic dynamic features that help us to better understand the ultimate reality. In the classical Greek view, there is a ruler who rules the world from the outside, an Alpha and Omega and a primary cause that precedes every existence. In Taoism, the controlling principles come from within. In fact, it is like a web that has no weaver. The Western human-centered approach has its advantages: it acknowledges humans' unique ability to reflect upon, question and reset their agendas, dogmas and worldview, constantly correcting and re-correcting their path.[38] But Western universalism has lost its superiority, not only in this general and philosophical sense, but also in a very practical, social, moral and political sense. This is true especially when it comes to demonstrating the significance and relevance of public affairs, common goods, and ecological assets.

Yet TAO is not only a way of knowing, but also another way of doing and being. Western thinking is positivistic and empirical. We emphasize what is visible and apparent and overlook what is missing. In this sense, Western thinking fears emptiness, as emptiness resembles its own shadow. However, it is exactly from this void or emptiness that everything emerges. Taoism values complementarities and identifies both the material progress and the void. In fact, whenever we claim that progress or an innovation occurs in one field, a shadow is cast or a void created in another field. Western thinking excels at highlighting progress and disruptive innovation, but has great difficulty in recognizing the voids resulting from this progress. For example, the invention of the printing press had an impact on oral memory; driving a car has an impact on walking, with consequent effects upon health; the use of antibiotics has led to multiple resistant strains; digitization has had an effect on jobs and so on. In short, whenever we progress in one area, we also "regress" in another.[39]

There is much the West can learn from Taoism. One such lesson is proportion, which reflects a kind of balance and harmony. Identifying the right proportions of things has the potential to reveal the natural pattern that we use to create and understand next to everything in nature and society. From a historical perspective, the concern with identifying the right proportions is older than any type of analytical or critical thinking. Identifying proportionality enables us to move from a merely analytical, linear, siloed, divided and dualistic worldview to one that embodies wholeness, oneness and unity. The purpose of proportion is to reconcile or resolve polarity into some kind of unity, wholeness or greater being. The well-known Yin-Yang symbol represents such a proportion. It is linked to the cyclicality of coming and going, appearing and vanishing. The more we become aware of this cyclicality, the more balance can be achieved. And each Yin—the passive, female principle of the universe, characterized as sustaining, associated with the earth, dark, and cold— also contains some Yang—the active male principle of the universe, characterized as creative and associated with heaven, heat, and light—and vice versa. When we begin to rebalance our thinking in politics, economics, and finance, we start tapping into a deeper understanding of the shadows we cast, the voids we ignore and the ignorance we are pursuing.

Another such lesson is how to reconcile opposites. The components that constitute the TAO are equal to each other, depend on each other and balance each other. They can exist only in relation to one another. Identifying the proper pairs of opposites is not necessarily a simple intellectual endeavor. Indeed, picking the wrong pairs could lead to the wrong conclusions and have ruinous consequences. Although right/left, female/male, up/down are easy to grasp, there are other forms of opposites where the right interrelations are more difficult to establish. For example, efficiency/resilience and equity/debt are frequently overlooked, yet powerful opposites on an archetypal level that hold particular relevance for the financial and monetary system, as we will see. So if we are to merge the East and the West, Taoism and finance, identifying the right pairs is important. These polarities should not be abandoned but contained, like in a battery, which contains both positive and negative poles. Failing to understand these polarities means an inability to harness the power or "electricity" of life (Fig. 1.9).

Taoism claims that the universe not only functions according to physical laws, but is based on moral ones, too. An individual's final destiny thus is fulfilled not only

Fig. 1.9 The well-known Yin and Yang of the TAO of Finance and its opposing values and forces. (Adopted from Lietaer et al., 2019). There are striking similarities between a matrifocal and patrilocal society, the features of the left and right hemispheres of the brain, and the financial system we propose later on in this text

by independence and freedom, but also by responsibility and caring. This caring universalism is fed by the understanding that everything is connected to everything everywhere and thus is fundamentally interdependent. This worldview provides a different understanding of humans, morals, society and nature. Taoism is less about transforming the world, as the Western view implies, but rather about understanding its inner dynamics: using this lens, humans become aware of the interrelatedness of all things, rather than creating and being the masters of their own destiny. TAO does not relate to scale or speed, to absolute or relative figures or benchmarking; it can be big or small, affect few people or billions, one single person or all of humanity. The TAO is always there, whether we study medicine or philosophy, psychology or astrophysics, macroeconomics or nanotechnology, Big Data or molecular biology, politics or engineering.

And the TAO of Finance, as we will describe in this text, can be such a path with greater balance and a deeper understanding of the economic process and human society as a whole. It can be a path with a heart—meaning with emotions, perceptions and intuitions beyond language and data but integrating them nonetheless, as we will see. And the TAO of Finance needs to exemplify and prove these opposite, mutually dependent features that cannot be reduced to but complement one another. Even more, the TAO of Finance needs to demonstrate that these components balance each other, addressing different parts in our inner and outer reality in order to achieve a more sustainable world. Only when the two parts are in equilibrium, each recognizing the other in their own right, with their own values, powers and entitlements necessary to complete wholeness and fullness, will we have accomplished the TAO of Finance. Only then.

However, talking merely about a transition or a transformation leaves us—the agents of change—with an unanswered question: in which direction are we to transit or transform? A Taoist rebalancing of the system provides a more objective pathway and orientation from the very beginning. Accordingly, we need to identify the components making up this balance. It is no exaggeration to state that if—and only if—all of these aspects of the TAO are met, we can call this approach the TAO of Finance. The following chapters will demonstrate that this is indeed the case.

In a letter to Kepler, Galileo (1610) stated repeatedly and urgently that the local authorities needed to look at the moon and the planets through his telescope, which they stubbornly refused to do. Galileo's argument was that if we want to discover new ground, we may have to look through the new lenses of such a new telescope. This was true for most discoveries and inventions in the past and will remain true for the future, too. It is one thing to state that our fossil energy-driven economy, our expansive economic growth pattern, endless disruptive technological substitutions and redistribution mechanisms represent explanations of our world; but another, broader view also looks at all the distortions, spillovers and negative externalities that our economic activities have generated at the same time. Asking different questions allows us to see and reflect on what we are missing out simply because our assumptions are too narrow.[40] If Albert Einstein was correct in saying that "we cannot solve our problems with the same thinking we used when we created them", then we need to look for a different understanding. The introduction of Taoist principles into our prevailing worldview might provide this different thought process, especially when applied to the problem of global common goods, which forms the topic of the next section.

1.7   Global Common Goods and the Sustainable Development Goals

In 2015, world leaders came together in New York under the helm of the United Nations to develop a road map for the future. Consisting of 17 Sustainable Development Goals (SDGs), this proposal aims to improve humanity, the planet, wealth, peace and partnerships.[41] The SDG agenda is based on hundreds of surveys, expert groups, panels and hearings, as well as millions of responses to population-based questionnaires. Most of the SDGs focus on common goods such as clean air

and water, universal access to health care, education (including preschool education), and maintaining biodiversity. Beyond the different political agendas all over
the world, which it seems highly unlikely we will be able to reconcile over the next
decades (democracies versus autocracies, failed states, asymmetric wars), the SDGs
can provide a sort of shared meta-narrative for all the different agents involved.
Instead of getting bogged down in a competition between different political systems, the SDGs offer us the opportunity to engage with a story that unites us
(Fig. 1.10).

None of the common goods referred to in the SDGs are exclusive. They should
be accessible to and enjoyed by everyone during their lifetime on this planet.
Additionally, none of these goals are separate from one another; they are all interconnected.[42] Achieving them requires a "non-siloed" approach: connecting North
and South, local and global, private and public. Looking at our issue from an insurance perspective, we see that an insurance can be designed either (1) to compensate
for unwanted future events or (2) as an instrument to reduce the likelihood of
unwanted events. From this point of view, investing in SDGs, although it appears
costly in the first place, relates to the second type of insurance. In fact, it would be
the largest preventive insurance campaign humanity has ever designed. There is
only one thing more expensive than investing in our future—not investing in it![43]
Within the current monetary framework, however, SDGs and their equivalent goals
have been chronically underfinanced. One reason for this is that they do not fit into
our current Western-oriented conceptual framework, where there is a fundamental
misalignment between our economic system and the nature of common goods. As a
consequence, we have neglected and overused common goods, in some cases to
their planetary limits, and this through no fault of their own. We therefore need to
design a monetary system that is based on the nature of common goods in order to
optimize their benefit for the planet and for humanity, not the other way around. The
TAO of Finance outlines a path with greater balance and a deeper understanding of
the economic process in relation to human society and the planet as a whole. In
order to embark on this journey, we must first change our mindset. Indeed, the
future of finance needs to be radically different from the past. We are facing unparalleled challenges for which silo and singular solutions are no longer adequate.
What we need is systemic thinking, and this shift in our mindset will lead to a
change in governance, technology, and the monetary system.

How are the SDGs to be achieved? Over 900 different multilateral contracts and
agreements on environmental issues have been generated globally in the last
40 years.[44] Over a dozen different approaches on varying levels have been proposed
to achieve the SDGs.[45] However, there continues to be intense debate on how best to
achieve these goals. The following graph summarizes the major proposals to achieve
the SDGs (Fig. 1.11).

Indeed, while the solutions proposed for the SDGs are all important, one has
been systematically overlooked: the role of the monetary system. The misalignment
between our current monetary system and the SDGs and our global commons has
led to their erosion and partial destruction. It has prevented their full economic
potential being achieved for the good of humanity. Our task is to adapt the economy
to conform to the nature of the commons for purposes of sustainability.

Fig. 1.10 The 17 Sustainable Development Goals (SDGs)

Fig. 1.11 The Sustainable Development Solutions. The grey area reflects solutions we have not been aware of. The monetary system (number 6) represents the missing gap

We will argue that the real tragedy of the (global) commons, which include social and ecological commons, is not the free-rider problem, nor their excludability; a common is a common, as fresh air, water, access to shelter, health care, food and education are human rights necessary to lead a life in dignity—and this regardless of the historical epoch or the dominant economic paradigm in place. We must adopt the economy to the nature of the commons, not the other way round. The real tragedy is that these commons have been encountering an economic reality, and a monetary system in particular, that does not take sufficient account of the value and benefits of common goods. It is the misalignment of the monetary system, rather than the commons themselves, that fails to contain, mitigate, encourage and unleash the economic potential of each common good for the benefit of humanity and the planet. We are stuck in a narrative telling us that only one monetary system can be used to finance our existence on the planet. This viewpoint limits and restricts us.

In summary, we have seen that the new era of the Anthropocene forces new requirements upon us—not only the requirement to take charge of our planetary fate, but also the new requirement of managing uncertainty. The narratives we have been telling one another, which up until now have represented an evolutionary advantage, no longer are suitable for this new era. If we wish to transform the way we live and take a more sustainable path, we need to be open to other ways of thinking such as Taoism, which provides another frame through which to see the world. This different lens must be applied in particular to our existing financial system, whose design is flawed in multiple ways. The next chapter will explore the advantages and limitations of this financial system.

Notes

1. P. Ehrlich's population bomb (1968), the misleading interpretation and reception of "limits to growth" Meadows et al., (1972), the "de-growth argument" that we have to cut down economic activities, leaving two thirds of the world population out of the equation, or the "material footprint argument" that the planet reaches its maximum extraction of resources at 50 Gt per year are just a few of many examples of how easily we get misguided, making wrong conclusions. Starvation and poverty have declined massively, the modeling of the Club of Rome has been approved, "poverty is still the greatest polluter" (M. Ghandi) and for the maximum of resource extraction there is simply no empirical evidence. If we start taking human creativity, entrepreneurship, technological innovation, science and the human capacity to wisely adapt to new challenges seriously, the entire story of our common future has to be re-written.
2. Crutzen, Paul, 2002. "Geology of Mankind." *Nature* 415: 23.
3. This is also called the *small-world paradox*: in a world where everything is connected, we already find ourselves confronted with complexity in the small world around us. Things become hyper-complex and we lose our perspective on how to act and respond in our daily routines (Perkins, 2014). The only way to overcome this complexity in the outer world is to increase the complexity in our minds.
4. Such *big loops* require a form of secondary-order adaptation that is completely different to primary-order adaptation to an environment. Irreversible non-linear tipping points and asym-

metric shocks, affecting even those who have done everything "right", force us to reframe our risk assessment in a world where everything is interconnected.

5. See Rathi (2017); this also refers to the so-called 10:50 rule: 10% of the richest people on this planet require over 50% of the resources; see also Otto, Kim, Dubrovsky, and Lucht (2019).

6. Complexity and connectedness of kinds always have been present in human history, but now they are enhanced, augmented and catalyzed, mainly through information technology, our lifestyle and the sheer number of people living on this planet.

7. In the Anthropocene Era, any fact turns into a normative statement, simply because we are forced to think about interconnectedness and boundaries. Traditional opposites like matter and mind, individual and society, society and nature take on moral and ethical dimensions. As long as we could afford to think in isolated units, the natural fallacy still held: facts do not generate a moral imperative. In the Anthropocene, this no longer is the case. From now onwards, we are enforced to reconcile our thinking and decision-making with reality (the facts). For example, when we examine a rise in global temperature or a loss in biodiversity, we must come up with a normative statement about this. This finding has significant implications for different disciplines: legal science needs to clarify a new line between private and public goods and determine the responsibility for private property in a new way; economists need to learn to quantify externalities and see how to internalize them, and assess to which extent the free market can generate a fair price according to uneven intra- and intergenerational patterns of distribution. In the field of political science, we need to learn to discuss new forms of local and global governance, their interconnectedness and how to reconcile short- and long-term incentives. In psychology, we need to better understand the components that will help us to transform our behavior, the impact of irrational framing, and how to cooperate. On a general level, we need to understand that interdisciplinary work will change: we can investigate well-nigh every single object from the perspective of every discipline.

8. Historically we could claim that whereas the first Enlightenment, the first axial time and the first Renaissance were about increasing the differentiation between the outer and the inner world, the second form of enlightenment we are facing now is more about integrating the results of that process of differentiation. This is sometimes called the "great convergence", following the "great acceleration". In this great convergence, politics, science, religion, thinking and doing are coming together and becoming reconciled with each other. The most powerful integrators in this process are information technology, spirituality and living within planetary boundaries in combination with a change in lifestyle. The "great convergence" relies on human beings' capacity for greater creativity, where identifying what we have in common is more important than searching to express each difference (see Baldwin, 2016; Von Weizsäcker & Wijkman, 2017).

9. However, the reality exists without figures and data. One of the achievements of Nassim Taleb's *The Black Swan* (2007) was its debunking of the false belief—held for centuries—that humans are capable of measuring uncertainty. The "black swan effect" refers to the problem that we tend to confuse statistical probability and any form of security. Weisberg (2014) accurately calls this a form of "voluntary ignorance".

10. The question here is: are experts in finance better at anticipating the future than ordinary citizens? There is now an empirical answer to this question, based on 20 years of research with several thousand controlled blind studies. At a time span of under one year, experts do better than chance. For forecasts longer than two years, experts generate similar results to statistical chance. Normal citations with a special interest in the field are equal or better than experts. What mechanism can improve prognosis? General intelligence is helpful, but more important seems to be the "group effect". Heterogeneous group samples with open-minded communication, a low hierarchy and failure-friendly environments can make the difference (see Tetlock & Gardner, 2015).

11. We are now significantly more skeptical about the future than 100 or even 200 years ago, despite the fact that we know more than in previous times. One reason for this finding is that we confuse wisdom and quantifiable information. The role of science is not to eliminate ignorance and uncertainty, as both are intrinsic to our outer and inner reality; its role is to solve

concrete problems. Uncertainty does not disappear once these are solved, but instead provides the terrain for further questions.

12. Such *social tipping points* occur when small changes in the environment cause large changes in our behavior. Four fifths of an average human's lifetime is shared with others. This is why we call our species a *zoon politicon*. Social tipping points are thresholds or a critical mass where minorities can flip into majorities in an abrupt and non-linear way. A social tipping point reflects a dynamic change in social convention. A small, but committed minority can cause and trigger cascading changes in behavior, and neither wealth nor authority is necessary to disrupt an established behavioral equilibrium. This is true for lifestyle changes, sexual harassment, energy consumption and public unrest. At the social tipping point, the given social fabric breaks apart and shifts from A to B; the capacity of self-organization or autopoiesis is reduced, as is the capacity to respond to external shocks. Science has identified the percentage of people in a group needed to trigger such a change. Empirically, it is around 25%. See Jasny (2018).

13. This *"tipping strategy"* was first investigated by economist Thomas Schelling (1971).

14. With regard to the financial system, the Amazon and the boreal forests are of special interest. The Amazon (two thirds of which lie in Brazil) stores up to 180 billion tons of carbon, while boreal forests (70% in Russia, 23% in Canada) store over 340 billion tons of carbon. These largest biomes on the planet are at risk from the global beef, timber, soy, paper, and mining industries. Recent research assumes that 25% of deforestation can trigger a tipping point at which vast amounts of carbon are emitted. The financial sector, on the other hand, is highly concentrated: only a few companies control 50–70% of the export value. Institutional investors with a long-term commitment should have a vital interest in protecting these biomes, as the costs of adapting to a post-tipping point scenario could be unpredictably vast. See Gaffney, Crona, Dauriach, and Galaz (2018).

15. For more in-depth readings, see Bardi (2017); Gladwell (2000); Meadows, Meadows, Randers and Behrends (1972); Wuebbles et al. (2017); Steffen et al. (2018); Otto et al. (2020).

16. One of the core constraints of our brain and our mind is that we are unable to appreciate exponential growth patterns. They are only accessible intellectually and require mental effort. Exponential growth does not mean fast growth, but growth that is unexpected based upon the underlying size. If a tree were 2.7 mm wide after one year and grew exponentially, it would be over 485 kilometers wide after 20 years. The rule of 72 is another rule of exponential growth: it characterizes the doubling time for an investment in relation to the growth rate. If the growth rate is 10%, the investment doubles in 7.2 years. Our annually adjusted economic growth rate is exponential; our compound interest rate, too. Take one cent and double the results each day, and after 30 days you have 5.3 million USD. See Meadows (2008).

17. One cognitive frame that will need replacing in the Anthropocene is speciesism or the so-called anthropomorphic frame: according to this frame, animals and plants are inferior and subordinate to humans. If we choose not to follow this linear backward-oriented evolutionary view, but instead assume that humans, animals and flowers exist in parallel worlds alongside each other, with different forms of perceptions in the micro and macro world that go beyond human perception, we would start telling our children a different story.

18. Harari (2014).

19. One example is the so-called *material footprint argument*: How much global resources do we consume in absolute terms and what share do individual regions have in this? However, the question is misleading in many respects and leads to the wrong political instructions. On the one hand, the calculations contradict the empirical findings of decoupling. In fact, the US economy has been decoupling itself sustainably from the country's GDP since 1970. In addition, even absolute electricity consumption has been decoupled from GDP for about a decade now, and CO^2 emissions have actually been declining. The material footprint argument is a kind of "omnibus term", which mixes different aspects and disguises the real challenges. One ton of sand, one ton of aluminum and one ton of copper are projected equally and then lead to a general increase to 80–90 Gt of resource consumption per year. But each ton of each resource has a completely different energy balance. At the same time, it is often claimed that a limit of

50 Gt per year globally is as much as the planet can sustain. We were unable to find sufficient empirical evidence for this claim, which the reader is simply expected to believe. The term "omnibus" then cannot be used to develop any real policy advice with regard to biodiversity, deforestation or air pollution, except for the indication that economic growth must be reduced (degrowth). But what are 80 Gt, are they good or bad, a lot or a little? They correspond to 0.000001% of the planet's continental crust, no more. By contrast, a differentiated measurement of individual resources per country is more advantageous. If we apply the right policy we learn that we can consume fewer resources and get more out of doing so: competitive market mechanisms, innovative technologies, public structural adjustments programs, a CO^2 tax and a change in monetary and fiscal policy. See the current debate around A. McAfee (2019).

20. See Beckert (2016).
21. F.D. Roosevelt was one the few US presidents able to understand the importance of telling the right story (Roosevelt, 1938). The major socio-economic parameters of American society remained the same throughout the Great Depression: neither resources, the hard-working labor force, the industrial infrastructure, the political institutions nor the market system changed. It was Roosevelt's story that created a shift on a subjective, not objective level, overcoming collective fear and loss of empowerment. This example shows that it is consciousness that makes the difference, not the given technology, demographic factors or governmental failure. Often, only a few individuals have been sufficient to change the course of history. In situations where we cannot see any way out, we should never underestimate the power of small groups to change the world (Mead, 1934).
22. In a larger context, such a narrative needs to be able to transcend the dichotomy of changes and necessities, pure coincidence and universal laws, where such dichotomies are combined and reconciled in a chaotic manner (see Jacobs, 2010).
23. This process of civilization was first described by Norbert Elias (1997); on the discrepancy between the pessimistic perception of our world and the objective data-based development, see Pinker (2018), Rosling et al. (2018), Schröder (2018) or the websites gapminder.org or ourworldindata.org.
24. See Brunnhuber (2016, 2018, 2019).
25. See Bourguignon and Morrisson (2002), Pinker (2018), Roser and Ortiz-Ospina (2018), United Nations (2019).
26. This parable has been adapted from the ancient one. The Indian parable of the blind men and the elephant tells the story of six blind men who go on a journey to explore the nature of the elephant and therefore touch the animal in different places such as its side, tusks, trunk, knee, ears, and tail. All of them gain a different impression of what the elephant looks like, as none of them have touched the whole animal. As John Godfrey Saxe (1936) later explained in the related poem, the truth is based on the sum of all the different findings rather than on one perspective. Some versions of the story mention a king or wise man who oversees the situation and finally concludes in a moral statement when he explains the situation to the blind men (for example Ireland, 2018). The modification of the parable in this book also refers to the commonly used expression of an "elephant in the room" that metaphorically describes "an obvious problem that no one wants to discuss".
27. To give further examples, political scientists tell us about the institutional framework within which autocratic or democratic decisions are made and how political legitimacy is enacted. Lawyers explore the legal framework within which we have to operate. Agronomists tell us about the impact of resource depletion, rare materials and the different forms of farming. Environmentalists warn us about the decline in biodiversity, melting ice caps and bleaching coral reefs. Neuroscientists create images of the brain, and clinical and social psychologists identify individual behavioral aspects and patterns of group dynamics in each of us. Then we have engineers, who generate the latest technological findings in nanotechnology, brain chips, new materials, IOT and automation. The experts on poverty and hunger, health care and education share their insights into the latest data and developments. The military experts tell us what is in the national interest and has to be defended and what does not. Politicians reflect public opinion on what is best. And finally philosophers shed light in the moral aspects of all

this. None of them are wrong, but each discipline is lacking the monetary and financial design and the helicopter view to put it all together.

28. Historically, over the centuries general knowledge became discipline-specific expertise, going from fewer than 10 disciplines taught at universities in the nineteenth century to over 150 in the twentieth century to several thousands of disciplines and sub-disciplines today (Braxton & Hargens, 1996; Bunge, 2003). This *compartmentalization* has expanded knowledge tremendously, but dissociates this knowledge from reality, producing masses of statistically significant, but in part irrelevant information (such as: *"Do we really need this study?"*) that is dissociated from knowledge in other disciplines (such as: *"Do they really know what is going on?"*) Any further cognitive specialization means that we risk losing our perspective of the whole (see also Karlqvist, 1999).

29. Can we achieve a 100% rate of renewables globally by 2050? Apparently we can, including grid, storage and curtailment. The costs for power would be cheaper by 52 Euro/MWh compared to 70 Euro/MWh in 2015 and this transition would generate millions of additional jobs. However, the transition to renewables is associated with the high initial costs of bailing out of the fossil fuel industry. See Ram et al. (2017).

30. See United Nations Environment Program (UNEP) (2013).

31. Despite the trade-off between ecological and social challenges, we should not overstretch the argument. The 12% of humans suffering from daily hunger can be managed with about 8% of our global food chain, and the 9% of humans lacking electricity would add a 0.2% additional burden to our global CO^2 budget (FAO, 2017; Holt-Giménez, Shattuck, Altieri, Herren, & Gliessman, 2012; IEA, 2017).

32. We tend to overestimate negative events in the short term and underestimate potential long-term exponential impacts, leading to false beliefs and conclusions on how to reconcile the real challenge of climate change with challenges of social needs. Empirically, negative events impress themselves upon the mind twice as fast as positive ones. So if we want to create a positive story, it needs to be at least twice as strong as its negative counterpart.

33. One response to this *non-trivial dilemma* is that we identify financial mechanisms that maximize our global commons, reducing negative externalities. Competitive markets consolidate and stabilize themselves through constant expansion and acceleration, mainly in an exponential way. Instead of deregulating and redistributing money to stabilize the system, we propose installing a parallel system that will partly downsize, but always "right-size" the conventional system to its adequate proportion. A parallel currency system can provide this mechanism, reducing the compulsion to grow, path dependency and lock-in effects and providing a rationale to cap and share in a world where physical boundaries and full-time interconnectedness are leading the way. How that works will be explained in greater detail below.

34. International trading, trafficking, financial flows and energy supplies all represent some sort of global connectedness, but remain pretty abstract in numbers. By contrast, *interconnectedness* is difficult to perceive on a global level for each individual. One way to look at this is: the amount of water and the amount of air on this planet have stayed the same throughout history (Berner & Berner, 2012). Each time we breathe in—and each person does this about 17,000 times a day, and there are 7.5 billion of us doing so—we are breathing in what previous generations over generations have breathed in (World Bank, Indicators, 2018a; Yuan, Drost, & McIvor, 2013). The same is true of every glass of water we drink. We were always connected with one another in the past, and in the future we will be connected even more. See for example Ford (2016), or Utke (1998). For an application of the concept, also see Capra (2010).

35. In fact, the cultivation of unique understandings of Taoism is an ongoing process that has led to diverse traditions. According to Kirkland (2004), this diversity results from an ongoing re-identification and distinct cultivation of "taoists of some stripes in some periods". Kirkland suggests that different generations construct their own forms of Taoism out of distinct elements, which leads to continuities and differences in the understanding of Taoism over time.

36. In fact, Western proportions of sacred geometry are similar (for example the "golden rule"), establishing an intrinsic link between beauty, proportion and goodness. In Greek philosophy we find the expression "kalos kagathos" which means "beautiful and good". This means that if we want to do the right thing and make the right decisions, we need to search for and should be exposed to the beauty of right proportions. The TAO represents such a proportion.

37. There is indeed a link between Confucianism and Western thinking, exemplified in communitarianism. In the West, we have enjoyed unparalleled experiences of individual freedom and self-realization, but these gains go hand in hand with ongoing losses. One of these is increasing fragmentation and the lack of a common narrative, leading to the question of the relation between the individual and society and nature as whole. This is addressed by communitarian social scientists such as Michael Sandel, Alasdair McIntyre, Charles Taylor, and Robert Bellah (see for example Bellah, Madsen, Sullivan, Swidler, & Tipton, 1985; MacIntyre, 1984; Sandel, 1982; Taylor, 1989).

38. Slaus, Giarini, and Jacobs (2013).

39. We could go further, stating that whereas in the West external technologies and empirical evidence are leading the way towards greater understanding, Taoism is more of an internal way that tries to identify and explore some sort of inner order. Since the Peace of Westphalia in 1648 with its system of checks and balances, the overall narrative in Europe and most of the world has focused upon the external, upon technology, upon balancing asymmetric forces. China on the other hand followed a tribute system, with the Chinese emperor in the center and the rest of the world circling around him—a hierarchical system that is center-focused, centrifugal and able to maintain its own balance (Kissinger, 2015).

40. See Walach (2019).

41. It was F.E. Schumacher (1973) who 50 years ago foresaw most of the developments we are facing now. Whereas any fossil-driven economy is based on an uneven distribution of oil, gas and coal, triggering political friction and a war-prone economy, renewables represent a more decentralized energy source that has the potential to create the basis for a peace economy. Renewable energy includes further components like "intermediary technologies", which are more in line with the human dimension, honoring the intrinsic value of nature and transcending human activities.

42. The concept of interconnectedness we are experiencing now in the era of the Anthropocene resembles the state of the ecology of the mind first described in detail by Gregory Bateson (1972). The context is what gives meaning. If there is no context, there can be no real meaning. Isolation and abstraction are a universal impossibility, as everything is interconnected with everything else. We frankly could study everything though the lens of every discipline.

43. There is a link to the Green New Deal (GND) Initiative: historically, the GND is rooted in F.D. Roosevelt's 1933 New Deal initiative to stimulate the US economy, mainly through public infrastructure programs. This agenda was based on F.M. Keynes's economy of public deficit spending. The Green New Deal then describes a political agenda that is trying to counter the ecological and social challenges of the twenty-first century using a similar recipe. The advantage of this is that the GND provides a framework that transcends isolated problems and starts to acknowledge the need for a change in the system. The challenge is to make sure that this term—GND—goes beyond "business as usual" and "piecemeal engineering", substantially upgrading the given operating system, "changing the rules of the game" and ending with a "new societal contract". This needs to include a reform of the care economy and social infrastructure programs, as well as investment in technological and digital infrastructure. To date, apart from the demand for "green investment bonds" (European Investment Bank), regulatory efforts and systemic changes to the financial system have not formed part of any national, EU or US program. If these "changes to the rules" are not considered, the heralded "just transition" into a new era will remain no more than a greenwashing process in which we appease one another but fail to make any meaningful change.

44. See Mitchell (2017)

45. To note: In the same year that the UN published the SDG agenda, Pope Francis published the encyclical *Laudato Si'* (2015), which in part complements the UN SDGs. Whereas the UN goals focus on management and global development, where regions have to "catch up" with the overall process of globalization, wealth and growth, *Laudato Si'* embraces a different perspective. Here, the commons are considered to be a gift to humanity that has to be fostered and cared for instead of managed. From this perspective, *Laudato Si'* is a declaration of interdependency, where all living species are interconnected with each other non-hierarchically and should not be subjected to the dictates of modern technology and finance.

Chapter 2
Beyond the Mantra of Traditional Finance: Significance and Limits of the Conventional Approach

2.1 The Relevance of Finance

Modern finance has profoundly influenced almost all aspects of human society and every aspect of our personal lives. To some extent it has become the basis of all economic decisions and investment strategies, social and ecological programs and even political decisions. Combined with new technologies, finance has become both the single most beneficial and the single most detrimental factor affecting the planet and our future. The 2008 crisis in particular revealed unanticipated but significant limitations to our financial system, which prevent us from better understanding and steering finance for the benefit of humanity and our planet.[1] These limitations are most evident where global commons are concerned. One of them is the idea of the rational market and its agents as possessing a utility-maximizing function.

However, new empirical findings in different disciplines—including in environmental science, psychology, systems theory and indeed finance itself—all seem to lead in the same direction, towards a world that is very similar to the view held by Eastern mysticism, especially Taoism: a world where everything is connected to everything, everything is in constant motion and everything needs to be balanced out in order to achieve a more sustainable future.

According to Thomas Kuhn,[2] paradigm shifts happen when too many anomalies occur within an academic field, scientific discipline or societal context, or when an increasing number of irregularities cannot be sufficiently explained within an existing scientific paradigm.[3] This requires a change both in mindset and in the modus operandi, that is, both in the way we think and in the way we deal practically with the challenges ahead. With regard to our particular topic of finance, the three most prominent challenges we are currently facing are physical risks, which include extreme weather, temperature and sea level rise as well as the impact of the loss of biodiversity and pandemics; then transitional risks, which describe the costs of

The original version of this chapter was revised. The correction to this chapter can be found at
https://doi.org/10.1007/978-3-030-64826-8_7

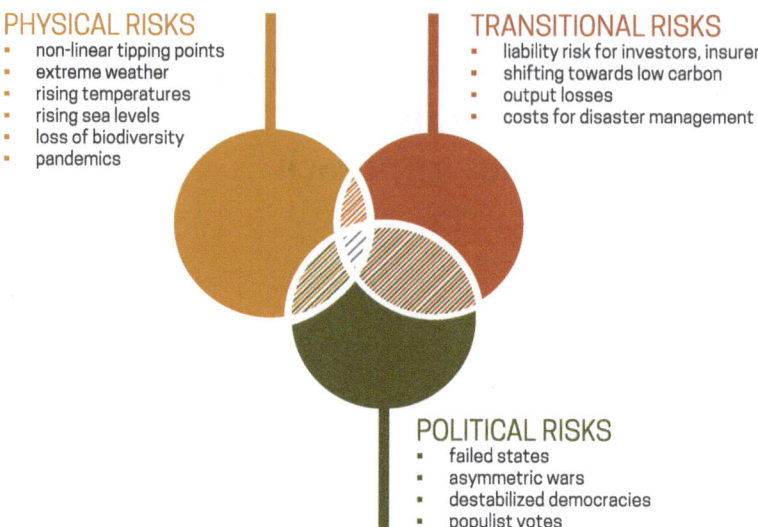

PHYSICAL RISKS
- non-linear tipping points
- extreme weather
- rising temperatures
- rising sea levels
- loss of biodiversity
- pandemics

TRANSITIONAL RISKS
- liability risk for investors, insurers
- shifting towards low carbon
- output losses
- costs for disaster management

POLITICAL RISKS
- failed states
- asymmetric wars
- destabilized democracies
- populist votes

Graph 2.1 Facing the risks

shifting towards a low-carbon economy, increased liabilities for investors and insurers, output losses and costs for damage control; and lastly political risks, which refer to potential asymmetric wars and failed states. The aim of this chapter is to demonstrate that an economic paradigm shift in Kuhn's sense of the word is required in order to finance commons. And this implies a change both in our way of thinking and in our way of doing things (Graph 2.1).

2.2 Money and Finance as a Social Construct

Money is neither a thing nor a natural law. It does not arise naturally in any given society, but is the result of a human invention, backed up by a narrative shared by billions of anonymous humans interacting with each other around the clock in order to improve the welfare of each individual and society as a whole. The more stable, reliable, and trustworthy this social construct is, the more powerful it will become to achieve the respective purpose each society has set itself. It is reciprocal trust and mutual tolerance that have the ability to catalyze greater human potential. The opposite is true, too. The weaker, more unstable, more speculative, unreliable and unfair a system is, the less capacity it has to exert its full positive influence on society and its members. This is the same for any social organization and invention such as language, the internet, or the legal system, which can be used for good or bad. The ultimate purpose of a monetary system should be that of promoting, facilitating and supporting human welfare, security and wellbeing. In this sense the financial system acts like a catalyst, enabling multiple interactions and infinite transactions between humans beyond space and time without becoming altered in the process. However, the more complex and interactive a society becomes, the more carefully the design of this invention needs to be scrutinized.[4]

In this sense, the financial system is one of the most powerful tools facilitating societal achievements that humans have ever invented.[5] Rather than rejecting the internet, our language, the marketplace, and governmental institutions when they serve less noble or ethical purposes, we try to improve their design or usage and minimize their negative externalities. This should also hold true for the financial system. Because the monetary system affects so many aspects of human activity, its steering power should increase benefits and achievements every time it is used. But money not only enables commercial transactions. It is able to facilitate human welfare from a much larger perspective, converting individual goods or services into almost any other desirable social good. It is the place where a bag of corn literally can be converted into a PhD or improved health, into a trip around the world or the construction of a house. In this sense, the financial system not only catalyzes and multiplies, but also potentially transforms our society, channeling the liquidity towards where it can create the most welfare for most people.[6] Historically, it is not the intrinsic value of the money itself, but the underlying real economy of goods and services that operates as the driving force to determine specific financial assets, monetary and fiscal tools and the required regulatory efforts.

The monetary system becomes even more prominent when a society has under- or

> Money is the road to freedom or to serfdom, depending on how it is designed.

unutilized resources. And there are plenty of these. Unlike in former times, when we did not have the scientific evidence or the knowledge to treat malaria, properly educate children or cope with global warming, and unlike times when systemic unemployment, poverty and hunger were considered a social given, we now have the means, the knowledge, the expertise and the technology to solve these challenges. To be more concrete: as a human species, we have demonstrated—on a regional level—how to achieve full employment and eradicate poverty and hunger. However, we have failed to set a reliable system in place to do so at a global level. This explains why unreliable employment still affects over 1.5 billion people globally, why 2 billion people are not even participating in the labor force, and why underemployment affects more than 75% of the labor force in some countries. In sum, over a third of the world's human capital is not being used properly to unleash the potential that lies in each individual.[7] Just imagine a social organization set up to meet all the requirements needed to unleash the full potential of humanity. Such mechanisms are still waiting to be developed, organized, channeled and distributed properly.

Our current monetary system thus operates far below the level necessary to achieve full employment and cope with environmental issues such as global warming and the decline of biodiversity while meeting basic needs such as access to health care, education and food for the global community. But it is precisely the design of this monetary system that can convert these challenges into opportunities waiting to be taken. By reversing our perspective and putting the individual with all her or his potential and possibilities at the center of the equation, we will be able to adapt our monetary system around the individual instead of adapting the individual to the monetary system.

Historically, the greatest achievements have been accomplished best when a social organization has put personal freedom and creativity, individual rights and entitlements at its core and spread this notion to the greatest number of people.[8] This human-centered approach not only is true for the age of the Renaissance and Enlightenment, but should also be true for the financial system: the ability to act freely, to self-efficaciously realize one's own aspirations, while simultaneously respecting and supporting the equal individual rights of others. Any monetary design should include such a human- or person-centered approach to promote societal welfare as a whole.

A human resource becomes a resource only when it is recognized as such by all of society. This is true likewise for all global commons: from fresh air to protecting biodiversity, from avoiding global warming to accessing health care for all, from achieving universal education to having full employment, shelter and peace—all of these can be acknowledged and recognized as global common goods. The power of the social construct of the money system lies in the fact that it allows humans to convert sand into silicon chips, organic matter into petrol, or molecular compounds into pharmaceutical drugs. But how does money come into the world?[9]

How does money come into the world?

- Money is a social invention, a legal act and a convention, not a natural law. Accordingly, we can change it.
- About 97% of the money in circulation is generated through the commercial banking system by a credit creation process.
- About 3% is created by the central banks (base money and/or cash). This 3% also acts as a loan to the commercial banking system.
- In modern times, central banks generate base or hot money as loans and purchase state or corporate bonds as collateral. This is how money comes into the world.
- This procedure increases their balance sheets, stabilizing our economy and our society as a whole. Theoretically, there is no limit to the amount of central bank loans possible.

The primary purpose of any money system is to create wealth for all in society. It has a quantitative aspect, measured in the volume of money injected and circulating in the economy, as well as qualitative aspects, measured by where money goes and what is does. However, adapting our current system for the good of humanity requires intellectual courage, scientific clarity and bold political decisions. The TAO of Finance provides such a path.

Our thesis is therefore: if we had a different monetary design—honoring the given system, but enlarging it towards a parallel optional currency system—mainly designed to promote global common goods, the currently untapped potential of humanity could be released, enabling us to live in a more sustainable, more peaceful and fairer world.

Traditionally, however, we have viewed sustainability only as a triad of social, ecological and economic issues, trying to find the smallest common denominator between the three components, and have left the monetary system out of the picture. This is misleading. Sustainability should rather be viewed as a funnel or an attractor in which the monetary system occupies a central role. And we will further demonstrate that the sustainability of living systems is more about achieving balance between their vital components than about searching for the smallest denominator. Any discussion about the future needs to include the role that money plays in that future. And contrary to popular belief, money is not tangible, nor has the form of a commodity. It is more akin to a law (G.F. Knapp 1924) that we have the ability to change. The following graph illustrates this (Graph 2.2).

It is thus not because of a lack of alternatives or a lack of intelligence that we are unable to establish a different monetary system; it is because of the false narrative we have been forced to believe. Although we repeatedly have witnessed the misalignment between our current financial system and the funding of global common goods, our deeply held belief in the narrative that there is only one form of monetary system has prevented us from questioning the design of the system itself.[10] So it is not left or right, Keynesian or Austrian, Marxist, institutionalist or behaviorist economics that will determine whether we can finance our commons. It is rather the psychological way we think and perceive the world through linear versus parallel thinking.[11]

In other words: if we seriously integrated the empirical evidence of systems theory, neurobiology, and both clinical and social psychology into our thought process, a completely different monetary system would emerge.[12] Rather than following the paradigm of economic growth first and partially redistributing revenue through taxation, fees or philanthropy to finance commons second, we argue in favor of designing a parallel optional monetary system that matches the nature of the global commons.

2.3   Conventional Financial Tools in the Era of the Anthropocene

In the era of the Anthropocene,[13] where everything is connected with everything, we as a species do not know when, where and to which degree we and our children will be affected by negative externalities. Unlike in the past, we do not have any real exit option, "Plan B" or "reset button", but are trapped within our world's planetary boundaries.[14] This fundamentally changes the way we are able to create the wealth of nations.

Money system
Real economy
Social world
Ecology

Ecology

Real economy

Social world

Graph 2.2 The missing link—the monetary system

The debate on how to finance our commons is closely connected to current economic debate. Multiple approaches exist on how best to stimulate the economy and create wealth to finance our commons, and the table below provides an overview of the most prominent scholars and their arguments.[15] Each perspective contains robust empirical, theoretical and intellectual arguments. If readers have the time and intellectual courage to dig into this complex debate, they either may become frustrated because the opposing positions cannot be reconciled, or they may end up with a halfway position where the expected results are suboptimal, expensive, inefficient and far removed from any Pareto-optimal allocation. We continue to buy into the stories of trickle-down effects on the political right or redistributive mechanisms on the political left as the main means of gaining sufficient liquidity and purchasing power to finance our future. These are both recipes of the past, not for the future. The future of finance needs to be radically different from the past, and this requires a shift in mindset. We are facing unprecedented challenges, for which such siloed and singular solutions no longer are adequate. Systemic thinking is needed, and this shift in our mindset will lead to a change in governance, in technology, in the monetary system. Not the other way round.

At its core, the intellectually complex discussion boils down to the controversy of stimulus versus austerity or supply versus demand economies. All of the above-mentioned arguments share a threefold bias: first, none of the positions explicitly consider the SDGs[16]; second, none of them question the structure of the financial and monetary system itself; and third, the arguments all use the same psychology. Additionally, these three biases share an overarching bias, which is that they use the lens of linear, perspectival thinking as opposed to parallel thinking (Table 2.1).[17]

Two tools traditionally have been used to achieve more growth: regulatory efforts to better control international trading and payment systems; and financial redistribution, or more specifically the manner and extent to which we distribute wealth to social and ecological projects. Financial redistribution procedures, of which the Marshall Plan[18] is a well-known example, represents what we refer to as "end-of-pipe" financing—generating revenue from the taxation of economic goods and services and partially redistributing it to social and ecological projects.[19] While regulatory efforts and financial redistribution mechanisms are both related, they take on a different significance when considered within a set of interventions—referred to here as a "six-pack". Their importance and sequence of use changes in view of the limited time for action available to us in the Anthropocene Era.

We can take this argument one step further. The body of research identifying the components of economic growth and so-called total factor productivity (TFP) now spans 75 years. It concludes that education accounts for about 14% of TFP and technological innovation for approximately 19%. The factors underlying the remaining two thirds of economic growth are in fact unknown. This is true not only for OECD countries, but for developing countries as well. Thus "bottom of the pyramid investments" have worked in some countries but not in others, without any specific reason for this having been identified. GDP growth is thus a means or a measure, not a goal in itself. The total factor productivity will continue to remain a mystery whether we have solved real problems or not. From an empirical

Table 2.1 The conventional debate on growth and wealth

Proponent	Position	Argument
Larry Summer (2015)	Secular stagnation	High savings and low consumption lead to low mass aggregate demand, leading to low growth rates, low interest rates, high unemployment and a high tendency toward deflation.
Alvin Hansen (1939)	Demographic bias	Aging (mainly in Europe, Russia and Japan) is leading to lower mass aggregate demand and therefore to lower growth rates.
Robert Gordon (2016)	Supply-driven approach	The lack of real technological innovation is causing low growth stimuli, reducing the leverage for distribution and wealth.
Barry Eichengreen (2014)	Human capital theory	Low public investment, mainly in education and on-the-job training, is causing low growth rates.
Ken Rogoff (2015)	Hyper-debt cycle	Following the 2008 crisis, states are overindebted. Ongoing deleveraging and credit restrictions prevent agencies from investing in the future.
Richard Koo (2015)	Balance-sheet recession	In the aftermath of the 2008 crisis, corporate/state balance sheets are overindebted, preventing them from investing in future markets. Premature budget constraints are prolonging this process.
Paul Krugman (2012), G. Friedman (2016), Friedman-Romer-Romer debate	Neo-Keynesianism	Declining aggregate mass demand requires a skillful intervention in the form of an expansive monetary policy and fiscal expansion. The controversy here is whether the stimulus is only short term or causes positive long-term effects.
James Galbraith (2014)	Structural Keynesianism	The lack of mass demand requires the institutional design to be strengthened, mainly through "big governance", including social security systems, trade unions and progressive taxation; raw material price volatility, dependence on fossil energy and technologies replacing jobs are causing a further decline in growth rates.
John Foster and Robert McChesney (2012)	Marxism/ Communism	The tendency toward global monopolization and financialization is what is causing stagnation in demand, growth and jobs.
Mitchell, W. et al. (2019)	Modern monetary theory	Monetary policy oversteers fiscal policy; savings and taxes are not the only sources of public funding; sovereign states can create money in order to solve real societal challenges as long as there is no inflation; zero budget approach.

standpoint, each economic growth episode appears to be historically and geographically unique. However, the underlying problems are the same: poverty, hunger, global warming, pandemics and so on. Traditionally we continue to solve problems by growing first and deciding how to redistribute the money through taxation and fees to solve them second. Because we remain unable to identify the major components of the economic growth process, we should, in all fairness, abandon our linear thought process and research in favor of a problem-centered approach that generates the liquidity required in a wise manner to solve the challenges of poverty, climate change, and loss of biodiversity and create reasonable jobs. Whether GDP is growing or not should then remain a statistical purpose.[20]

2.4   The Six-Pack

Up until now, development needs have been financed primarily through crowding-in private sector financing, conventional public sector funding and philanthropic commitment. Yet the public sector is over-indebted, over 15 trillion USD in state bonds are returning negative yields, more than 40% of corporate bonds are issued with negative interest rates (up to 2020), private cash deposits of over 12 trillion USD remain unproductive, and institutional investors are sitting on a carbon bubble exceeding 40 trillion USD, forcing them to write off substantial parts of their assets.[21] In fact, we are in a paradox, deflationary situation: on the one hand, we have millions of unemployed people, social challenges on a global scale (access to health care and pre-schooling, gender inequality, hunger and poverty) and unprecedented universal challenges (global warming, biodiversity loss, air pollution).[22] On the other hand, there is a lot of liquidity, but it is either unproductive, unsuitable or unavailable to finance our future. Conventional financial engineering appears to be insufficient in scale, speed and scope to meet these pressing financial needs. Instead, the world community is too busy repairing, stabilizing and refunding the existing system to address the problem. The financial gap has become so large that we need to discuss fundamentally new ways of financing and identify fundamentally new channels to support this agenda. As there is a search for private and institutional investors finding new future markets, there are plenty of options. Some of these markets will be small, others large in scale, for both small and big money. The following list illustrates some of these new future opportunities ahead:

New future green moonshot for small and big money

1. Care economy (nursing, kindergartens, social work, teaching)
2. Implementation of basic needs (food, shelter, security, sanitation)
3. Investment in regional smallholders in agriculture (irrigation systems, extreme weather insurance, seed provision)
4. Public infrastructure (sewage, public transportation, land registry, financial and tax offices)
5. Investment in renewables including decentralized storage and power grid
6. Ocean clean-up programs
7. Reforesting the Sahara (including humus formation, protecting local biodiversity)

However, all these new future green moonshots are hybrids that no longer fit into the conventional financial operating system. Achieving them will require new investment tools and financial engineering. But before we can describe such new tools, we first find ourselves confronted with the carbon bubble.

2.4.1 Monetizing the Carbon Bubble

The carbon bubble is part of a larger picture expressed in the UN SDGs (2015). Fossil fuels generate CO_2 emissions that lead to global warming, and global warming is now considered to be the single largest threat to humanity. Over 80% of our primary energy supply comes from CO_2-producing fossil fuels and biofuels, which are deeply enmeshed in our global economy; this percentage has not changed since 1971.[23] This means that any increase of 1% in disposable income is still associated with an increased energy demand of almost 1% on a global level, despite local and regional differences and efforts to reduce the carbon load. However, since the 70s, the total primary energy consumption has tripled in absolute terms. Robust scientific evidence has shown that going beyond the 2 Degree Scenario (DS) will cause huge disruptions to our planet in the form of extreme weather patterns and the loss of biodiversity and natural habitats. It will significantly affect human life due to forced migration, a rise in uninhabitable regions and food insecurity due to harvest loss, to name but a few factors. While we traditionally use a linear perspective to look at future trends, we will increasingly find ourselves confronted with non-linear tipping points, where no return to the earlier status quo is possible.

If we take the 2DS as a political benchmark, then the so-called carbon bubble represents the financial correlate to this scenario. It will affect approximately 23–100 trillion USD in assets over the next two decades. This large range in estimation relates to the extent to which the fossil fuel value chain is taken into account. The graph below illustrates the following: there is a 60% chance of remaining within the 2 Degree Scenario if we burn 1500 Gts. Of the 2000 billion tons of fossil reserves still available and already accessed on this planet, only 1000 Gts can be used before our likelihood of remaining within the 2DS drops below 90%, even with future food production and deforestation calculated in. The rest of the fossil fuel reserves consist of stranded unburnable assets that need to remain in the ground.[24] Would we be ready to step on a plane with a 60% probability of crashing? (Graph 2.3)

This means that most listed companies will have to depreciate their balance sheets by up to one third or more. Institutional investors with skin in the game in assets dependent upon fossil fuels will be forced to write off substantial parts of their investments.[25] Investment in carbon-lowering measures is required. Table 2.2 provides the top ten out of the top 100 CO_2 drawdowns.

Flogging a dead horse: The collapse of the carbon bubble will lead relatively quickly to a depreciation of large cohorts of pension funds and privately funded social security systems, in particular those of the baby boomers. But as long as no alternative scenario is available, rational investors will stick to their assets as long as possible and resist change—even if the horse they are flogging is already dead. In the period up until 2017, only 2.5 trillion of the estimated 23–100 trillion USD carbon bubble was divested.[26]

Much has been written about the UN SDGs, but only little about how to finance them. Currently we are following the protocol of reverse engineering: the financial capacities of our cash positions, the claims and the corporate script of the given

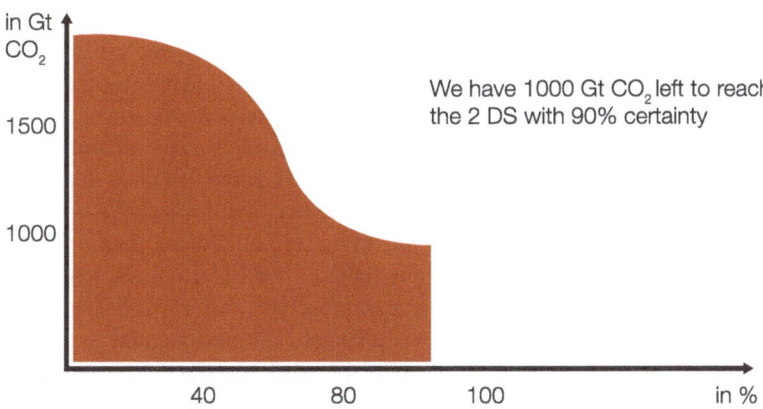

Graph 2.3 The budget left to meet the 2 Degree Scenario

Table 2.2 Top 10 out of the top 100 CO_2 drawdowns until 2050 with the potential to reduce the CO_2 load by up almost 600 gigatons. (Project Drawdown 2019)

		Total atmospheric CO_2 EQ reduction in gigatons by 2050
1	Refrigerant management	89
2	Onshore wind turbines	84
3	Reducing food waste	70
4	Plant-rich diet	66
5	Tropical forests	61
6	Educating girls	59
7	Family planning	59
8	Solar farms	36
9	Silvopasture	31
10	Rooftop solar panels	24
	Total	580

institutions come first and the SDGs are adopted accordingly. This is true for almost all institutions involved—WB, IMF, UNCTAD, WTO, UN DESA, IATF. The goals come last. As the donors are exclusively nation states, the most prominent question of all NGOs and IGOs is: which SDG can we best resell to our customer or client? National donors' preferences shift and are heterogeneous by nature. For example, erasing poverty (goal 1), reducing inequality (goal 10) and increasing peace on earth (goal 16) have had little success in finding the right donor states. This leads to a partly conflicting, asynchronized process, where the different priorities of member states are expressed in different forms of commitment and impacts accordingly. This finally leads to unilateral biases, where the poor regions are left behind. We are going to describe a social invention that is able to overcome these biases.

As we will discuss in greater detail later on, calculations demonstrate that the world community requires an additional 4–5 trillion USD every year to finance our future. About one third of the SDGs are suitable for private investment, while two thirds refer to global commons. If we had endless time, our options would be unlimited. We keep pretending that we are in such a situation—but we are wrong, of course.[27] We have 10–15 years at most to significantly change the course of this planet for the better or for the worse. We do not have limitless time for academic discussions, further field studies, randomized controlled trials, or political propaganda or maneuvering, nor for endless expert panels or manipulated fake news campaigns. As our time is restricted, our options too become limited. We must carefully choose the tools and interventions with the highest likelihood of changing the course of this planet for the better. And we may have to make bold decisions and adopt a multi-step approach to enable the world community to shift towards a more sustainable future. The longer we wait, the more limited the options and the window for opportunities will become. In the following, we will introduce the so-called "financial six-pack". It provides a rationale for operating within the given limits and will allow us to shift our society towards a sustainable model, ensuring our grandchildren's and great-grandchildren's survival:

The financial six-pack

1. Regulation–harmonization–transparency
2. Taxation, fees and subsidies
3. Impact funding
4. Ex-swap strategies
5. Private-public partnerships/private-citizen partnerships
6. Parallel currencies

A mix of policy instruments is necessary to tackle the challenge of financing our future. The six most relevant financial engineering tools to do so and establish a more sustainable common future at the same time are structured like a staircase (see graph below). This stepped approach is sensitive to time, to the capacity for collective action, and considers a balance between current and future generations.[28] It builds upon the wisdom and experiences we have gained in traditional finance in the past (regulatory efforts, taxation, impact funding) and extends that wisdom and those experiences into the future, adapting and enriching the instruments in question according to the challenges ahead. In general it has the following rationale: the more time available and the stronger and denser the multilateral agreements on which global transactions are built, the more likely it is that the lower, more traditional steps are favored. Conversely, the less time we have and the more multipolar or bilateral our world becomes, the bolder and more unconventional the monetary and financial decisions must be, as embodied in the higher steps.

Whereas literature and empirical evidence concerning the lower steps is increasing, there is less awareness of the upper steps of our staircase. In fact, the phrase "tragedy of the horizon" (M. Carney 2015, 2016) has been used to describe this issue. There is a 25- to 30-year time lag between initial carbon emissions and global warming, the resulting climate impact and the discount of any future impact. If this is not taken into consideration, the future will be over before it has even started.[29] As neither the Paris Agreement nor the UN SDGs contain any politically binding criteria, a multi-step approach is required.

2.4.2 Regulation—Harmonization—Transparency

Since 2008 in particular, efforts to regulate the international payment and trading system have gained momentum. Most, if not all academic and political attention has focused on regulatory efforts that seek to avoid, prevent and manage future crises. There is general agreement that financial crises, especially idiosyncratic ones, cannot be predicted, and that systemic crises require additional regulatory efforts to insulate the real economy from these more intrinsic perils. There has been a wealth of proposals, most of which focus on singular codes of conducts and rules, and some of which suggest replacing the entire system with an alternative—past examples include the Chicago Plan in the 1930s, the introduction of gold standard, and its abandonment in the 1970s.

Discussions cover aspects such as greater transparency and accountability, increased sound regulation, international cooperation and reinforced institutions, Basel III (plus),[30] the recapitalization of the International Monetary Fund (IMF) and the World Bank (WB), a shift to more macro-prudential policy tools, and more surveillance strategies such as early warning exercises, mutual assessment programs and peer reviews. This debate also refers to a variety of contributions on a different set of risk assessments, like market-to-model versus market-to-market, the so-called "too big to fail" argument, bonus programs for top managers, the impact of bail-in strategies along a liability cascade and contagion effects (from stock owners to borrowers to clients to the taxpayer),[31] whether rating agencies should serve as a public good and so on. This list is not complete nor fully up-to-date, as regulatory efforts since 2008 alone would have filled a volume of some 35,000 pages. And this process has not yet come to an end. The argument on regulatory efforts needs to be more general and fundamental: is regulating the monetary system currently in place the best way to achieve a maximum of output with regard to resilience, efficiency and sustainability? Regulatory efforts tend to be behind the curve, despite their ability to adapt to historical events. What if all these regulatory efforts produce a false sense of control over manifest reality? What if all these preventive regulatory efforts fail? What if regulation of the given system is a suboptimal or even wrong approach, like trying to put toothpaste back into the tube, making the overall system even less resilient to future adverse shocks? If we cannot predict idiosyncratic and random crises and events like black swan effects, but want to stop them from becoming systemic risks, then regulating the given system may produce only limited results. It is somewhat like operating on the heart of runner in an "Iron Man" competition while he is actually running. However, regulation has a moral and economic point to consider: a completely unregulated market means no protection for children or the vulnerable ones, and hence is like forcing your six-year-old child to work on the streets shining shoes instead of going to school and becoming an MD, a teacher, an engineer or a physicist.

When we constantly regulate a system, we admit that we are unable to rely on its self-regulating or autopoietic power, and thus implicitly admit that there is something wrong with the system's design. Regulation is just the first step up the staircase.

2.4.3   The Beauty of Taxation, Fees and Subsidies

Generally speaking, taxation and subsidies reflect the explicit relation of each citizen to the state and the implicit relations between each citizen. Both reflect how we redistribute our wealth and economic activities among ourselves.[32] There are dozens of very clever and thoughtful taxation schemata on how to refinance social and ecological goods and invest in commons, and the debate of the last 50 years has demonstrated the intellectual power of these schemata. During the post-WWII period of high growth rates, redistribution mechanisms involving fees and taxes successfully provided additional sources of revenue and income to finance social and ecological projects and public infrastructure. However, in the absence of high growth rates, redistribution via taxation and fees in a global context has become more problematic.[33] For example, if the poorest 20% of Scandinavian citizens are richer than the richest 20% in developing countries, and if private wealth of 4200 USD already qualifies the owner as belonging to the upper 50% of the world population, the well-established and conventional way of redistributing money through taxation, fees and subsidies may be one political tool among others, but does not have the ability to finance our future.

To further clarify the argument: most financial experts and academics agree that a carbon tax is the best redistributive measure.[34] Theoretically, it would be the mechanism to shift corporations, consumers and states away from the fossil age towards a low-carbon economy.[35] But the argument has several flaws. Firstly, implementing a carbon tax would require a high level of global consensus, as states and corporates would otherwise be incentivized to avoid the tax. Secondly, a carbon tax would have a massive impact upon the entire value chain.[36] Currently, the carbon pricing in the EU ETS countries is below 10 USD per emitted ton of carbon dioxide. To remain within the 2DS, a barrel of CO_2 would need to cost between 75–100 USD.[37] And this increase would need to happen within the next 10–15 years and requires huge alternative investments. This means that most products along the value chain would face massive price and cost pressure, with hugely disruptive social consequences that are next to impossible to anticipate. Finally, fiscal policy is growth dependent: when there is no economic growth, there is nothing to tax.[38] The International Monetary Fund (IMF) estimates the gap between current taxation and the required taxation to be up to 5 trillion USD annually.[39]

In other words, the dilemma is the following: we need to increase the carbon tax and reduce the direct and indirect subsidies for all fossil energy, which will make it possible to lower CO_2 emissions in the atmosphere on a global level. At the same time, we also need to reduce the tax burden and increase subsidies for renewables on a local and global level. Both of these strategies interfere with social and ecological trade-offs on a local to global level, such as overcoming poverty and hunger and protecting biodiversity among others. In such a complex, mixed and unforeseeable situation, technology, taxation, subsidies and regulation are part of the solution, but they are not the primary solution.[40] Focusing only on taxation and regulation overlooks and partly trivializes the speed, volume and magnitude required to ensure the shift we need. Instead, this focus generates endless so-called "socio-ecological paradoxes" and forces us to engage in multilevel re-regulatory efforts to compensate for unwanted social impacts. Such paradoxes are created when we want to do good and avoid harm, but end up creating the exact opposite. For example, if a nation representing 3–4% of the global burden of atmospheric CO_2 decides to exit the fossil age, the corresponding drop in demand for fossil fuel would trigger a decrease in its price, which in consequence would very likely increase consumption in other parts of the world. This so-called "green paradox" (H.-W. Sinn) describes the dilemma of carbon leakage in a global market. Any activity to reduce the dependency on fossil energy is valid only as long as the CO_2 remains in the ground. As long as there are insufficient equivalent alternative investments available, reducing fossil consumption unilaterally is logically counterproductive. What is more, any rational producer of fossil energy will be incentivized to over-extract their resources short term in order to maximize their portfolio and reinvest the revenue elsewhere.[41] And any intervention in the real economy alters the multiple equilibriums of prices and volumes, demands and supplies in the market in multiple ways. In this sense, taxation, fees and subsidies can cancel each other out or neutralize their original intention, resulting in a next to zero net effect. It is similar to prescribing a drug. If a doctor prescribes more than three or four drugs simultaneously, potential interactions and side effects cannot be ruled out completely. The result will remain unclear and fuzzy to some extent. The given forms of taxation (carbon tax, heritage, wealth) are end-of-pipe strategies, where we do whatever we want in the first place but tax the results and then try to do good second. Instead of using the taxation schema as a tool of punishment, we should design it as a positive reinforcement measure. Each time we generate additional liquidity, yields or revenue and tax them, we enhance the initial process towards greater sustainability.

2.4.4   The Impact of Impact Funding

Ratings are a wicked problem. On the one hand, it is crucial that we learn to differentiate between "green" and so-called "brown" or "black" investments. However, studying corporate reality reveals that only about 20% on average of all tangible and intangible assets as well as short-term and long-term spillovers can be managed and mitigated within the corporation.[42] Anything above this would cause the business to collapse. We can differentiate between three levels (Table 2.3).

The following graph illustrates the proportion and the dynamic between the three elements (Graph 2.4).

Corporate profits are near a record high, but are realized on the basis of huge, unpriced negative externalities. These negative externalities are transferred to taxpayers and governments. We have seen above that SCR measures are able to deal with at most 20% of spillovers, meaning that 80% need to be managed on the systemic level. Disruptive and involuntary systemic changes can lead to unprecedented suffering and costs.[43] Any change by design is better than by disaster. It is important to separate the signs and symptoms from the overall root causes. While rating refers to symptoms in the form of further transparency, information and documentation, the root causes lie in the monetary system itself. A systemic change such as this does not mean that we have to do everything all at once and at the same time, but we do have to consider (almost) everything to ensure this integral change.[44]

Generally speaking, investing in something is a commitment to the future. So-called impact investments epitomize future commitment because they consider not only the return in terms of money, but also the social and ecological "impacts" of these investments.[45] The higher the impact, the better. In the last years, capital worth 250 billion USD was divested from the fossil fuel sector and invested in the green sector. The taxonomy of impact funds (brown or black versus green) differentiates between good and bad investments in relation to their impact on social and environmental welfare (a "good" investment would involve no tobacco, no weapons, no coal, no alcohol, no child labor etc.). In this respect, impact funding is the right choice. However, several aspects demonstrate that the matrix underlying impact funds is flawed. Firstly, the volume of funding is far too low and the speed too slow to guarantee any significant shift. Secondly, the approach is too siloed and too micro, maximizing lobby interests without seeing the full picture on a macro level. It thus fails to balance and reconcile the many different invested interests with one another. Thirdly, the impact funding strategy is skewed towards parts of the world with higher SCR (social corporate responsibility)—standards. This occurs at the expense of more vulnerable regions on the planet, where liquidity is most needed. Fourthly, the shift towards green bonds will put a risk premium on the old brown and black bonds, which will make conventional investors resistant to changing their portfolio, or encourage them to simply greenwash their assets. Taken together, this will create further regulatory and documentation requirements but do little to nothing to change the negative impact on the environment.[46] Impact funds remain a complex, well-nigh unresolved story of excluding or banning industries. In 2019, the value of such impact funds, where capital is primarily divested from the fossil sector and moved into the green sector, totaled 502 billion USD.[47] There is even a strong argument for remaining invested in critical industries, in order to maintain control over the executive management and steer them towards greater SCR and higher ESG (ecology-social-governmental) standards. Whereas the difference between a "green", a "brown" (fossil) and/or a "black" (guns, drugs, alcohol, child labor) investment is easy to make in theory, in practical terms such a taxonomy has to take into account all the different business models and corporate shares and interconnected corporate participation. In short: is Volkswagen or Apple green or brown? Is SAP or Deutsche Bank green, brown or black? Those corporates who fail

Table 2.3 Social Corporate Responsibility (SCR)—Sector—System: a three-step approach

1	SCR and ESG criteria on a corporate level.
2	Sector level that implies value chains, customers and clients as well as the social and ecological environment by proxy.
3	Systemic level that requires a shift in the incentives to make it happen.

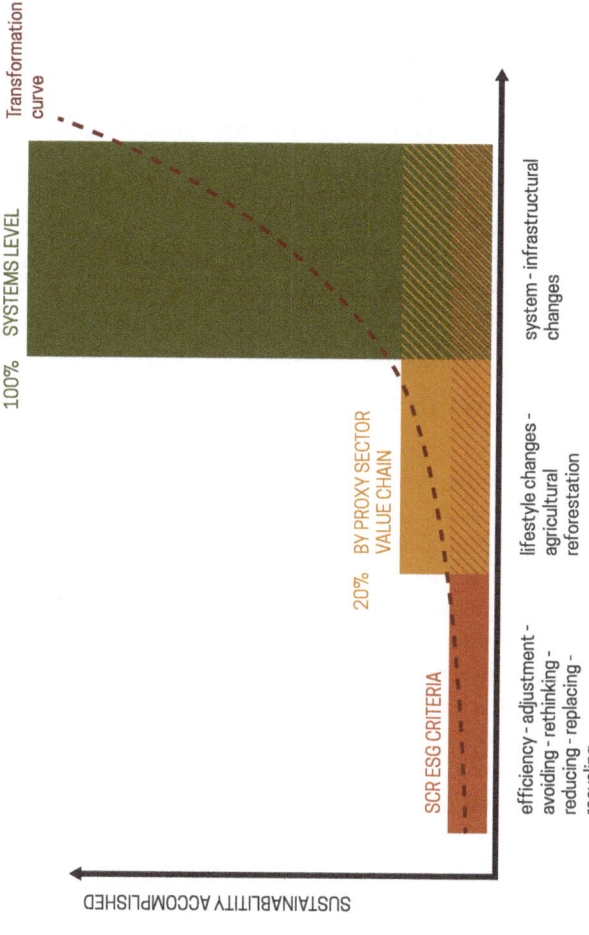

Graph 2.4 From social corporate responsibility (SCR) to sector value chains to systems level

to achieve the "green" label will withdraw their collaboration for fear of paying a higher risk premium on their assets. Finally, the strategy behind impact funding risks having virtually no effect upon the 2DS, as we will see below.[48]

Private vs. public financing of commons: From an investor's perspective, agents who invest in state bonds, pension funds and/or private equity and who are involved in impact funds represent clients' selective interests. These interests are fundamentally mismatched with those of the global commons.[49] Financing the SDGs requires an agent or co-signer with provision and revenue interests representing the global commons themselves. The United Nations, the World Health Organization, and the World Bank are three examples of such agents. In addition, the more connected we are, the more we need to invest in common goods. A real initial impact investment would honor the fact that commons come first and private investment second; it would honor the fact that taxation, fees, donations and other forms of redistributive financing are too slow in speed and too low in volume to ensure the required change. Financing the commons should not be a transitory measure adopted in times of economic crisis, but a constant monetary intervention that ensures ongoing societal transformation towards a sustainable future (Graph 2.5).[50]

2.4.5   From Derivatives to Hybrid Ex-swaps

In the last two decades, derivatives were the new kids on the block. In an unstable economic environment, it was rational for investors to buy first-, second- or third-tier derivatives in order to reduce the risk of failure. The "hot potato" could be handed over to someone else, and at the end of the day, someone always paid the bill—usually the taxpayer. These times are over. The greater the extent of our global interconnection, and the more "systemic" in nature the risk, the less a derivative can help to leverage or hedge the investment. Put the other way around: as long as a risk remains local or sectoral, a derivative is a rational instrument to hedge microeconomic risks. This is due to the fact that buying a derivative can leverage diverging expectations regarding a risk. However, the rise of our global interconnectedness results in risks being shared at a systemic level, where they can no longer be geographically or sectorally isolated. Future expectations, such as pricing in the impact of global warming, are more likely to converge than diverge. This explains the increase in asymmetric shocks, where despite having done everything "right", the agents in question were still hit by the unexpected consequences of negative feedback loops and fat tail events with widespread repercussions. In this situation, using a derivative of any sort as a general global remedy is an irrational financial decision, because instead of reducing risk, they produce further systemic risks and lead to additional costs. A rational investor in the era of the Anthropocene fully understands this risk assessment and therefore requires a different financial environment in order to become invested.

NIMBY (not in my backyard): When the Vatican, for example, switches from brown to green investments, it clears its own balance sheet. However, the situation

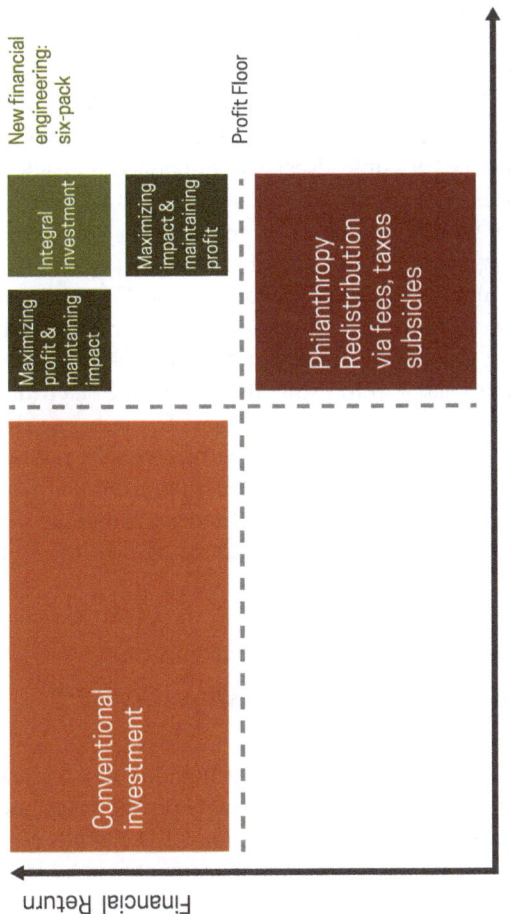

Graph 2.5 Integral view on different investment strategies (adapted from Bozesan 2020)

in the real world has not changed at all, because the brown or black investments—for example a coal site, mine production or child-labor intensive products—from which it has divested will still pollute the air and kill humans, nor will this divestment change the working conditions of the children, whose labor is now under different management that may be less competent than the former. This hot potato will thus be handed on repeatedly, but its ecological and social impact will remain unchanged.[51] In an unstable non-linear complex scenario, only a so-called ex-swap asset makes sense: swap the asset and close down and exit the previous one as fast as possible to avoid asymmetric shocks, non-linear feedback loops and increasing costs for damage control.[52] To be more precise: Because approximately one hundred companies account for 71% of the global carbon footprint, CEOs of these fossil-fuel related companies could receive an executive incentive to encourage them to shut down operations as fast as possible. Respective maturities would be considered. Such an exit strategy is part of the overall solution, as otherwise assets simply change ownership with little to no impact on social or environmental burdens.[53]

If such a global exchange bond or a global swap were created, where brown fossil fuel investments could be swapped over for large-scale green investments, companies and investors would not face extinction but rather experience a very steep transition to different types of investments and businesses. These large-scale projects could include things such as reforesting the Sahara, the electrification of Africa, and many others put forth by various organizations. To overcome shareholder value maximization, most ex-swap assets require a contract with the public sector, providing a co-signer with a long-term perspective. As seen from that perspective, reimbursing and incentivizing the owners of oil, coal and gas across the world community could be cheaper than all the negative spillovers being paid for by the taxpayer or future generations.

2.4.6 Hybrid Private-Public Partnerships (hy-PPP)

The standard argument is that there is abundant liquidity in the market and that we must simply create an environment that will enable private investors to make green investments. Indeed, there are close to 300 trillion USD's worth of financial assets, 150 trillion USD of which are assets under management held by institutional investors. Yet less than 2% of these assets are invested in infrastructure and more than 5% have negative yields.[54] If we think this proposal through to its end, we end up living in a privatized world: the investors' interest is to provide as much purchasing power as possible to fuel the consumption level of the baby boomer generation of the Western world. As mentioned above, this is indeed a feasible scenario for about one third of the SDGs, but not for the other two thirds. These other two thirds are (global) commons and require an entirely different financial approach to ensure our common future. One way to guarantee the financing of the commons is a co-signer principle, with a public protagonist's skin in the game; a protagonist following a different agenda than that of privatizing the world. The federal public sector and the international multilateral development banks (European Investment Bank, World Bank, Asian or African Development Banks) are such candidates.

In a fully connected world, there is no private without public, and hybrids are increasingly common. In fact, this situation requires a closer look at the agents and protagonists involved. In a country with low income, a low tax base, low tax collection and a high debt burden, there are a variety of possibilities for the private and the public sector between them to generate additional liquidity to finance public goods.[55] Each possibility follows a different protocol, risk assessment, liability and type of politics. Done the right way, they reverse short-termism towards a long-term view, reverse maturity towards long-term yield and honor and foster the relevance of public goods and infrastructure for a common sustainable future.

Take the generally accepted UN human right to access to fresh potable water for every human being. Should we privatize this right, so that all freshwater springs become a private equity and these equities are then sold with a private yield, which then increases the wealth of the owners of those springs? As in 2015 over 800 million people did not have access to drinking water,[56] the owners of these springs would have to be taxed to generate sufficient revenue to ensure that those 800 million can exercise their right to drinking water. Instead of this linear process of privatizing commons and taxing the private yields, we could start creating a hybrid private-public partnership (hy-PPP), where 5% of the asset is private and 95% public, for example. The public money comes from a monetary source in the form of parallel green additional liquidity (earmarked for this specific right, see details below). This combination can bring private entrepreneurial expertise and risk assessment together with a public co-signer (like a governmental body or an international development bank); yields, maturity, liability and risks are split respectively and both agents (private and public) have a long-term interest, creating a win-win situation with a constant flow of private revenue and more healthy people, meeting public interests at the same time: there will be fewer negative social spillovers, like health care costs for the treatment of diarrhea. A healthier population can attend school, do business, pay taxes, extend their lives and increase their own wealth and the wealth of nations in parallel. This is true for all global commons: fresh air, access to basic health care, schooling, protecting biodiversity, and reversing global warming among others.

A common is a common and remains a common as soon as we, as a world community, declare it a common. A private equity is a private equity as soon as we, as a world community, declare and define it as a private asset. However, the tools required to finance the two are different. Financing commons as commons requires an entirely different approach than turning them into private equity. Do we want to live in a fully privatized world? No, we don't. Instead of violating the nature of commons, we should adopt the financial architecture to the nature of the commons and not the other way round. This requires a shift in our mindset and a shift in the architecture of our monetary system.

End-of-pipe financing and redistributive measures: The most commonly advocated form of financing our commons is so-called co-financing, which constitutes the core argument in most, if not all economic proposals on financing social and ecological commons.[57] So far, our six-pack staircase has followed this rationale. Co-financing has the following rationale: goods and services freely traded on the market are taxed and this revenue becomes the main source of finance for common goods. In this widely accepted practice, financing commons is secondary and sub-ordinate to the activities of the free market. It is only when the market generates sufficient liquidity and the political will is strong that common goods can be financed. This co-financing strategy is a form of end-of-pipe technology, well known in engineering science: a technology, lifestyle or economic activity that harms our environment (polluting fresh air, for example) is implemented, and a fil-ter at the end of the process (i.e. at the end of the pipe) is subsequently added to avoid too much damage. The co-financing strategy always follows the same ratio-nale. Within any given economic value chain process, humanity is left with a lim-ited, end-of-pipe procedure that eventually dedicates and distributes 0.6–2% of GDP to SDGs or commons.[58] Here, we have to be economically productive first and then can redistribute the "leftovers" to social and ecological projects. But what if we started thinking in a parallel way?

> It is easier to enable new thinking than to get rid of outdated practices. Such new thinking occurs when we leave the well known behind and become involved in new practices.

2.5   Filling the Gap: Parallel Currencies

So far we have been working our way up the six-pack ladder, defining new financial engineering in the Anthropocene. One step—probably the biggest one—is still missing: a parallel currency system. We can define a parallel or complementary cur-rency system, one where something other than the given conventional currency sys-tem is approved as a medium of exchange and a means of payment in order to match unmet needs with underutilized resources. This is necessary because the first five steps of the six-pack staircase are unable to guarantee the volume of liquidity required, the speed we need to generate sufficient purchasing power, and the accu-rate targeting of SDGs necessary to finance our future.[59]

We will see that such a parallel currency system, also referred as a monetary ecosys-tem, offers additional, optional, targeted liquidity or purchasing power; runs in parallel to the given system; is partly designed differently to the well-established monetary sys-tem; uses new technology (mainly distributive ledger technology) with a smart contract; is earmarked to finance primarily our global commons; and lastly operates through complementary monetary channels. Introducing this additional monetary mechanism would make it possible to steer economic decision-making, stabilize the overall econ-omy and orient our entire society towards a sustainable future in a coordinated way.

A parallel currency system could be implemented through new third- or fourth-generation blockchain technology in digital form only, competing with bank depos-its and conventional cash money as a medium of exchange, as a store of value and as an international unit of account. It would operate in parallel to existing currencies and be eligible for the payment of taxes and wages. In the following chapters, we will see that preliminary empirical findings by central banks, communities and the cryptocurrency scene already speak in favor of considering or even implementing such a parallel currency.

The introduction of such a system can achieve a significant welfare effect through targeted and earmarked output.[60] This can happen through several alternative channels: for example as a "citizen dividend", where the additional money is given to private households either directly or via tax reductions, stimulating consumption.[61] Or the money is given to the public sector, stimulating public infrastructure (education, security, health).[62] Besides this "public channel", there are other channels. Here, the money is given to non-governmental organizations (NGOs), small and medium enterprises (SMEs) or local community organizations. In the traditional perspective, we generate unspecific, expansive growth in a first tier and then battle with regulatory efforts and transfer payments systems (fees and taxation) to generate enough money to finance ecological and social projects in a second tier. In this new approach, the money is distributed first. It is this pre-distributive design rather than a redistributive mechanism (end-of-pipe financing) that has the potential to shift and transform our entire society, moving it in the right direction: it will increase the overall welfare effect in the form of millions of green jobs, fewer illicit transactions, additional green growth, an enlarged green tax base, and reduced costs for negative spillovers and disaster management among others. Such a parallel optional currency mechanism would provide targeted, programmable, identifiable, recordable financial transactions and earmarked and dedicated funds, avoiding fraud and corruption. This would create a new parallel marketplace for the 75% of the world population who have not benefited from the existing operating model. And this new mechanism would eventually become intertwined with the traditional sector and would provide central bankers with an additional monetary tool to achieve price stability, employment and the global commons at the same time. We are going to explain this parallel currency approach in more detail in the next chapters. The following graph illustrates the stepped approach (Graph 2.6).

We can further differentiate these findings and come up with a variety of additional financial tools to finance our future. Some examples, where conventional financial tools can be developed further using the parallel mechanism to stabilize and steer our society towards a more sustainable future, are summarized in the table below (Table 2.4).

Let us take this argument one step further. Catastrophe bonds (CAT bonds), pandemic emergency facilities (PEF), forced migration facilities (FMF) and harvest default bonds (HAD) all operate along a similar principle: a region signals a hazard and asks the World Bank for financial insurance assistance. The World Bank or the IMF then issues bonds with an interest rate and a complex contracting agenda to the private sector, which buys up the bonds. The contract determines when and how the private sector must commit to paying for the hazard or alternatively is reimbursed if the hazard has not occurred. Examining harvest default bonds more closely, we see that two thirds of global farming are small enterprises operating for

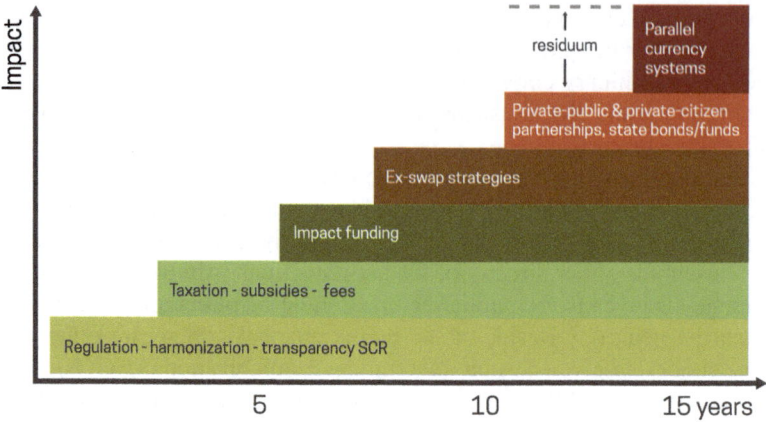

Graph 2.6 The multi-step approach to a sustainable future: the six-pack

Table 2.4 Further concrete examples of how a parallel optional, digital monetary system can help us to finance our future and cope with asymmetric shocks

Green bonds	Catastrophe bonds (CAT bonds) Pandemic-emergency facilities (PEF) Forced migration facilities (FMF) Harvest default bonds (HAD)
Green credit easing	**GreenTLTRO (Targeted Long-Term Refinancing Operations):** Conditioned lending for SME, private households and public sector entities to finance green investment, consumption.
	Green repurchase agreements (Repos) Green assets are eligible to borrow liquidity from central banks. They serve as collateral for financial institutions for short-term refinancing and operate as a criterion in case of a "haircut".
Green quantitative easing	Additional base money issued for developing banks/EIB, operating as financial intermediaries for conditioned green lending.
Green private-public partnerships (PPP)	Performance contracting between the private and the public sector, where the public infrastructure remains in public ownership, and the management runs through private companies.

self-sufficiency. Once a drought occurs, HADs come into play. However, it is unnecessary to loan money from the private sector and reimburse it with a risk premium. A supplemental digital currency, as explained in this text, operating through a non-profit cooperative banking sector and monitored by the UN, could take over this task with less risk and higher yields for the community. In each case, the World Bank's balance sheets increase in the first place. In the case of a harvest default, the World Bank will need to write the event off and decrease its balance sheets in the second place, but millions of farmers are saved from insolvency and able to continue their business. Or take the TLTRO (Targeted Longer-Term Refinancing Operation) programs, well known in Europe and already run by several central banks. In its traditional guise, a TLTRO is a form of conditioned lending to SMEs, private households or public entities. A green TLTRO would then steer additional credit easing towards green investments.

In fact, well-nigh unlimited permutations are possible, as each of the financial facilities is backed up by development banks (such as the EIB or World Bank), funded by central banks, monitored by the UN and enabled through domestic and national agencies. If we are prepared to change our mindset and the underlying narrative about money, unlimited options are possible.[63]

To note: In a general sense, it is about increasing the liquidity available in the market, instead of only transferring money from the given GDP in order to finance our common future. This is expressed in the graphs below. Using this approach, the higher the global consensus is to achieve the lower steps, the lower the necessary effort becomes to achieve all the further steps. For example, if we can come up with a global agreement on regulating tax havens, common accounting standards, harmonized ESG criteria (ecology-social-governmental) and a global carbon tax, the need for ex-swap asset strategies, public contracting and a parallel currency system is then lower. However, the lower the global consensus on the lower steps, the bolder the decisions will have to be regarding the higher steps. Assuming we end up with next to no global governance consensus, but still want to finance our future, we will need to make the effort to install additional parallel liquidity to ensure the transition from a high-carbon society to a low-carbon one (Graph 2.7).

2.6 Conclusion

What is required to finance our future in the era of the Anthropocene is to devise an exit strategy to rapidly phase out high carbon emissions while funding socially critical projects. This will not only guarantee the end of our high-carbon economy, but also lay out a plan to shift to a low-carbon economy while consolidating existing collaterals such as pensions, private insurance and so forth. This procedure requires a new financial mechanism that differs from the approaches taken in the past, such as hedging, leveraging and derivatives.

The Scope, Speed, Scale and Symmetry (4-S) of the challenges ahead should match the 4-S of the solutions. Unprecedented action must be taken or we will have to bear unprecedented consequences. Thinking the unthinkable will be our most advantageous and rational strategy. A successful risk analysis requires us to overcome the executive myopia and linear thinking that currently dominate corporate and public leadership, beyond the "least drama" and the "lowest common denominator" scenarios. These "business as usual" scenarios have simply become far too expensive. What is required instead is an emergency-like transition to a post-fossil era. Finding the fastest and least disruptive way to do this is key, as time is not on our side. The new financial mechanisms described will make the world safer, more resilient, more foreseeable and more certain. Traditionally we have gone to vast effort to regulate the given system with taxed economic activities and increased charity, philanthropy and private pledges, and have redistributed that money to social and environmental projects—with reasonable but still insufficient results.

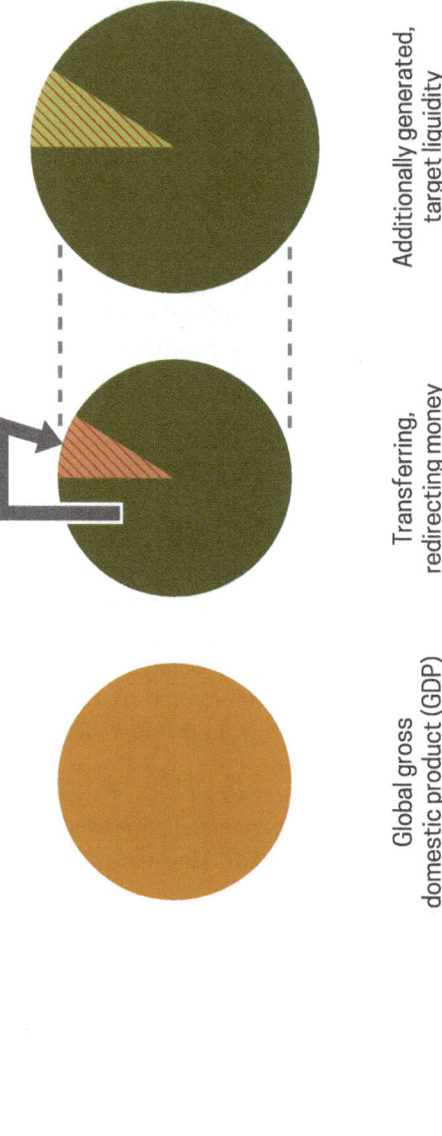

Graph 2.7 Additionally generated liquidity earmarked towards our commons

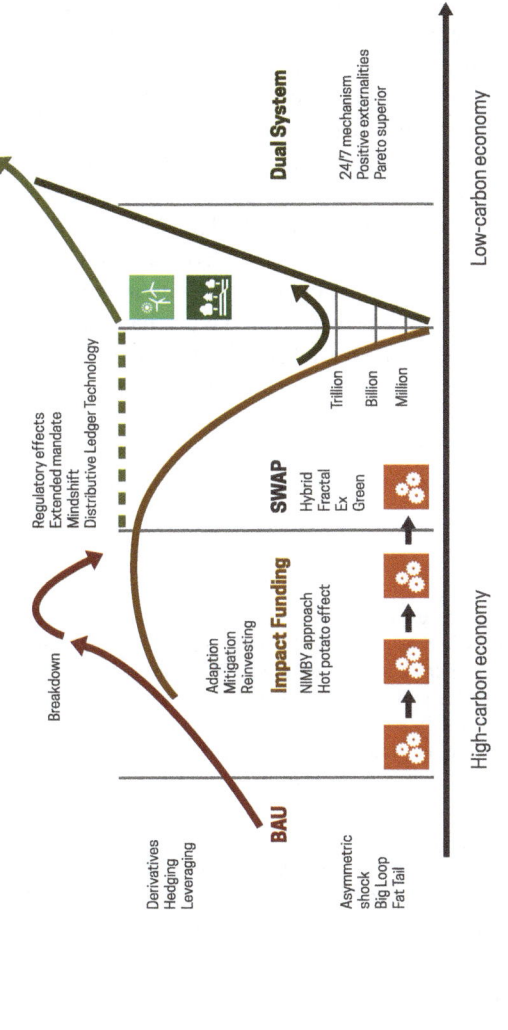

Graph 2.8 New financial engineering to shift from a high to low carbon economy

In conclusion, the multi-step approach presented in this chapter includes: regulatory efforts (consisting of stress tests, agreed accounting systems and total cost approaches); prudent taxation and targeted subsidies; private impact funding with relative benchmarking; a negative ban list and case-to-case management; new ex-swaps that guarantee the phasing out of the fossil age; and lastly hybrid-PPP. Only this combination strategy will allow a longer-term perspective to finally achieve the necessary, but hitherto lacking liquidity and purchasing power through a parallel currency system. Taken together, these steps provide the rationale for such a multi-stakeholder approach.

Considering the 15-year timeline left to achieve the SDGs, the magnitude and additional volume of liquidity required (equivalent to 4–5 trillion USD annually), and the fact that half of the world population either live in autocratic regimes or failed states, achieving a global democratic mandate seems unrealistic. A bold and unorthodox approach on how to finance our future is required. As a world society, accomplishing these six steps in view of the limited existing leverage at a corporate and sectoral level would be possible through systemic change. And if this change is carried out in an intelligent manner, a situation beyond the classic tradeoff between social and environmental challenges would be generated. We would end up with millions of jobs, a cleaner environment and a better world in which to live. The mechanism presented here, or a very similar one, will be the fastest and least disruptive way to ensure this change. Before we start to explain the characteristics of such a parallel complementary monetary system, we will first take a look at the insights that traditional Western thinking provides in support of our argument. The graph summarizes some major new financial engineering to shift from a high to a low carbon economy along a time line (Graph 2.8).

Notes

1. The 2008 crisis was on the expensive side, costing over 10 trillion USD to repair. This includes 40% in lost output, 40% losses in asset values and 20% in banking write-offs (Otte 2019). Traditionally we have spent a huge amount of effort and resources to regulate and stabilize a fuzzy and fragile monetary system. The reality is that the real economy is facing additional costs of up to 2% and the financial sector of up to 20% for these regulatory efforts. And each time there is another crisis, humanitarian and environmental projects fall off the cliff. We should learn to dance with the system instead.

2. See Kuhn (1962).

3. P.A. Hall (1993) took up this idea, applying it to economic and policy procedures, differentiating between first-, second- and third-tier changes. In this explanation, first-tier reflects normal policy changes, second-tier moderate changes and third-tier a paradigmatic shift.

4. One of the remarkable characteristics of the monetary system is that over time it has become more and more subtle and less material, as well as more and more democratized in the sense that more and more people are benefiting from it: from regional barter to bank accounts, to credit lines, to global fundraising and crowdfunding, to microcredit, to electronic payment systems, to regional currencies and cryptocurrencies.

5. See Jacobs (2016); Jacobs and Slaus (2012).

6. Historically we can argue that it was not the Industrial and the French Revolution that triggered the major divergence between Europe and the rest of the world, but innovations in the financial sector, namely paper money, the credit creation process and the fractional money creation process, which were inaugurated by the Swedish Reiksbank and the Bank of England

in the second half of the seventeenth century. These inventions enabled human-centered wealth creation, entrepreneurship and both private and corporate planning and investment that were not possible before.

7. The OECD defines human capital as "the knowledge, skills, competencies and attributes that allow people to contribute to their personal and social well-being, as well as that of their countries" (Keeley 2007). At the bottom line, unemployment or underemployment in a society reflects this society's inability to make full use of each citizen's potential. However, unemployment is not a natural law, but an artifact of the chosen economic system. Each economic transaction sooner or later leads to some sort of human activity and an associated job, otherwise these economic transactions would have been useless to begin with. The equation is the following: assuming 4–5 trillion USD additional liquidity with a multiplier of 2 and a 40-hour workload per week, 2 weeks of sick leave and 4 weeks of holidays with a 5-day working week. With an hourly payment of 8.50–14.00 USD, 350–500 million full-time jobs can be generated. If we further assume 170 million unemployed and 140 million underemployed people globally (ILO 2019), this would match the volume required to finance the SDGs. Not to mention that there are regional differences in purchasing power.

8. Most of the components for change were available already, with one exception: by 1820, human societies had invented the wheel and the printing press and were able to handle fire. We had nation states in place, a banking system and taxation. Mathematics, astronomy, religion, music and arts and knowledge of the human anatomy had been established. Copper, iron, wheat, meat, vegetables and fruit, bread and butter were available too. Most components of daily life were there. Despite this, until 1820 human conditions had not changed very much for centuries if not millennia. Human life remained the same from birth to death and societies as a whole evolved according to a so-called Malthus cycle: economic growth was triggered exclusively by demographic factors. But around 1820, roughly 30 years—just one generation—after the French and American Revolutions, something astonishing happened that unleashed a whole new process different to anything seen before in all of human history: the social empowerment of individuals to use their critical minds, their creativity and new forms of social cooperation. This human-centered approach basically changed everything.

9. De Grauwe (2019).

10. This also called the Goodhart rule. For every regulation implemented, there will be an innovation and efforts to overcome it, rendering the initial regulation next to useless (Goodhart 1984, 2008; Freeman and Soete 2009).

11. See Kahneman (2011).

12. Within a Pareto optimum, any investment in a (non-excludable) common good, whether financed through fees, taxation or philanthropy, is a form of goodwill or charity made to appease guilt that causes suboptimal allocation and inefficiencies, as underfunded commons lead to suboptimal yields in the private and state sector. We will return to this issue in greater detail in Chapter 5, as this argument is significant for a better understanding of the relevance of a dual currency system.

13. See Crutzen (2002); Crutzen et al. (2011).

14. See Rockström and Klum (2016).

15. See Eichengreen (2014); Foster and McChesney (2012); Friedman (2016); Galbraith (2014); Gordon (2016); Hansen (1939); Koo (2015); Krugman (2014); Rogoff (2015) and Summers (2015).

16. We need to admit that we have already lost about 30–40 years in this whole debate. In 1990 it would have been possible to steer towards a different future. After the collapse of the Soviet Union, the world community would have had the chance to utilize the military expenses associated with the Cold War to achieve greater peace, fairness and sustainability on this planet. But instead of using this "peace dividend" for good, the world decided to sign up to the Washington consensus (Williamson 1993), which pursued greater liberalization, privatization and deregulation. We should not repeat the same mistake—privatizing, deregulating and liber-

alizing the world. The result would be to privatize all gains while society as a whole operates as a backstop, making all losses public should a failure occur.

17. Here, psychologists refer to so-called "confirmation bias": we simply reconfirm what we already know, find only what we see and see only what already has been done in the past. Some scholars call this bias one of the most powerful and misleading forms of thinking and concluding (see Oswald and Grosjean 2004; Wason 1968).

18. The *historical Marshall Plan* (European Recovery Plan) had a volume of 13 billion USD in 1948. 10% of this was invested in Germany (Hogan 1989; Sorrel and Padoan 2008). Translated into today's money, the volume would need to be more than 10 times larger, at least 130 billion USD, and the transfer sum would be 13 billion USD (Bureau of Labor Statistics 2019).

19. The *global Marshall Plan* (Gore 1992), a prominent initiative, will only work if the whole financial system remains relatively stable and all actors are able to rely on the expected transactions. This was true after WWII for Germany and also to a large extent when the EU enlargement to the East occurred (Sorel and Padoan 2008). However, the current financial framework operates on highly speculative ground, with offshore havens operating globally (representing around 10% of world GDP according to Alstadsaeter et al. 2018), recurrent currency and banking crises, besides an ever-increasing dark pool and shadow banking sector, high frequency trading, fraud and corruption. Taken together, these factors make reliably sourcing the funds to finance our global commons a near impossible endeavor.

20. Banerjee, A. V. and Duflo, E. (2019).

21. There is a strong argument that focusing on the 2DS and whether global warming is man-made or nature-made is partly misleading. There are at least four other reasons why we need to leave the fossil age behind, beyond its impact on heating up the atmosphere: first, a more decarbonized world that is more dependent on renewables will be healthier for all of us; second, the shift towards a non-fossil economy is cheaper, especially when we tag the price for all the negative externalities involved; thirdly, this new energy source is available in unlimited form (sun, water, wind and geothermal energy) and there will be no "peak energy" for humans; and fourthly, renewables are decentralized and available to everybody. This reduces the potential trading of and military conflict over energy sources and provides a kind of "peace dividend" for the world. In conclusion, even if one is skeptical about global warming and its man-made nature, there are more than enough other arguments to support the shift towards a non-fossil age. For the current discussion, see especially Randers et al. (2018); my thanks to Philipp Schöller for personal comments and remarks on this topic.

22. This can be called a *volcano effect:* imagine a volcano eruption affecting 800 million people on the planet. Within a short period, this population would be living below the poverty line, without shelter, water, sewage, power, limited healthcare and an estimated damage equivalent to 2.3 trillion USD. In such a situation, how is a government to raise the necessary funds? Taxing the existing economy to redistribute money to the 800 million people is not an option. Rather, the 2.3 trillion USD need to be newly generated to finance emergency measures and rebuild infrastructure. Would this measure be inflationary? Not necessarily, it would simply boost the world economy. And it would rebuild the lives of 800 million people back to where they were the day before the volcanic eruption occurred. If there were a tsunami or an asteroid impact we would certainly do the same. However, in the absence of a worldwide catastrophe affecting 800 million people, what would we do? This describes the situation of the "bottom billion", and the answer is that we should do exactly the same. Creating the 2.3 trillion USD in the proper way would boost the world economy with green technology.

23. World Bank Indicators (2015).

24. Citigroup (2015); Lewis (2014); McKibben (2012). If we further consider that the indirect (social) costs of the fossil economy are about 10 times higher (4.9 trillion USD), then it becomes obvious how difficult it will be to detach the insane relations between fossil energy and direct and indirect subsidies. In this calculation, the world community as a whole is subsidizing every ton of CO_2 with about 150 USD. The exact social costs of carbon depend on the

discount rate put on these future costs. The higher that rate, the more the future is discounted or devaluated. Under the Obama administration the rate was 3%, under President Trump it has been increased to 7%. See the informative contributions of Ottmar Edenhofer (2015), Carney (2015), and McGlade and Ekins (2015).

25. To be more precise: an estimated third of oil, 50% of gas and more than 80% of coal reserves must remain unused in order to meet the Paris Agreement. See McGlade and Ekins (2015).

26. Modeling (for example DICE; IAM, UN, Kompas, Stern, IPCC, SSPs) reveal a high range of costs, ranking from 2% of GDP until 2100 to 40% over the same period. This is among other factors due to the implemented discount rate (ranking from 1.5% to over 5%). The higher the rate, the higher the costs we have to bear today. It seems to be next to impossible to come to a consensus for political decisions. The point we would like to make is the following: we don't know the cost (exactly), due to non-linear tipping points. But we know that regardless of whether it is only 2% of GDP or far more, a low carbon economy can generate more jobs, is healthier for the planet, renewables will be cheaper, and as renewables are more decentralized than fossil energy, it will generate a "peace dividend" for all of us. See for the debate: Kompas (2020); Stern (2016) or Nordhaus (2019).

27. We can look at the issue from a time perspective. How highly do we value our future? In psychological terms, a present benefit weighs more than a future one. If we have to forego something now in order to gain something in the future, our instinct is to devalue the future and seek instant gratification. Representative studies from 76 countries covering 90% of the world population reveal that our future is discounted significantly. When asked to postpone a present benefit for one year, study participants demanded a return up to 50% higher. In numbers: how much do we think should we be reimbursed in 10 years' time in order to give up 1000 USD today? Empirically, it is 329,000 USD on a global average; when postponing the benefit 20 years, this sum increases to 3 million USD. The willingness to postpone a present desire for a future one is vanishingly small. Any policy that is built on renunciation, sanctions or punishment in the present in order to gain more benefit, gain or profit in the future will fail. People are simply not prepared to pay that price. Accordingly, we should build our strategy for a common, more sustainable future on different monetary incentives than the ones we are currently operating with. And the TAO of Finance provides precisely these different incentives (Falk et al. 2018).

28. Sachs (2015), Orlov et al. (2018), Claringbould et al. (2019) and Heine et al. (2019).

29. The New York Times special issue *Losing Earth* recently demonstrated that we have lost decades of constructive climate policy (Rich 2018). William Nordhaus (2018a) calculated in the DICE model that a 2DS is unfeasible as it would require "extreme virtually universal global policy measures".

30. See Knight (1933). Harmonizing EU Regulations is not a goal in itself, but a tool to achieve something else. The more we level up regulation on an EU level, the more we streamline the economy and social security systems. This requires huge regulatory efforts that make the system more efficient but less resilient at the same time. Any time there is an asymmetric shock anywhere, it affects other countries unintentionally. For example, a capital market union requires a harmonization of the domestic insolvency law, which is different in each EU country (the discharge period in Germany is three to six years versus one year in other countries, and follows different liability rankings). The same is true for any EU unemployment security. Currently each country is financing this asset in a different way, requiring a huge amount of political regulatory effort. Take the SBBS (Sovereign Bond-Backed Securities), which are bonds that solidarize domestic risks and liabilities, normally issued to create security for society as a whole. In short: the harmonization of regulatory efforts is not impossible, but remains partly unviable or infeasible and puts additional constraints on the system dynamic (ESRB 2018; Esser et al. 2013; McCormack et al. 2017; Véron and Wolff 2016).

31. In particular, the bail-in regulations since 2016 have generated a liability cascade that is new for the banking system. Traditionally and historically, banks have been saved by governments

when they got into trouble. Following the 2008 crisis, the governments have little to no leverage to do so because of increased public debt. The new bail-in strategies basically affect billionaires and ordinary people with small assets in a similar manner. They are both sitting in the same boat and will potentially lose their wealth when the next crisis occurs. New technologies beyond the given banking intermediaries (mainly distributive ledger technologies), alternative investment strategies (tangible assets) and new financial engineering (hybrid swaps, parallel currencies, impact funding) are a rational and expected consequence of these bail-in regulations. See European Commission (2016).

32. Björklund Larsen (2018).

33. Several dozens of proposals on different taxation schemas are available: progressive income taxation, wealth taxation and heritage taxation are the most prominent (see for example McCaffery 1994; Schenk 1999). They are all valid, but are chronically difficult to realize in a democratic political system. For example, if we decide to implement a progressive income tax, we risk those with high incomes leaving the country (Piketty and Saez 2013). If we tax wealth, we are confronted with an endless list of corporate shares that are affected by this tax. This can easily end in a higher price for the consumer, greater unemployment and perhaps lower tax efficiency. These are all forms of regulating, taxing and redistributing money within the given system. If we had a second parallel system in place, at the same time, our leverage to finance our future would increase rapidly and significantly. For the debate see also Saez and Zucman (2019).

34. The most prominent ones are W. J. Nordhaus on carbon tax and the DICE model: the actual price of a ton of CO_2 is between 3–10 USD. The social costs for any additional ton of CO_2 in order to remain below the 2DS are over 230 USD. Nordhaus proposes a Climate Club and classifies the CO_2 load as a club good. EU, NATO or multilateral agreements would create such "clubs", in which members pay dues and can be excluded and non-members are penalized through tariffs on their exports to the club. Club members additionally have economies of scale or public good. See for example Nordhaus's Nobel prize lecture (2018b).

    There is another proposal. Take the numerous calculations demonstrating that *if* we tax international currency transactions (Tobin 1978) or *if* we reduce military public spending (Klein 2015) or *if* we tax the upper 0.0001% ultra-high net-worth individuals (UHNWI), we would gain a certain amount of liquidity that then could be redistributed towards global common goods, such as ending poverty, hunger etc. None of these approaches are wrong, they all have their point and they are all well calculated. But there are several biases at work: there is no global governance that could implement a yield from any global economic activity, and tax procurement remains national. Most taxation, once set up, requires huge regulatory effort to compensate for its negative social spillovers. The current price of CO_2 per ton is an example. We would need an increase in price to over 200 USD globally to ensure a change of the magnitude required to remain within the Paris Agreement. Such a price tag would require tremendous payments to individuals with low incomes, who could not afford to pay the carbon tax. Indeed, taxation is not impossible, but it leaves the dynamic of the current production and consumption chain untouched. The implementation of a dual currency approach changes the playing field: those with a high income are responsible for their asset investment themselves and global commons are financed through different monetary channels, some of which are explained in this text. See also Lietaer et al. (2012).

35. Already discussed in Stern (2006); see also Heal and Schlenker (2019); European Commission (2018) Action Plan.

36. The idea goes back to Pigou (1920), who first introduced environmental taxation as a way to internalize social costs caused by negative externalities. Furthermore, William Nordhaus (2018b), who received the Sveriges Riksbank Prize in Economic Sciences in Memory of Alfred Nobel 2018 for his macroeconomic investigations taking account of climate change issues, mentioned the impact of carbon taxation in his Nobel lecture.

37. See Carbon Market Watch (2017). However, in the period up to 2017, only 5 trillion of the estimated 28–100 trillion USD carbon bubble was devoted to divestment (Arabella Advisors

2016; Citigroup 2015; Lewis 2014). If we take into account the fact that we currently have around 8 trillion USD in cash, 17 trillion in debt yielding a negative interest rate, and over 25 trillion USD invested with and interest return of less than 1%, there is plenty of private money in circulation (Aigner 2019; Desjardins 2017; Van der Knaap and De Vries 2018).

38. If we want to rely on the steering effect of any CO_2 taxation schema towards a low-carbon economy, we need to be aware that the CO_2 tax is a general-purpose tax. Unlike taxing alcohol or cigarettes, issuing a speeding ticket and fining the wrong disposal of waste, fossil energy is part of almost every product or good along the value chain. This means that avoiding CO_2 requires an alternative strategy. Under the current energy mix in OECD countries, a CO_2 tax would have next to zero steering effect. The upper class would simply pay the bill and continue to follow their consumption pattern, while the lower class would be reimbursed through the tax, but have little leverage to change their consumption pattern. The middle class will be affected most by the CO_2 tax, but part of their initial offset will simply be compensated by multiple rebound effects. In net, this taxation program would create a huge and costly administrative apparatus with little net effect on the climate.

39. Parry et al. (2014).

40. Korzeniewicz and Moran (2009). For accurate numbers on the global wealth distribution, see Shorrocks et al. (2018), or Credit Suisse Research Institute (2018). To note: subsidies and taxation—as two major forms of regulation—both can distort the given price equilibrium in a free market economy, mainly due to crowding-out effects, lump-sum taxes and deadweight losses (Freedman et al. 2010).

41. Empirically, the CO_2 load in the atmosphere has increased in absolute terms for 50 years and oil prices have been relatively stable since 1970 (!). In fact, regional withdrawal from the fossil energy supply can cause a so-called "green paradox", as mentioned above in the main text. This describes the undesirable effect that we are unable to cancel out the global supply of fossil energy with a policy that encompasses only saving energy. A regional reduction of demand by saving energy thus lowers global market prices. This could make things worse. In figures: Germany creates 2.3% of the global carbon footprint. China and India generate 60% of their power supply through coal, Poland 80% and South Africa 88%. If Germany were to withdraw from coal, these countries would be at a competitive advantage, leading to even a higher consumption of coal and a greater carbon footprint overall. Resource owners will pre-emptively extract their resources even faster to get most of their business today, as their future business model is threatened. Within the current environmentally friendly policy framework, we aren't slowing down climate change, but accelerating it. The "green paradox" can be overcome, but it requires the combination of an "exit" strategy with hybrid swaps, parallel currencies, smart impact funding and a variety of public-private partnership contracts. See in more detail Sinn (2012); for an example of greenhouse-gas accounting see Kander et al. (2015).

42. See Dixon (2003, 2006, 2019).

43. Three of the more hidden forms of negative externalities are *land grabbing, virtual water* and *the import of CO_2*: in Europe, the current annual rent for an acre of arable land ranges from 20 EUR (Latvia) to 320 EUR (Netherlands), while in Africa arable land can be leased for less than 0.5 EUR per acre per year over a duration of 99 years (Bloomberg 2019; Eurostat 2018). Around 40 to 200 million hectares globally have been affected by land grabbing, and more than half of these are located in sub-Saharan Africa (Batterbury and Ndi 2018; Hall 2011; Oxfam 2011; Rulli et al. 2013). Up to one third of arable land in Africa is affected already. Globally, over 4 million hectares of land are used to produce goods that then are exported. We have enough robust evidence showing that the production of food is highly water-sensitive. For example, 1 apple requires 80 l, a cup of coffee 140 l, a hamburger 2400 l, a portion of crisps 185 l and so on (Hoekstra and Chapagain 2006). If such products are produced in countries exposed to water stress, mainly in the southern hemisphere, this amount of water is then lacking for local communities. The same is true for the CO_2 load. While OECD countries have been able to reduce their CO_2 burden nationally, this has taken place mainly by exporting the

production of goods and energy. The products imported to supermarkets in OECD countries should carry the hidden costs of land grabbing, water depletion and an increased carbon footprint. See also Hoekstra and Hung (2005); Liu et al. (2017).

44. Taxonomy is key to ensuring private equity impact funding. There are initiatives by different stakeholders (NGOs, politics, the corporate world, science) with different interests and objectives, all of which have to be reconciled. Essentially, we require a matrix that allows us to evaluate, measure and compare the entire expenditure of human economic activities. This includes a *total cost analysis* (TCA) upstream and downstream along the value chain, *integral accounting*, *improved comparability* for mergers and acquisitions, *measuring and evaluating* the impact not only on profit, but on human wealth in general. In addition, we need a *relative benchmarking* for different sectors (like aluminum, cement, agriculture) and between sectors, facilitating comparability as well as improving corporate decisions (de-risking) and public awareness on different levels (OECD, EU, G7, G20). Finally, we need an *enabling environment* for harmonized regulation and taxation that would set up a new global accounting system for every agent involved. Initiatives such as these that seek to better incorporate natural, social and human capital have been around for at least 30 years. However, most of them already fail at the stage when the different stakeholders provide completely different views on the topic. For example, international accounting firms already have different opinions on how to evaluate and measure the upstream impact of child labor or water pollution on the corporate balance sheet. We might end up with three findings: relative banning, relative benchmarking and single case-to-case approaches.

45. Initial Public Offering (IPO) has decreased continuously over the last 15 years from 7000 in 2004 to around 300 in 2019. In addition, corporations are more interested in recalls of their own stocks than in investing in long-term projects, as dividends are higher than the potential profit retained. Both aspects lead to decreased opportunities for conventional investors to become involved. As most of the money is held by institutional investors, whose clients are the baby boomer generation, the likelihood of reinvesting in risky alternative assets is low. This is one reason why we need a strategy that combines de-risking with new investment strategies.

46. See for further examples and calculation Randers et al. (2018), who discuss the acceleration of renewable energies and the productivity of the food chain, reduction of inequality and the investment in education, family planning and health; or the new Club of Rome Climate Emergency Plan (Club of Rome 2019), which marks carbon pricing and exit strategies, women's education, exponential technological innovation, circular economy, regenerative land use and higher material efficiency among others.

47. Mudaliar and Dithrich (2019).

48. Bozesan (2020); for updated and more precise figures see the comprehensive report of Henderson et al. (2019).

49. Private equity funds historically have a high yield ranging between 19–25% (Kaplan and Schoar 2005) annually. In a world where GDP is growing by 2–3% (World Bank 2019) but private investors demand 10 times more, this revenue has to come from somewhere. In fact, most of it comes directly or indirectly from the lack of financing for public goods. This means that instead of funding public preschooling and collective health care, protecting against pollution, eradicating poverty and hunger, and averting the collapse of biodiversity, the money instead goes into the private sector, where HNWI (High Net Worth Individuals) realize additional returns. A 19–25% return for private equity, even with additional impact funding, is an unrealistic scenario in a world where the wealth gap is increasing and public common goods are underfunded. Private equity is a small part of the solution, but it is not *the* solution.

50. If market solutions are presented as the main answer to social problems, we might end up with what Anand Giridharadas (2018) calls the "winner takes all" effect: the "giving back" or "pledge campaigns" of the elite are well meaning but remain non-starters. Here, we need to take two aspects into account: first, the social and ecological damage caused by the elite when building their fortunes. Second, the existing mechanisms that fail to address the root causes of the problems. Philanthropy and charity are not bad things, but we should be aware that they

treat symptoms, not causes, and also serves to keep the system as it is instead of changing it. The global net result of these campaigns might be still negative. They will help to appease the consciences of the elite, but not improve the lives of people in the future.

51. 200 fund managers globally manage roughly over 47 trillion USD in assets, which is more than 50% of the global GDP (Investment & Pensions Europe 2019). So, if we want to gain momentum for a change towards a low-carbon economy, we need to get these 200 fund managers in one room and tell them what to do.

52. This ex-swap asset might include a specific bonus program for the executive boards of the companies in charge of liquidating their own company and provide an alternative investment for the shareholder instead.

53. See Griffin (2017).

54. Aigner (2019); Ro (2015).

55. Private-public contracting allows a long-term perspective, especially in critical infrastructures such as energy, health, education, and telecommunications. In 2017 90 billion USD were contracted globally, down from a peak in 2012 of 140 billion USD. The World Bank advisory offers blueprints and guidance on how to contract private and public sector interests. However, the devil is in the detail. De-risking is the major issue, where both sides have to clarify who is going to take on the risk in the case of "force majeure", such as natural catastrophes, terrorism or state failure. Who is the insurer of last resort? How to determine payments and who is fully and who is partly compensated? What is the very nature of the financial assets (bond, bank financing or corporate financing)? The International Center of Settlement on Investment Disputes (ICSID) associated with the World Bank seems to be just one institutional alternative among others. In order to de-risk the project for the private sector and make it bankable for the public sector, both sides have to give in: the private sector has to surrender its high yield expectations and its short-termism, and the public sector has to tackle corruption and bad public management. There is currently a tendency to partisanism and to advocate for private-sector money instead of public procurement. See Eurodad (2018); World Bank (2017).

56. World Health Organization (WHO), Unicef (2017).

57. The term co-financing is used especially in reference to international development projects such as those in developing countries (Asian Development Bank 2019). According to Law (2014), co-financed loans are characterized by a partnership between "commercial lenders, especially banks, [and] a government or a government sponsored organization."

58. The ratio goes back to Tinbergen (1962). In order to achieve 5% economic growth in developing countries, 0.3% in private capital flow and 0.7% in official development aid (ODA) is required. The Harrod Domar equation specifies this further (based on Domar 1946; Harrod 1939). If we look more closely at the concrete and actual spending on ODA, we see that there is double use and double counting, including prioritizing domestic industry. Roughly one quarter of the 0.3% of GDI, which is only 50% of what has been approved (0.7%), is going into real ODA (OECD 2017). In addition, there is a constant negative net flow of money from the global South to the North. Whereas the global North transferred roughly the equivalent of 1.3 trillion USD to the South in between 1980 and 2012, developing countries lost about the equivalent of 3 trillion USD in the opposite direction due to interest payments, capital flight, corruption, miss-pricing of trade and income, and corruption (Kar and Schjelderup 2015; personal communication with Prof. Dr. Jan Kregel, September 2019, New York).

59. A short history of the first 1000 years of dual or parallel currencies reveals that for most of that millennium, dual currency systems were the standard, whereas a monetary monoculture was the exception. One of the two currencies was designed for long-distance trading (mainly backed up by a metal that had the additional function of storing value), while the second was mainly designed for local and regional exchange. This made for flexibility, but also created social asymmetries in exchange, often increasing transaction costs and generating economic rent. Any time these currency systems broke down due to unregulated money creation and/or unregulated convertibility, the societies started again with a dual system and not a monocul-

ture. It is only in the last 100 years that a monetary monoculture has been favored exclusively. Taking the default design (lack of regulation) into account, at the beginning of the twenty-first century we now can do better. In light of new distributed ledger technology (blockchain-associated), a deeper understanding of the system dynamics of dual systems (resilience, anti-cyclical steering, cost savings due to the stimulation of regional economic activities), and more empirical evidence on the role of monetary regulation (price stability, convertibility and impact of regulatory efforts), re-establishing a dual currency again for the wealth of nations seems only natural. See e.g. Rössner (2012, 2018).

60. See the UN World Food Program as a *first proof of concept.* A smartphone interface with a biometric identification system prevents misuse and fraud. This creates greater security and privacy for the clients enrolled, as sensitive data are not shared with third private parties, like social media firms or banks (World Food Program 2017).

61. The idea of a "citizen dividend" represents calls for a "social credit" system where commons are distributed equally amongst all citizens (Douglas 1924). An exemplary proposal for the "public channel" was given by Jeremy Corbyn in the UK. His "people's quantitative easing" proposal aimed at spending newly created money directly on public infrastructure projects (Berry and Guinan 2019).

62. Other proposals refer to a roll-over of state bonds to central banks, infinite credits without maturity, credits without interest, or credit lines that modify their conditions and facilities while rolling over from central banks to states and vice versa (Turner 2015). As convincing as all these arguments are, none of them address the resilience of a dual currency system and therefore stay within the given paradigm.

63. Dag Hammarskjöld Foundation (2019), Breitenfellner et al. (2019) and NGFS (2019).

Chapter 3
Western Thinking at Its Best: Systems Theory and Psychology

Our financial system has been analyzed, dissected and examined through many lenses. However, two major contributions of Western thinking—systems theory and the field of psychology—have not featured prominently in these analyses. In this chapter, we will first try to answer the following questions: firstly, what are the components required to make a system more sustainable? And secondly, how can we better deal with the unknown, with uncertainty and complexity? Nature serves as our example: living systems have an astonishing capacity to stay within a window of viability over extraordinarily long periods of time. This chapter will demonstrate that beyond the various schools of economics and finance, systems theory can provide a more comprehensive approach. Besides systems theory, findings in psychology and neuroscience then help to support the idea that humans have the capacity to access and operate within two systems simultaneously. This is because we have two cerebral hemispheres that represent two different ways of interacting with our environment. This dual capacity of the brain and of the mind is reminiscent of the Yin and Yang of Taoism.1 In conclusion, we will refer to six components that can help us to change our behavior on a personal level.

3.1 On Dancing with the System: Dealing with Uncertainty

Dance is not an algorithm or rule to be followed, nor an action that unfolds on auto-pilot. It requires the right music and rhythm, the right pairings of and interplay between people. Dancing is a complex skill that we need to train. If we consider the finance sector as a system and we want to learn how to dance with that system, we need to take these factors into account. One of the most detrimental beliefs we hold onto is that we are able to control, predict or fully regulate the complex financial

The original version of this chapter was revised. The correction to this chapter can be found at
https://doi.org/10.1007/978-3-030-64826-8_7

system we have developed. In reality, the system is objectively uncertain, "open" and full of unexpected surprises. Financial networks are not closed. They interact constantly with their environment and self-organize in a non-linear and chaotic way, where single cause–effect correlations are the exception, not the rule. This generates ongoing feedback loops that delay, enhance or counteract the initial intervention, rendering the results partly unpredictable. This process will always remain incomplete and prone to failure, especially if crises, defaults or shocks occur that challenge the integrity of the system itself. So instead of seeking vainly to maximize the system's efficiency and transparency, would it not be better to listen, ride and learn to dance with the system to our own advantage, honoring its complexity? This requires different tools and a different mindset, and these systems theory can provide. We then can learn to better understand the system's dynamic, its interconnectedness, how every part depends on the whole, and how the whole impacts each part.[2]

> Complexity means that it is impossible to separate a system from its context, an object from its measuring instrument and a thought from its action.

3.2   Efficiency, Resilience and Robustness

The challenges we face can be compared to the differences between the captain and the designer of a ship. A bad captain can damage even the best-designed ship. However, a poor design can make any ship unsafe, such that even an excellent captain has difficulty safely sailing it. Statistically speaking, 80% of a ship's direction is dependent upon its design and 20% upon the captain's experience. In short, the design of a system prevails over the system's operator.

Applying this image to our financial context, we see that while conventional monetary policies, proper regulatory efforts and rules, increased transparency, stress tests to prevent further damage in case of crisis, and the management of non-performing banking credits all are undeniably important, the design of our monetary system is fundamentally flawed. This explains why it fails repeatedly, despite appropriate interventions.

Generally speaking: what maintains a system's integrity, or what is the sustainability of any living system? The theory behind complex, open-flow network systems, where reciprocal causalities predominate,[3] is able to provide some answers. Applying these findings to the financial sector means asking: what are the variables that keep a monetary system stable, sustainable, reliable, viable long term and shockproof at the same time? What design is required, even if the monetary regulators are wise and experienced "captains"?

From a systemic perspective, we need to introduce a new way of looking at the monetary system's dynamic. We will start to look at the efficiency and resilience of a system state and differentiate it from its robustness. These are complementary aspects that correspond to one another, rather than being reducible to one another. The efficiency of a system is best described as the capacity to manage an optimal throughput per unit. It streamlines its components and increases potential outcome in the short term. The robustness of a system state, on the other hand, describes its resistance to shocks and unforeseen events. A resilient state, however, means that the system is able to recover and regain its previous "normal" state after a shock. Regulatory efforts such as Basel III and the Financial Stability Board as well as attempts to obtain additional information through data mining all aim to increase the robustness and resilience of the financial system.

These variables are intertwined: a system's resilience is enhanced by greater diversity and a higher number of pathways (or greater connectivity) because there are numerous channels of interaction to fall back upon in times of trouble or change. Diversity and connectivity also play an important role in throughput efficiency. However, here they have the opposite effect: efficiency increases as diversity and connectivity decrease. Placing too much emphasis on efficiency sacrifices resilience and diversity. This automatically results in systemic collapse or crisis. The opposite is true as well. If too much emphasis is put on resilience at the cost of efficiency, the system will not be viable either and will become stagnant. Such findings have already revolutionized a wide range of fields, including geophysics, engineering, demography, ethology, biology, medicine, acoustics, and electronics. The power grid, airline security measures, nuclear power units, and agricultural monocultures versus biotopes are further examples. In this vein, suggestions for redesigning the financial system need to strike the right balance between efficiency and resilience and then remain within an optimal "anti-fragile zone", where the system can learn from failure and consequently improve its overall integrity and contribution to society as a whole. Anything outside this zone is either too brittle (too efficient) or too stagnant (too resilient).[4] By contrast, any intervention that supports remaining within the anti-fragile zone will provide us with the tools to learn from failure and to improve the system's dynamics and integrity. By following a path of efficiency first and foremost, we are currently operating outside this financial anti-fragile zone.

3.3   The Anti-Fragile Zone

The optimum state in which efficiency and resilience are reconciled is where the financial sector benefits most from each. We can call this the "financial anti-fragile zone". In this state, the system reaches an optimum where all information, future prognoses, uncertainties, risks, liabilities, potential costs and yields, private, public, short- and long-term strategies merge with the two variables of efficiency and resilience.[5] Anti-fragility refers to a system's capacity to learn from shocks and continuously improve its ability to respond to future shocks or unforeseen events. Anti-fragility is more than robustness. An anti-fragile system exposed to shocks not only resists, but even improves through the exposure to volatility, randomness and stress. Once a system is in an "anti-fragile zone", it does not merely passively adapt to the environment, but rather perfects a systemic response to disorder, aversive events, volatility, shocks and failure, harm and stressors. This means that a system's performance improves through anti-fragile features.[6] In order to strike the right balance between these components, we need to take this argument one step further.

More concretely: it is anti-fragility that provides us with the proper understanding of how finance should be organized. In order to make decisions in a complex world we do not fully understand, and to start learning from failure without the risk of the system collapsing, finance needs to become anti-fragile. Rather than trying to forecast a future that will always remain unpredictable, attempts to become anti-fragile and learn from randomness, stressors, volatility and the "unknown unknown" are the way forward. Anti-fragility in a financial system is achieved by diversifying capital structure through more options, channels, or opportunities that are less prone to error. In order to maintain the system's integrity, a balance needs to be achieved between these components (Graph 3.1).

The following table illustrates this and provides a perspective beyond the existing controversy between economic schools. To note: the optimum of the anti-fragile zone is shifted slightly towards resilience. This asymmetrical emphasis shows that resilience is more important for maintaining the system's integrity than increased efficiency. The following table explains the interrelation between efficiency, resilience, robustness and anti-fragility as complementary, opposing pairs (Graph 3.2).

As it becomes more efficient and processes are gradually streamlined, a complex flow system builds up a kind of self-organizing momentum that eliminates diversity. In general, increasingly efficient systems tend to become more directed, less diverse, and consequently more brittle over time. This is a profound point with far-reaching

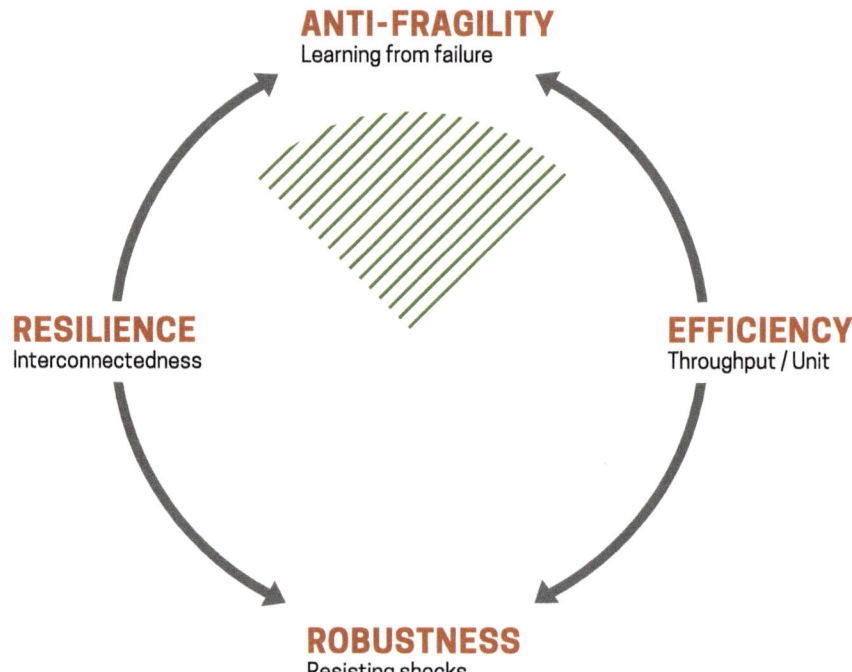

Graph 3.1 Opposing, complementary pairs: robustness—anti-fragility—efficiency—resilience

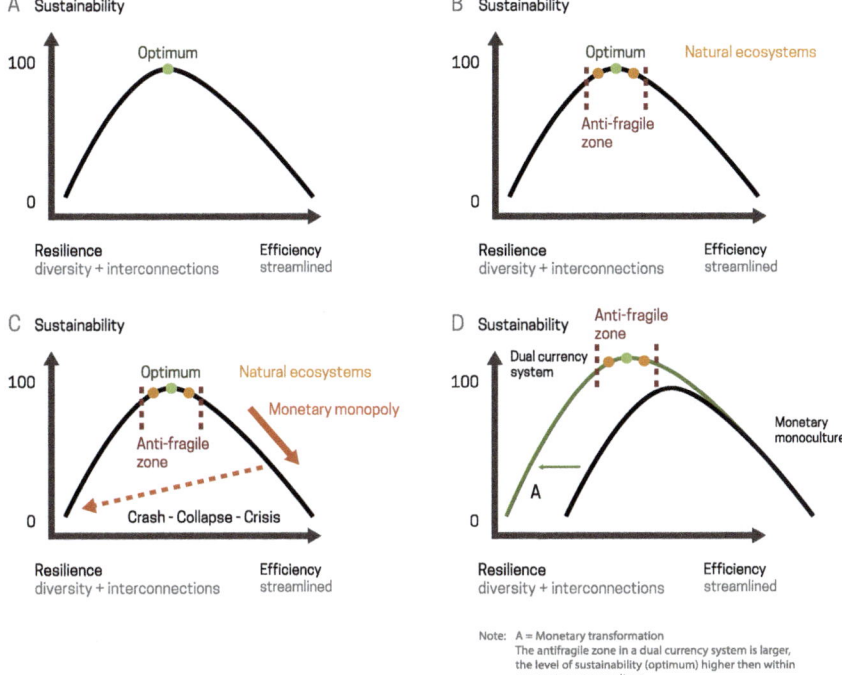

A: Sustainability curve mapped between the two poles of efficiency and resilience. In nature, resilience is accorded more importance than efficiency and the curve is steeper on that side of the graph. This explains the asymmetry of the curve

B: In the real world, all networks corresponding to natural ecosystems operate around the optimum point within a specific range called the "anti-fragile zone". Individual parallel currencies reflect states along the curve, as we will demonstrate below

C: However, regulatory efforts within a monetary monopoly will tend to overshoot the "anti-fragile zone" towards more efficiency, sooner or later leading to a crash, collapse or catastrophe

D: A fully established parallel, optional, complementary money system will realign the international trading and payment system towards an "anti-fragile zone". To note: introducing a parallel currency system will shift the entire curve towards a higher level of sustainability, a wider "anti-fragile zone" and greater resilience at the same time, sacrificing part of the system's efficiency

Graph 3.2   Laws of sustainability: a systems theory perspective

implications for all complex flow systems, including our global economy. The increase of monopolies in the world economy reflects such a development. Since resilience and efficiency are both necessary but pull in opposite directions, nature tends to select those systems that have an optimum balance between the two.[7] This complementarity between efficiency and resilience is not a metaphor or an analogy, but rather a natural law. This complementarity is independent of what flows through the system. Complex systems themselves respond with these two variables efficiency and resilience to create long-term viability or sustainability. Finding the right balance between collapse and stagnation is what provides us with a window of viability in the anti-fragility zone. Such an approach leads to less efficiency in the first place, but results in higher stability and resilience in the long term. We are learning that in complex systems there is no single cause–effect correlation. An obstacle in one place could be a driver, catalyzer, or tractor in another place or become another obstacle, objective or challenge in yet another one. It depends on the questions we are asking. What then are the practical implications of these concepts for financing our future?

Box 3.1   Efficiency and Resilience in Food and Land Use

If we take our food chain and food consumption as a prominent example: currently we are trying to increase efficiency through industrial agricultural, BIG Farming and genetically modified organisms (GMO) to feed the world, but we are still wasting over one third along the food value chain globally. And this pathway is subsidized by governments with 600 billion USD annually. Going down that path might be efficient for each single agent operating in the food and agriculture industry, but it becomes extremely expensive if we take all the additional hidden costs into account. The market value of the entire global food system reflects about 10 trillion USD. If we start discounting the hidden health costs (underfed and overweight, pollution and antibiotic resistance) of 6.6 trillion USD, the environmental costs (greenhouse gas, biological diversity, species extinction) of 3.1 trillion USD and the socioeconomic costs (food loss, waste) of 2.1 trillion USD, the net benefit for the world community of our current food and land use is negative with an amount of 1.9 trillion USD. The impact of waste and losses along the value chain alone represents 3.3 Gt CO_2, which is the third largest polluter after China and the US and it represents about one fourth of our water consumption, equal to 250 km^3, which accounts for four times the water consumption of the US annually. Finally the waste reflects about one third of our agricultural land globally. Reversing these unhealthy leakage trends alone, which cost over 240 billion USD, would require additional investment of 10 billion USD, creating huge economic opportunities of up to 240 billion USD until 2030. Ending hunger and feeding 9 billion people until 2030 does not necessarily require additional production, but a transition of our agricultural value chain away from more efficiency towards more resilience, where different channels and logistic pathways are prominent. The financial incentives described in this text provide a mechanism to enable this.[8]

3.4   Financial Instability Explained

Looking at the monetary domain from a systems theory perspective, we see that we currently have a worldwide monetary monoculture where the same type of medium of exchange is circulating in every country: a single national currency created through bank debt, highly efficient, enabling firms, states and private households to invest and trade, irrespective of the potential damage generated by these investment

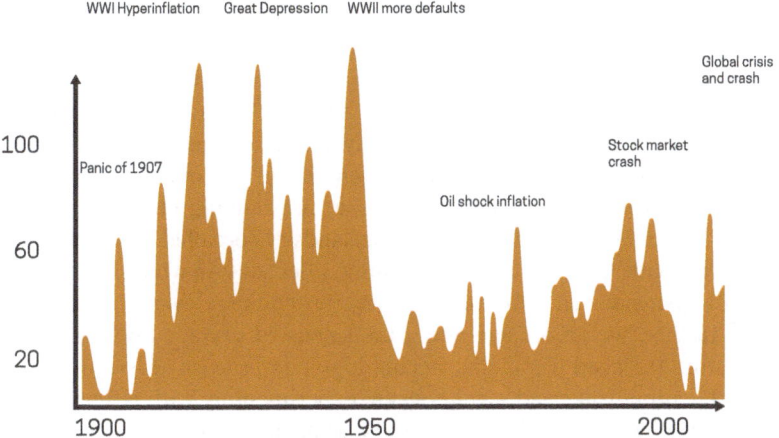

Graph 3.3 Financial instability—a never-ending story in a world of a monetary monoculture (see: Reinhardt and Rogoff 2009)

or consumption patterns.[9] This monoculture results in a brittle and unsustainable system. In this sense, efficiency provides a short-term perspective, favoring quick fixes and private revenue. Resilient features, on the other hand, favor a long-term view and provide a reserve or fallback position where public and common goods are predominant.

The hundreds of systemic crashes that have occurred over the past 40 years demonstrate that our system is inherently unstable.[10] Whereas small crises do play a relevant role in self-correcting the market, larger scale financial crises have a destructive impact on society as a whole. The optimum balance between efficiency and resilience has been overshot significantly. Since 1970, there have been 186 debt crises, 66 sovereign state crises, over 147 banking and 218 currency crises worldwide. If we further consider the consecutive output losses, direct and indirect costs, the additional debt burden and fiscal costs, the pre-post gap for the pension system and the defaults on ecological projects, we see that reconsidering the monetary design could make our world more efficient and resilient at the same time, and would definitely make it cheaper.[11] In our current situation, currency and derivative markets remain highly speculative, offshore and off-sheet transactions[12] have become a normal procedure, and banking, state and currency crises occur repeatedly—not to mention unregulated dark pool, high-frequency trading und shadow banking. In this situation, traditional co-financing and transfer payments constantly encounter an unstable system and incorrect price signals (Graph 3.3).[13]

While there is recognition that the pre-2008 phenomenon of being "too big to fail" should never have been allowed to happen, the ten largest banks in the USA now control over 40% of the market as compared to less than 30% before the 2008 crisis. In view of this fact, we can predict with almost absolute certainty that further systemic crashes will occur in the future. This lack of resilience regarding interconnectedness or the lack of a back-up system will leave the world economy, future generations, nature, developing countries, tax payers and citizens—including the "winners" in our monetary system (if indeed there are any)—with higher efficiency, but also with a much higher bill to pay. If W. McDonough is right that "the need for regulation is always a sign of a faulty design", it is this faulty design that determines the negative outcome rather than its users or agents.[14] The structural solution needed to give sustainability a chance, albeit totally unorthodox, is then to offer a higher degree of resilience by diversifying the given design and creating a monetary ecosystem, where at least one or more currencies are running in parallel to the given system. In actual fact, there are already thousands of so-called community currency projects worldwide that have been operating for decades, in which thousands of citizens, small businesses and communities have tested the relevance of such a parallel system;[15] further, we are experiencing thousands of cryptocurrencies worldwide, demonstrating the need for another technology and process of issuing money; and we see that central banks and regulators are experimenting with different currencies or so-called CBDCs (Central Bank Digital Currencies). These movements, albeit all incomplete, simply prove that the design of the given monetary system is being questioned and that we need something else beyond the given financial infrastructure. This holds true for the proposed mechanisms described in this text as well. We will get back to these Proofs of Concepts (PoC) and their implications in the next chapter.[16]

However, the rationale behind the monetary ecosystem we propose follows a different logic. We define a parallel currency as the agreement of a given society to accept something other than the conventional currency as means of payment. It should be designed in such a way that the society is able to match underutilized resources and unmet needs and force its members to do so, too. And as such parallel currencies are not considered to be a substitute or an alternative, but rather a complement to the given financial system, the parallel currency we propose will aim to complete the existing system, balancing out its negative side effects, weaknesses, spillovers and constraints in one way or another. In this vein, we should focus on its capacity to create a longer-term perspective, increasing social capital and trust, operating in an anti-cyclical manner, favoring public, common goods and basic needs and providing positive externalities instead of negative rebound effects.[17] Such a monetary ecosystem would also serve as a necessary back-up system, which while prevalent in the information technology sector is as yet non-existent in the financial realm.

In other words: we can learn from nature that any time we push a living system in one direction or another—whether more towards efficiency or more towards resilience—and leave the anti-fragile zone, we start generating multiple unwanted self-enforcing feedback loops that endanger the system's overall integrity. This is true of any monoculture in farming, where we need to fight back with chemicals. This is true of any economic monopoly causing higher prices, lower quality and the misuse of power, requiring antitrust laws and democratic rules. And this is also true of the financial system. Here, we find ourselves confronted with a monetary monoculture, where increased efficiency is causing additional regulatory efforts, spillovers and crashes. In order to improve the capacity of the financial system to better self-organize and reduce instability, we require conditions that allow the system to learn by doing, to learn from failure and improve at the same time.[18] A dual-currency system should provide the conditions to achieve this.

In summary, a more sustainable financial system must be neither too efficient nor too resilient. Most human-designed systems, and certainly the monetary domain, are focused on maximizing efficiency at the expense of resilience. Banking and currency crises, state failures, increased market concentration (monopolies), deflationary tendencies, chronic unemployment and increased costs for disaster management are some of the symptoms of a faulty design.[19] If we want a sustainable financial sector, we need to steer away from our current monetary monoculture towards a monetary ecosystem. Although less efficient, it will allow us to remain within the anti-fragile zone and help us to deal with uncertainty of the Anthropocene.

3.5   Two Ways of Thinking: Dual Processing

Whereas the previous section focused on a systemic view, emphasizing a top-down approach, this sub-chapter adopts a bottom-up perspective to better understand the impact of human behavior and individual responses within groups. This approaches the topic on an individual level, highlighting the personal view with all its potential and limitations. We will focus on the phenomenon of dual mental processing. Dual mental processing is seen both in the brain, through the specific capacities of the right and left hemispheres, and in the mind, which has the capacity to think in a parallel as well as a linear fashion. This dual thinking has implications for the way our financial system is organized.

Traditionally, we have believed that our way of reasoning is a given. However, it is not.[20] While we all have daily experiences, evidence shows that humans do not act, respond or behave in a rational manner. In fact, the opposite is true. For example, intellectually we are able to grasp that a long-term view is preferable, but we still tend to act in view of the short term. We know that eating less meat, riding a bike and using public transport is the right thing to do. However, in many cases, we choose to do the opposite. These well-documented findings on irrationality demonstrate that when it comes to the future of humanity, we cannot rely on individual choices alone to create the change we wish to see. Rather, we need to establish mechanisms and structures to ensure that each individual acts in a sustainable manner.

From an individual standpoint, day-to-day experiences provide freedom of choice. When it comes to organizing complex common goods, individuals are not conscious of all the consequences and feedback loops associated with their daily actions—much like the elephant and the blind experts in the room. This why we, as humans, need to honor our imperfections and work on social mechanisms that ensure a path towards a common future. Relying on unregulated, individual choices, which are often irrational, will not get us where we want to be.

Most people want to make the right choices for themselves without harming the planet and others. However, individuals and their decision-making are too fragile a basis to formulate general monetary and fiscal policy. From unawareness to awareness, to contemplation, to planning, to initiation, to continued actions, to long-term maintenance—at each stage, individual behavioral changes can miss the target.[21] This is because we tend to overestimate individual human responses to moral imperatives, nudging, voluntary commitment, corporate social responsibility and good resolutions. Likewise, we overestimate our capacity to effectively change our behavior on a permanent basis. In reality, our minds are also affected by irrational framing such as overconfidence and non-consequentialist conclusions, as well as by convenience, mindless automatism, regressive and addictive behaviors and constant distraction.[22] Additionally, because we live in a complex, chaotic and connected (3-C) world, we require a complex, chaotic and connected 3-C mind. However, only a small proportion of humans, perhaps 3–5%, are capable of generating sufficient internal complexity, non-linear thinking and interconnectedness to ensure a personal behavioral shift on a constant level. For the majority, personal shifts in consciousness are caught up and trapped in endless paradoxes, mental frames, and double binds, preventing us from making rational decisions. With most of the conclusions we draw, we remain unaware of the potential consequences.[23] The vast majority of humans require an extrinsic, external institutional support system to ensure a permanent shift in behavior. The design of such a system needs to consider findings from neuroscience, clinical and environmental psychology, behavioral economics and systems theory. In doing so, it will favor parallel rather than linear processing, non-linear rather than causal thinking, holistic and integral perspectives rather than siloed views.[24] We must be the transformation we want to see in the future, regardless of whether this transformation is mainstream or heterodox, convenient or disagreeable. Transformation is not an endpoint but a pathway, not a utopia but a reality, and not a singular but a plural—some call it a "pluriverse".[25]

However, a personal, microscopic and individual approach is not a systemic, macroscopic and collective one. In order to reconcile both of these levels, we need an intermediary between the micro and the macro world. This means that external support, rules, and institutional incentives that ensure and guarantee ongoing behavioral shifts for 8 billion people, 24/7, are required. The monetary system is able to act as such an intermediary.

In the field of neuroscience and clinical psychology, thinking does not necessarily equal thinking. Humans have at least two ways of thinking, both of which are necessary.[26] This is true of both the "brain" and the "mind".

> Primarily, what we have is not a crisis about global warming, loss of biodiversity, poverty or pandemics, but a crisis of our mindset, our critical thinking and our consciousness. Looking within will help to reveal our interconnectedness, limits and fragility, where profit, people, purpose, passion and the planet come together, embracing paradoxes, uncertainties and opposites and shifting towards greater wholeness.

3.5.1 Linear Versus Parallel Thinking and the Divided Brain

At first glance, the two ways of perceiving the world, managing problems, evaluating challenges, paying attention and so on are rooted in the properties of our two distinctive cerebral hemispheres. Why did evolution provide us with not one single brain, but two partly separate, partly twisted, partly asymmetric brains that are inter-connected via the corpus callosum? One of the main reasons that evolution has favored this form of asymmetry or lateralization is that both hemispheres operate and perceive the inner and the outer world differently, and thus provide the human species with two potential modes of thinking. The size of the corpus callosum in relation to the hemispheres has decreased over time, demonstrating that intercon-nectivity is more important than size or volume. It is said that we have more poten-tial interconnections in the human brain than there are elements in the universe! The hemispheres partly operate in parallel, partly inhibit one another and partly are interconnected. Each offers a different view of the world, self and other, differing less in what they do than in how they do it and how they process the world.[27]

Similarly, a vast body of clinical research initiated by Daniel Kahneman demon-strates that the "mind" also operates using two systems—system 1 and system 2.[28] This dual mental processing offers the inherent selection advantage that humans have access to two completely different perspectives on the world in order to solve problems and reflect upon themselves. Both perspectives have their advantages and disadvantages and both systems are interconnected, meaning that in order to operate at their optimum, a flexible use of each system is required.

3.5.1.1   The Left Brain and System 2

The left hemisphere of the brain allows us to engage in focused attention and logical and analytical thinking. It enables us to reduce complexity and emphasize facts and frameworks over contexts and individuals. The left hemisphere measures, weighs, counts and calculates the world, which appears linear, causally linked, sectoral and fragmented. Details predominate and distinct static objects are investigated.

Similarly, the system 2 mode of our mind allows focused, linear, analytical rea-soning, which leads to slower, discursive thinking. Because the effort required through this thought process is significant, the capacity of the working memory is reduced and the results are path dependent. From an evolutionary perspective, sys-tem 2 is the younger system. The advantage is that we end up with accurate, precise results. System 2 is also the preferred system when it comes to interpersonal com-munication using language.

Sequential thinking and processing is self-limiting and self-referential. It creates the conditions for experiments, cause-and-effect procedures, and solutions that are often short-term, fragmented and detail-oriented. Once the tasks have been carried out, an answer is given and the process comes to an end. Each step needs to have been accomplished before the next is begun. These linear and sequential procedures provide us with a specialist view, where we are able to dive into detail but lose the overview. This type of thinking is a bit like a person with autistic syndrome or a high-performing athlete. Both possess highly specialized knowledge or skills, but do not have a helicopter view of the full spectrum of skills available. This sequential thinking measures, weighs and counts the world. The discovery of vitamins, the periodic system, DNA, and space flight would have been impossible without this analytical, linear, left-hemispheric approach. This approach provides a map of the world, but it is not the world itself. It remains reductionist, manipulative and inter-ventional—as indeed most technologies and scientific experiments are.

The thought process of the left-brain is a closed system or hermeneutic circle, with a tendency towards self-enhancement and self-mirroring. We only do what we see, and we only see what we are looking for. We only search for what we know, and only know what we thought in the first place.

In the world of the left-brain, words and data predominate and everything else is banished into non-existence. The left hemisphere's role is to de-contextualize data, manipulate it and then intervene. Technology, bureaucracy, regulation, administra-tion, and analytical experimental science are prime examples of left-brain endeavors.[29] Such a world is more digital than analog, more abstract than concrete and more virtual than real. But this represents only half of the brain, of the mind, and of the world as a whole.

3.5.1.2 The Right Brain and System 1

By contrast, the right hemisphere is focused on integral, holistic and fractal process-ing. Here, parallel processing predominates, and perception is guided by the exter-nal real world. This perception is both metaphorical and contextualized. The right hemisphere's role is to contain uncertainty and embrace ambiguity. Unlike the left hemisphere, which is precise and slow, the right brain is fuzzy and fast. It can pro-cess larger volumes of information and is more implicit, non-verbal and intuitive. From an evolutionary perspective, the right hemisphere is older and therefore pre-determines the left-brain functions. Similarly, when we are in system 1 mode we operate intuitively and automatically. Decisions are made quickly, associatively and context-specifically. Here, a lot of information can be processed, but the results are less accurate and more fuzzy. Most information in the brain and the mind is pro-cessed in parallel. Creativity, humor, face-to-face brainstorming, cooking, going fishing, playing an instrument, climbing, "Gestalt" perception, and complex prob-lem awareness are examples of system 1 mode.[30] Just to note: by a ratio of 1:1 mil-lion or more, parallel processing is the de facto thinking process and prevails over linear thinking. Nature has differentiated these two complementary forms of per-ception, and we need both of them. Through the two hemispheres, humans are per-manently being synchronized to synthesize the world, increasing their adaptability and therefore their chances of survival. The following table summarizes the two properties within the so-called "divided brain" (Table 3.1):

However, when one hemisphere predominates, a self-destructive aspect ensues. The left hemisphere currently is dominant in our Western society, favoring siloed and linear thinking that reinforces itself over and over again and is unable to self-correct. This leaves us with the illusion of control, of being able to manipulate the world, of generating grand technologies, endless growth and administrative solu-tions for problems that might have required a different worldview prior to interven-ing in the system. We end up only seeing what we have searched for and only find what we have reflected on in the first place. If we restrict our thinking and

Table 3.1   The divided brain: features of the two hemispheres

Left hemisphere	Right hemisphere
Focused, narrow attention, reductionist	Broad attention, integral, looks at the whole, fractal
Explicit, verbal and literal, representational	Implicit, nonverbal, nuanced, metaphorical
Closed systems, perfection, neglects complexity, abstract	Tolerates and acknowledges ambiguity and diffuse and contradictory information
Logical and analytical, thinking in terms of dichotomies	Contextualized, living embodied entities
Sequential, dogmatic, following rules	Parallel processing
Good at processing predictable, narrow, isolated events	Good at processing new and unique events
Manipulative, interventional, practical utility, fixing things, surveillance, regulatory	Observational, descriptive
Self-referential, autonomous	Connected to the outer real world
Types, categories, facts, generalities, frames, references	Unique, individual meaning, particularities, multiple perspectives
Sticking to mistaken conclusions, path dependency, confirmation bias, rigid	More flexible, adapting to new experiences, changing, detachment
Serving function when balanced with the right hemisphere	Mastering, commanding function when balanced with the left hemisphere
Tends to respond to positive feedback through reinforcement	Tends to respond to negative feedback and balance it out

processing towards a linear and sequential mode, the problem solutions we generate remain solely linear and sequential, too. However, the world is only partly constructed in a linear and sequential way, and such cause–effect correlations are an exception rather than the rule.

In summary, in complex, life-threatening circumstances, humans need the mental ability to focus intently on a specific situation and at the same time pay attention to the larger overall situation with regard to side effects, feedback, and externalities in real time. In humans, the capacity of the two systems is mainly located in the prefrontal cortex and is greatly enhanced by it.[31] When we start to use the full capacity of both hemispheres and begin to think in a systemic, integral, holistic manner, our perception will change as a result, and furthermore our personal gravity of consciousness will shift towards a more integral perspective.[32]

Indeed, all psychological properties (thinking, feeling, perceiving, deciding, motivating, behaving) require both systems and are located in both hemispheres. It is the relative difference between the two that determines how we understand and act in the world and among ourselves. However, the way the world is processed is different in each system. To explore and survive in the world, we need both processes that are detailed and linear as well as processes that are fuzzy and holistic. This asymmetry or lateralization must offer some sort of selection advantage to our species, otherwise humanity would not have been able to survive with such a complex anatomical device for thousands of years.[33]

To provide a concrete example, imagine a mother bird trying to feed her offspring. If she were to rely only on her left hemisphere or system 2 for thought processing, she would have the executive aim to target a worm, catch it and fly back in a linear fashion. However, in the absence of her right hemisphere, she would be unable to filter the potential dangers around her (system 1—right hemisphere) and thus potentially would be eaten by a predator while wholly focused on the worm (system 2—left hemisphere). In this case, the mother bird's survival and her ability to feed the next generation is possible only because she operates using two separate and intertwined systems. This dual parallel processing system has offered an evolutionary selection advantage for millions of years, and so we as humans need to pay attention to this design tool if we are to survive in the Anthropocene.[34]

System 1 and system 2 thus reflect a basic principle that can be applied to economic science: we need to access both modes in order to fully balance out the capacities of our brain and our mind, and what is more, balance out ourselves and our world.[35] Both systems can reciprocally inhibit one another, dysfunctionally dominate one another, or be balanced according to demand.

If we process everything predominantly through the left hemisphere and system 2, we remain unaware of the full potential humans can apply to solve problems. This means that as long as we are not tapping into the full potential of our brain and mind—just using half—we cannot expect to solve global problems of such complexity as global warming, poverty, or even simply providing enough jobs, public infrastructure, education and health for the majority of the people on this planet. In other words: the world as seen through the lens of the left hemisphere or through linear thinking has a substantial bias. What we see is an incomplete and lop-sided representation of the world, providing only suboptimal solutions.[36] The following table summarizes the main features of system 1 and system 2, both illustrating two different but complementary ways on how we perceive, operate and change the world (Table 3.2).[37]

We will see that so-called Pareto-optimal solutions requested by economists, where the allocation of goods and services has reached a maximum, do not require a different market system, better governance and state-driven interventions, nor do they require greater regulatory efforts or different forms of disruptive technologies. Rather, they require a new way of thinking.[39] Misinformation, anxiety, time pressure and stress reduce our capacity to integrate and make use of both systems, resulting in false conclusions and suboptimal solutions.

Systems theory and psychology converge in that they are both based on a dual and intertwined structure: systems theory uses bipolarity or efficiency and resilience, which balance out in the anti-fragile zone; the brain has two asymmetric interconnected hemispheres, which are macro-anatomically complementary and present a selection advantage; clinical and behavioral psychology has the dual system of system 1 and system 2. This duality is also what Taoism represents. Why should our financial system not also be set up with this duality in place?

Instead of maximizing one system, we should try to achieve a balance between the two. It is this capacity—the fact that humans are able to access two separate and irreducible worlds, parallel to each other, in a simultaneous way—that provides a selection advantage for survival in a complex environment. Living in the era of the Anthropocene in a fully connected and increasingly unpredictable world requires less control and less singular efficiency and greater adaptability, flexibility,

Table 3.2 Aspects of parallel thinking (system 1) versus linear thinking (system 2)[38]

System 1	System 2
Unconscious reasoning	Conscious reasoning
Implicit	Explicit
Automatic	Controlled
Low effort	High effort
Large capacity	Limited capacity
Rapid	Slow
Default process	Inhibitory
Associative	Rule-based
Contextualized	Abstract
Domain-specific	General
Older in evolutionary terms	More recent in evolutionary terms
Nonverbal	Linked to language
Includes recognition, perception, orientation	Includes rule-following, comparisons, weighing of options
Modular cognition	Fluid intelligence
Independent of working memory	Limited by working memory capacity
Emotional and associative	Logical reasoning
Parallel	Serial

resilience and diversity. The link between these two different thought processes and our financial system forms the basis for introducing a parallel currency system to finance common goods. Equipped with some basic knowledge about our brain and our mind, the next sub-chapter will look at how aspects built into our current monetary system—when it is not in crisis—shape individual and collective behaviors (Graph 3.4).

3.5.2 Our Financial System Is Not a Neutral Veil

If we had more of a helicopter view (or what psychologists call a meta-cognitive view), we would see that our current financial system conditions us in many ways. It is obvious that monetary or financial crises can be highly destructive and are not necessarily compatible with the concept of sustainability. More difficult to perceive, however, is how some aspects of our monetary systems shape our individual and collective behavior. Among its positive effects, our modern monetary system should be credited with triggering an explosion of unprecedented entrepreneurial, expansive economic growth and scientific innovation. However, far from being a behaviorally neutral and passive medium of exchange as is generally assumed, conventional money profoundly shapes a range of behavioral patterns, six of which are incompatible with sustainability.[40]

Graph 3.4 Our Resilient Brain—Two ways of thinking, perceiving and acting in a complex world enable survival

Box 3.2   Six Behavioral Patterns Induced by the Current Monetary Design, Preventing us from Achieving a more Sustainable Pathway
Unsustainable behavioral patterns triggered by our monetary system:

1. Amplification of boom and bust cycles: Banks provide or withhold funding to the same sectors or countries at the same time, thus amplifying the business cycle towards boom or bust. This amplification is detrimental for everyone, including the banking sector itself. In the worst-case scenario, banks stop trusting one another.
2. Short-term thinking: "Discounted cash flow" is standard practice in any investment evaluation. Because bank-debt money carries interest, the discounting of all future costs or incomes inevitably leads to short-term thinking.
3. Compulsory growth: The process of compound interest or interest on interest imposes an exponential growth pattern on the economy. However, in a finite world, exponential growth is unsustainable by definition.
4. Concentration of wealth: The income and wealth gap continues to increase, with most of the wealth flowing to the top and growing rates of poverty at the bottom. Such inequalities generate a broad range of social problems and are detrimental to economic growth. Beyond economic issues, the very survival of democracy may be at stake.[41]
5. Devaluation of social capital: Historically, social capital such as mutual trust and collaborative action has been difficult to measure. Nevertheless, whenever measurements have been made, they reveal a tendency towards an erosion of social capital, particularly in industrialized countries. Recent studies show that money can promote selfish and non-collaborative behavior—behavior that is incompatible with long-term sustainability.
6. Rebound effects: A rebound effect describes the reduced impact or benefit of technology-induced resource efficiency due to behavioral changes. Empirically, such rebound effects vary up to 80%, meaning that a significant part of the efficiency gains are lost. Any increase in efficiency either reduces the price of the good and thus enables increased consumption of the same good (price effect) or it provides additional income, which is then spent on another good with a similar negative impact. For example, combustion engines increased their efficiency over the last decades, but these gains were either used to drive more or to use the additional income to fly more. Either way, the initial benefits from resource efficiency have been lost.[42]

These six behavioral patterns engendered by the design of our monetary system thus affect the future of humanity. Because we have the equivalent of a monetary monoculture, we have been led to believe that the monetary system is a natural law. We behave like fish swimming in water that never question their situation. As humans, however, we are able to escape our glass bowl, evaluate the characteristics of the water and decide to change if we wish. But faced with the supremacy of our

Table 3.3 Behavioral complements to the existing monetary system

Unstable	More stability
Pro-cyclical	Anti-cyclical
Short-termism	Long-termism
Forced growth	Qualitative growth
Income disparity	Equality and fairness
Reduction of social capital	Increased social capital
Negative rebound effects	Positive externalities
Global and universal	Regional and sectoral

current monetary system, which is designed and manufactured as a currency monopoly, is issued by central banks with scarcity criteria, and uses only one throughput channel—from the central banks to the commercial banking system into the real economy—, we do not consider questioning it. This often overlooked, but tremendously important aspect of our monetary system has significant consequences regarding human behavior and decision-making.[43] Indeed, by adding the non-neutral aspect of human behavior to the inherent instability and universal character upon which our monetary system is built, different complementarities emerge. We will need to take them into consideration in order to upgrade, redesign or simply balance the given financial and monetary system. Table 3.3 describes some major complementarities to the current system that any future financial system will require.

Our monetary system thus is not a neutral veil between the economic agents involved, but through its design determines the nature of our investments, consumption patterns, saving strategies and our risk assessment. It is as water is to a fish. Fish take water as a given. But we humans are able to step out of the water and gain a more integral view. If we want to fly to Mars or invent 6-G, we honor the advantages of the conventional system. However, if we want to finance our commons—fresh air, a stable concentration of CO_2 in the atmosphere or overcoming poverty—we need to start thinking differently. Any complementary monetary system should be designed to foster greater stability, equality and fairness, encourage a long-term view, favor qualitative rather than quantitative growth, promote social capital and prioritize regional or sectoral value chains. These qualities also describe what common global goods need to exist. So what specific aspects need to be included in the design of a new complementary monetary system? After digging deeper into the art of behavioral changes, we will present these aspects in the following chapters.

> It is not about replacing the protagonists in the game or improving the existing rules. It is about changing the narrative for the protagonists, and this will allow them to change the rules of the game.

3.6   The Art of Change or Why We Have to Do Things Differently

We have lost the capacity to trust our own evaluation and perception, to cope with unpredictable challenges, and to create a future we would like to live in. If we leave the question of what to do in regard to the upcoming hazards up to the global population to answer on its own, or focus solely on technological solutions to solve our global challenges, we will end up with a scenario that is incompatible with a peaceful sustainable future. Arming ourselves with the tools to enact fundamental social change means empowering people to regain their self-confidence, self-efficacy and trust in their own evaluation of the world. This change requires a deeper understanding of human drives, motives and tasks on the one hand and of the measures and rewards to encourage them on the other hand.[44] Traditionally, as is well known, we have differentiated between intrinsic and extrinsic motivation. Extrinsic motivation means that a behavior is triggered in order to avoid punishment or to earn a reward. Intrinsic motivation instead means that an activity is undertaken for its own sake. Both extrinsic and intrinsic motivation are valuable and can encourage humans to change their behavior. Which of the two—or which balance between them—is most effective depends on the challenges ahead.

From a behavioral perspective, there are three major types of intervention that make humans change their behavior. The first type is represented by sanctions, negative reinforcement or punishments, such as taxation or fees. These can cause a change, but fail to provide the candidate or the cohort with an answer to the question of what to do instead. In addition, negative reinforcement without further direction and rewards causes multiple rebound effects. The second type of intervention is positive reinforcement. Positive reinforcement or positive stimuli, such as subsidies, generate positive predictability and expectations. The downside is that they trigger adaptation and accommodation effects. The third type of intervention is positive intermittent reinforcement. Such interventions occur unexpectedly and can cause behavioral changes beyond the well-known rebound effects and adaptations. Positive intermittent reinforcement can generate long-lasting shifts in human behavior.

Where rule-based procedures and tasks such as doing the laundry (yes or no), sorting one's garbage, or the need for more linear and algorithmic routines are concerned, extrinsic motivation can be successful. This includes the well-known carrot-and-stick approach, where external sanctions and positive reinforcement can steer human behavior towards a certain goal. Subsidies versus fees and taxation are well-proven fiscal interventions that help us to respond in the desired way. Empirically, such extrinsic motivations work best when delivered as intermittent positive stimuli, such that the person or institution receives unexpected positive feedback after having engaged in a certain behavior. However, extrinsic motivation—whether with or without intermittent reinforcement—is obligation-based and liable to be adapted quickly. Thus interventions based upon extrinsic motivation remain short-term and unstable. They can trigger repeated unwanted rebound effects and the need for increased administration.

The situation for humans changes significantly when the required task becomes more complex and creative solutions and problem-solving prevail. Urban gardening, lifestyle changes, sports, and mastering an instrument are all examples of more complex tasks. In these cases, external interventions are less successful. Self-efficacy, the search for purpose and constant improvement are more appropriate psychological tools to ensure changes in behavior. This form of intrinsic motivation applied to complex problem-solving offers longer-term prospects. It requires discipline and passion and is motivated by self-actualization. It is what psychologists call an "autotelic flow": pursuing the task is an end in itself and does not require external stimuli. In these cases, the use of external motivations through a carrot-and-stick approach is counterproductive because it fails to acknowledge the intrinsic motivation. This distinction is essential because different tasks and motivations require alternative forms of incentives. Our monetary system is a social mechanism that can incentivize or avert certain human behaviors. Extrinsic motivation, which favors different forms of conditioning to accomplish more mechanistic procedures, treats humans as the equivalent of chess figures, acting and moving according to pre-defined rules. Intrinsic motivation, however, favors self-efficacy to carry out more heuristic tasks and challenges. In these cases, humans are more like basketball players, applying existing rules creatively and responding flexibly to the needs of the given moment, motivated by their love of the game itself. Achieving the SDGs with their intrinsic complexity requires incentives that lead to intrinsic motivations, such as those that motivate the basketball players. In the following chapters, we will see that the proposed monetary ecosystem is based less on the fees, taxation and subsidies typical of the conventional system and rather on unleashing the creativity and self-efficacy in each of us, supported by positive intermittent reinforcement. In order to counter the current biases in our current monetary system, as well as the inherent biases that exist at the individual level, six elements should be built into the design of any new financial engineering tool:

The personal approach to human behavioral change

1. Context-bound information over mere facts
2. Identify interlinkages
3. Seek out complementarities rather than causality
4. Favor cooperation over competition
5. Intermittent positive reinforcements
6. Synchronizing peer groups

1. Favor context-bound, relational information rather than isolated, clear-cut facts. While the use of context-bound information does not reduce or overcome the uncertainty inherent to the system and to our thinking, it helps us to cope with it better. This information might generate additional paradoxes and uncertainties, where things are not neatly lined up in a row but are ambiguous, fuzzy and contradictory. The change begins with an interest in understanding the system's capacity to self-organize, self-realize and become self-conscious.[45]

2. Identify interconnections by processing the world in a parallel, non-exclusive way, where macro-, meso- and micro-levels are interlinked. This requires a shift in dealing with uncertainty, which then no longer triggers flight or fight responses, play-dead reflexes or unproductive avoidance strategies, but rather mindful (mind-full) reflection and time out for critical reasoning. We abandon the mechanistic determinism of daily routine with its illusion of control and avoidance of random-ness and enter a sphere of "tolerance for ambiguity". We become more aware of the synchronicities happening simultaneously around the word. Instead of being righteous, ego-driven or seeking simple and reductionist solutions, we learn to listen to one other, embracing our counterparts and opposites. In such a context, the opposite of complexity is not simplicity but reductionism.[46]

3. Seek out complementarities rather than causality. We often presume that causal relations in the financial or societal realm can be explained, but then end up endlessly debating who is right or wrong. For example, we assume a direct causal link between inflation and money supply or between money supply and interest rates. However, empirically no such causal link exists.[47] Causal relations in a non-linear complex system are very rare, if they occur at all. Instead of searching for the invisible, we need to identify complementary relationships.[48] This difference is key and represents a major shift in mindset, reflecting a shift from linearity towards complementarity. It is this complementarity that provides the best solution to our search for a new balance for finance and for the future.

4. Favor cooperation over competition. Abundant evidence from game theory shows that humans at baseline favor cooperative behavior and fair results. It is only when conditions for cooperation are abandoned that the second-best behavioral interaction of "tit-for-tat strategies" is adopted. Only when these strategies fail do humans start competing and finally become aggressive towards their own species. Our mindset will start to favor collective, cooperative solutions rather than singular, individualistic, competitive behaviors. In fact, cooperative behaviors and solidarity multiply in much the same way as competitive and selfish behaviors. Empirically, even if people have not been involved from the start, cooperative behavior spreads from person to person. This behavior is contagious and causes random unknown acts of solidarity and generosity with a cascade of up to three grades.[49]

5. Use intermittent positive rewards as a catalyst for behavioral change. Humans are the species with greatest ability to adapt quickly to new, disruptive, unexpected and ever-changing environments. This is true of individuals, groups and large cohorts. The good news is that we are able to adapt. The bad news is that we can easily adapt to adverse and self-destructive behaviors, where the flexibility for behavioral change is lost or generates paradoxical responses. The use of positive, intermittent, unexpected reinforcements as a mechanism to establish individual and group behavioral change is best known from addictive behaviors, such as gambling.[50] This mechanism works much better and faster than punishment. Intermittent positive reinforcements are necessary because if people are sanctioned only, they know what they ought to avoid but are then left to find out what to do on their own. The positive stimulus needs to be intermittent and unexpected, as the human brain quickly adapts to positive expectations, which will reduce the motivation to make further changes.[51]

> Personal and individual lifestyle changes are pivotal, but will remain singular, incomplete silo effects as long as they are not embedded in an approved social mechanism that enables 7.5 Billion people to act in a positive way 24/7.

6. Use social peer groups to effect large-scale change. In addition to positive intermittent reinforcement, a second parameter exists to effect change for the better. Humans are more comfortable with changing their behavior if they can do so within a peer group and to act in a synchronized way. For example, when humans have the chance to dance, sing or walk together and synchronize their behaviors accordingly, this increases pro-social values, such as trust and solidarity, giving, support and cooperative attitudes. Belonging to a group and doing something in an intentional and synchronized way further reduces the so-called free-rider effect. Apparently such cultural practices have the inner property of acting as a selective competitive advantage. The monetary system represents one of the most powerful tools ever invented to intentionally synchronize human behavior in large cohorts.[52]

A better understanding of the conditions for behavioral change is crucial. However, while a shift in our personal gravity of consciousness, our mindset and our behavior is necessary, this alone is not enough to ensure our common future. Such a personal and individual approach to change is simply too unstable and unreliable to guarantee the consistent transformation required. Advocating personal change as the solution to our problems trivializes the need for systemic change and places all responsibility on the shoulders of the individual. This can easily generate paradox, unproductive or appeasing behaviors. For example: faced with global warming, people could conclude that it is better to enjoy their current lifestyle as long as possible or withdraw from any commitments due to the magnitude of the challenge ahead. Any change in our mindset therefore must be built into the design of any new financial engineering as a fundamental precondition. This design needs to take account of what we can call the "six Ps": it should honor positive intermittent reinforcement, provide purpose and profit for all agents involved, generate some sort of pleasure and pro-social activity, empower people and be proxy enough to ensure that all of us, all around the clock, can become committed to a better future. But before we identify the "six Ps" in the monetary domain and on a systemic level, we first need to describe the nature of the global commons and how to unleash their full potential.

To summarize: Adaptability is in fact one of humans' key characteristics. Humans are the most adaptable species on this planet. Throughout human history, we have been able to adapt and come up with creative solutions. Adaptability is coupled with an increased capacity for knowledge, learning, and wisdom, which in consequence changes the rules of the game and finally modifies our awareness and our mindset. In short, adaptability offers a selection advantage through failure-friendly strategies to solve problems.

Here are some striking empirical findings that demonstrate the human capacity to overcome such adverse events. In 1920, roughly 500,000 people died due to natural catastrophes such as wildfires, flooding, hurricanes and so on. In 2020, the absolute number of humans dying from such natural catastrophes has reduced to about

20,000 per year. This reflects a reduction of over 95% due to the improved capacity of early warning systems and increased economic growth, which has led to dam building and higher levels of education. This constitutes a truly dramatic improvement, considering the increase in our global population over the last century. Take rising sea levels: if we do not adapt to rising sea levels, about 180 million people will be affected directly over the next 50 years. But if we adapt, the number reduces to less than 300,000. This number is lower than the people who decide to migrate from California each year. Another example: following latest IPCC modeling, climate change will cost about 0.2–2% of our GDP over the next 50 years. This is a challenge, but not a disaster. If rich countries (OECD) were to stop their economic activities immediately and bear a recession over the next decades, the impact on our climate will be an increase of 0.3 degrees Celsius by 2100, with tremendous costs for human societies.[53] Instead of a false apocalypse, collective anxiety and alarmism that prevent wise responses to such asymmetric shocks, triggering wrong mental frames, causing us to make wrong political decisions and priorities, we should change our mindset. Humans will be able to identify creative solutions to cope with all the challenges we face. Increasing asymmetric shocks require such new forms of adaptability. We have to learn to prioritize and compromise between different goals. And one of the key mechanisms at our disposal, which we have ignored for decades, is the financial and monetary system. We can go even further. If resilience becomes more important, then shareholder value maximization, resource allocation and capital accumulation become less relevant in a world where asymmetric shocks prevail. This is because individuals, firms, communities, or societies that aim to achieve more such efficiency in order to gain a higher competitive advantage simultaneously will become more fragile and brittle in face of the next shock. It is adaptability and learning from failure that will determine the survival rate of an individual, a firm, a community or a society as a whole. Calls to avoid or prevent high blood pressure, depression, or an infectious disease do not mean that we would abandon hypertensive drugs to adapt our blood pressure, avoid using an antidepressant to adjust our serotonin levels, or refuse to use an antiviral vaccination to cope with Covid-19. We would always request both prevention and avoidance on the one hand and managing the side effects and symptoms on the other. This has substantial consequences for any sustainability strategy and the redesign of our monetary system.[54]

To put it in other words: it is like dismantling an omnibus. In this context global warming seems like an omnibus, containing multiple challenges and heading towards us. Not all of its components are directly connected with one another, but they all affect our lives. There are dozens of these negative effects associated to climate change that only in part have a causal link to climate change. But they are kind of like passengers on that bus. If we start dismantling this omnibus of global warming into smaller pieces, it will become less frightening and more manageable. Although we still face the impact of climate change beyond 2 degrees, we will then find wiser forms of adapting to parts of the problem, instead of facing the entire omnibus heading towards us, something that seems unbearable. Redesigning and differentiating our monetary system will help us in demystifying this process.[55] The following graphs (a-c) provide some components of that omnibus and how to overcome the obstacle (Graph 3.5).

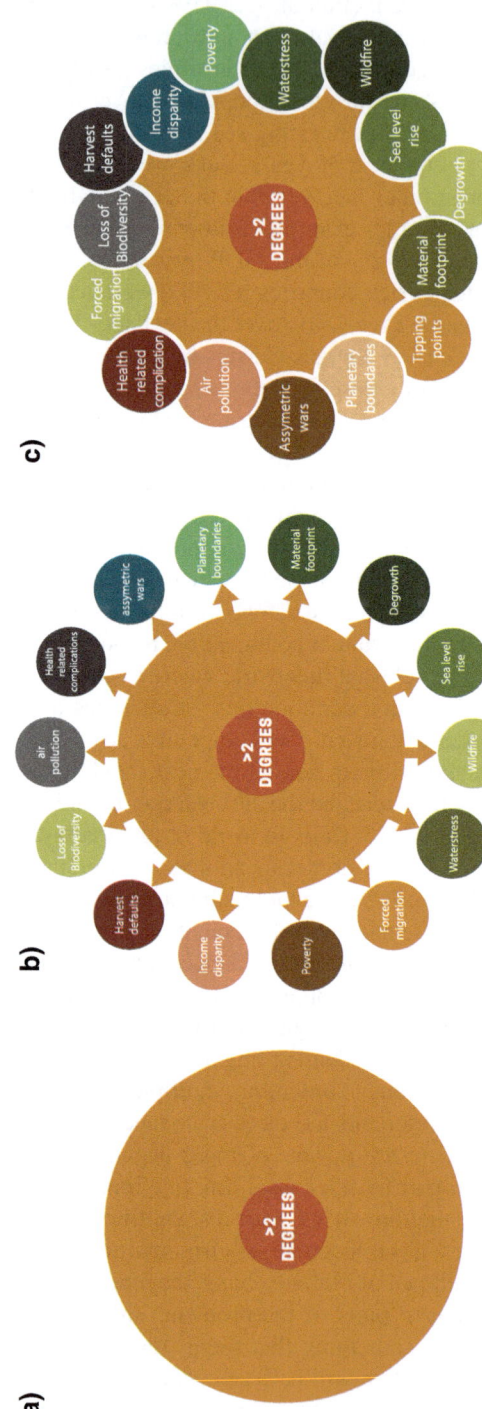

Graph 3.5 Dismantling the omnibus heading towards us: (a) global warming beyond 2 degrees; (b) associated impacts of the 2 Degree Scenario; (c) slicing the challenges: global warming does not go away, but becomes less of an unsurmountable mystery and more of a manageable problem

All the challenges are very likely to occur if we do not adapt wisely. And we don't know whether we will adapt, but we surely know that we can adapt. If we start slicing the magnitude of the challenge, regaining self-efficacy and control over its complexity, continue prioritizing and start thinking out of the box we have a good chance to rise to the challenges. And again the design of the monetary system will become key.

Notes

1. Empirical findings in the Western psychology of wisdom basically confirm major ancient findings of Eastern mysticism. What makes a human wise? It is the capacity to tolerate uncertainty, accepting the relativity of values and norms, adopting a longer-term perspective, allowing more complex and contradictory emotional states, developing the capacity to distance oneself from one's ego state and becoming more mentally balanced towards day-to-day experiences while remaining curious about the miracles the world has to offer. We should take account of these parallels when talking about redesigning the financial system; see for example Sternberg and Jordan (2005).
2. See D. Meadows (2002).
3. A good summary of intertwined causality is provided by E. Laszlo (1996). For a definition and discussion of the implications of mutual causality, see J. Macy (1991).
4. In fact, open-flow network systems operate with many more variables: they generate fractals, i.e. scale-independent isomorphic states. Such systems are best understood first through fuzzy logic, then through discrete and clear figures: it is not black and white, nor 0 and 1, but everything in between that counts. Most open-flow network systems are further characterized by non-linear, non-reductionist and complex features. Such systems mainly develop crossover scale modalities, meaning that they generate new emergent qualities from one scale to the next. And finally such open-flow network systems are able to learn from failure, disaster, losses and crisis. This is called "anti-fragility". These systems have the tendency to create more inner order and act negentropically (e.g. like a cell compared to sub-cellular components). However, despite all the parallels that most if not all systems have in common, there is at least one component that differentiates biological systems from social ones: social systems are able to reflect upon themselves. If we do not take all these components into account in our attempts to better understand the complex financial system, we run the risk of misinterpreting fundamental economic data and drawing the wrong conclusions from it. See Meadows (2008), Soros (2015), and Taleb (2012).
5. Goerner et al. 2009.
6. See Laeven and Valencia (2013). Anti-fragility is more than resilience, as a system that is exposed to shocks not only resists, but improves through exposure to volatility, randomness and stressors. In this understanding, a parallel currency system is an anti-fragile feature. In finance, this is known as the Barbell strategy: "A dual strategy, a combination of two extremes, one safe and one speculative, deemed more robust than a 'monomodal' strategy; often a necessary condition for anti-fragility" (p. 428).The heterogeneity of capital structure and additional optionality increase this form of anti-fragility. More options (optionality) means that errors cause less harm. We start to benefit from uncertainty. The more complex a financial system, the higher its uncertainty, the higher the preference for optionality rather than predictability, teleological thinking or the creation of additional information. All this is expressed and favored in a parallel currency approach to creating a more sustainable future: creating positive feedback loops by gaining from disorder.
7. The exact balance varies depending on the system under investigation. Therefore, we propose a working definition of sustainability as the optimum balance between efficiency and resilience.
8. For data see food and land use coalition (2019).

9. See also the work of Beinhocker (2006), where the author demonstrates the fallacy of modern economics being misclassified as closed systems.

10. Instability is like a house of cards. From a speculator's perspective, it might be interesting to bet against the next financial crisis. From a systemic perspective, where most parameters are interlinked in a complex, non-linear manner, the next collapse of that house of cards could be caused by anything. Nobody knows what this will be in advance, although everybody will have known better in hindsight.

11. This is extremely expensive, requires 3–5% in direct and indirect costs (over three to five years) to partially restore, reshape and stabilize the system so it can fulfill its function of serving the real economy (risk allocation, intermediate function, maturity transformation). These costs are borne exclusively by present or future taxpayers. This money is then not available for social and ecological projects. See Laeven & Valencia (2013); Lietaer et al. (2012).

12. Up to 10% of the global GDP, equaling approximately 7–10 trillion USD, are held offshore; see Alstadsæter et al. (2018), Saez and Zucman (2019a).

13. Just as a reminder: at the 1992 Earth Summit in Rio de Janeiro, the global community decided to invest 0.7% of global GDP in foreign development aid. Apart from some of the Scandinavian countries, no country has ever achieved this ratio in the last 35 years (Grubb et al. 2019).

14. Regulatory efforts normally increase the homogeneity, contagion effects and co-linear amplification of market behaviors (like mark to market-effects). Additionally, we are regulating a complex system of which we are not fully in control. This fact must be taken into consideration to adjust our expectations concerning the extent to which our monetary system can be regulated. Regulation remains limited and it might be more beneficial to shed this illusion of control and simply start learning how to deal with uncertainty. See McDonough and Braungart (2002).

15. Currently there are over 4000 complementary, parallel currency projects in operation worldwide (Lietaer and Dunne 2013). None of them have any macroeconomic significance, but they all demonstrate that such dual systems work: from B2B, Lets, local barter, to regional money, B2C, C2C etc., they all have a social, sectoral or ecological target built in and are able to solve concrete, local problems. For example, the Bristol Pound is a regional currency with an exchange rate of one to one with the British Pound. The mayor of Bristol is paid completely in this currency, a fact that seeks to demonstrate at least two aspects: users can pay local taxes with the Bristol Pound, and the wealth created in the region stays in the region. The payment of taxes is crucial to *any* money system, as it closes the loop between state, households and corporate sector.

16. Lietaer et al. (2012); Lietaer and Dunne (2013).

17. See Haldane and May (2011), where the authors state that "homogeneity breeds fragility" and a financial ecosystem requires "system-wide characteristics of the network" (pp. 351–355).

18. If we take interconnectedness seriously and apply it to the financial sector, a systemic view requires us to confess honestly that we need to stop bashing the corporate and political worlds. For example, corporates and investors are managing the money of millions of workers who waive parts of their salary for their future pension, which is invested in corporates and state funds. And in Western democracies, politicians represent the average will of their citizens. In short: *we ourselves* are the politicians and the investors we are criticizing. A systemic view requires a systemic change that includes all of us.

19. Another way of looking at this phenomenon is the so-called "opportunity–cost approach": these are the costs of non-realized alternatives. Money could have been spent on something else more valid instead of repairing damage. When a roof is broken, we have to repair it. The same is true of any damage control costs. We only see where we have spent the money, but do not see where we could have spent the money instead. As damage control has become tremendously expensive and will be even more expensive in future, we might have to look for a mechanism that prevents us from causing further damage. For detailed theoretical explanations of the concept of opportunity costs, see Buchanan (2008). For example, the cost of ending poverty in 20 years is 175 billion USD per year (Sachs 2006). The opportunity costs of unrealized human potential are at least 10–15 times higher. The general counter-argument is "better than nothing", meaning it is better to transfer 0.5% of GDP than nothing at all. As true

as this argument is, it is irrational in economic terms, because the cost of not financing the commons will be higher in the long run. See Brunnhuber (2015).

20. From an evolutionary perspective, this is the result of a developmental process in which analytical, logical, critical, perspectival, ego- or self-centered thinking is the product of an ontogenetic and phylogenetic process. In short: the mind evolves, and this process is not random, but follows predictable steps and stages. Volumes of empirical evidence prove that this applies to all properties of the mind (motivational, cognitive, affective, learning, sensomotoric, kinesthetic, spiritual, social etc.). One of the core findings is that ego- or self-centered thinking is not the last evolutionary step. There is more to come. Psychologists sometimes call these states of consciousness integral, holistic, transpersonal, post-conventional or transrational. See Wilber (2000) or Brunnhuber (2016, 2018).

21. See Hertwig and Grüene-Yanoff (2017), or Cane et al. (2012).

22. Daniel Kahneman (2011; Kahneman and Tversky 1982) classified this way of thinking as "reference class forecasting" or "external view" bias: as humans, we tend to look at the future too optimistically and classify risks and probability incorrectly. Potential risks are systematically undervalued, whereas potential gains are overestimated. We mainly follow a "confirmation bias", tending to stick to what we know and extending this information in a linear way.

23. See Darwin (1859).

24. Additionally, behavioral science describes at least six factors that increase the likelihood of sustainable behavioral change. If we look at behavioral changes from a personal perspective, we should consider what we call the "big six" or "six Ps": Pleasure, Purpose, Positive intermittent reinforcement, Prosocial commitment, Profit and the by-Proxy effect: First we start identifying a "purpose" in what we are doing, we draw "pleasure" and satisfaction from it, operating within an environment that enables "positive" intermittent reinforcement instead of sanctions, and providing a rewards for "pro-social" commitment, which goes beyond an egocentric view; empowerment and "profit" will help us to gain control over what we are doing and get a return from it; and finally, the change requires a mechanism in which not abstract theory, data or metaphysical beliefs, but a "by-proxy", step-by-step approach guarantees transformation. Any future financial engineering needs to take this into account.

25. See for example Escobar (2011, 2015).

26. See Byers (2014) or Dewey (1910).

27. McGilchrist (2009).

28. See Kahneman (2011).

29. This is especially prominent in the left prefrontal cortex. The prefrontal cortex provides humans with the capacity to distance themselves from the world instead of acting through mere reflex. This generates control over evolutionarily older neuroanatomical systems through mental probing, reasoning, the use of tools and language. This allows us to investigate ourselves and the world without an automatic and immediate reflex loop following a given stimulus. For the first time, we have the possibility to avoid, refuse and negate things. Besides these cognitive properties, we have evolved the capacity to feel empathy, creating a social brain that allows us to better understand the other. See LeDoux (1996, 2000).

30. See De Giacomo and Fiorini (2017).

31. See Miller and Cohen (2001).

32. We should note that system 1 and system 2 are not identical with the right and the left hemisphere. However, they do demonstrate a general finding that can be adapted usefully to finance: a dual processing or asymmetrical, lateralized entity with two optional sub-systems that interact with one another, each offering different features for problem solving, is superior to a monoculture, one-brain or one-mind feature. See Kahneman (2011), McGilchrist (2009), and Taleb (2012).

33. To note: most scientific findings occur where it has become possible to connect unconnected, ambivalent components, such as objects and the law of gravity (I. Newton), electricity and magnetism (J.C.Maxwell), or acceleration and gravity (A. Einstein).

34. This design is like a master and his emissary (see McGilchrist 2009): the operating system provides an impulse, an idea, a command or a drive. It is a master who never intervenes in the

world, never manipulates, but rather retains a helicopter view. The master requires an emissary who transmits the message or does the job. And it is the linear, sequential system that does this. We could assume that if such a duality is in place, there must be kind of a third system, integrating system 1 and 2 or the left and the right hemisphere. This system 3—so to speak—is not about fast or slow, rational or intuitive, parallel or sequential, but about a mode that offers a multi-directional, multi-perspectival, complementary and non-dual way of perceiving, thinking, acting, deciding and living, prior to any differentiation into two systems. For thousands of years, the world's mystical traditions have provided empirical evidence of such a third system.

35. Most thinking happens within a given conceptional framework, and most (if not all) scientific discoveries occur when this rule-based conceptual thinking is questioned and transcended. Irregularities, ambiguities, anomalies and paradoxes are dissolved and new connections and insights become visible. W. Byers calls this state "deep thinking" (2014): opposites and irregularities can be contained, and complementarities, fractal correlations, creativity and new learning occur. If we replace outdated technologies but our thinking remains the same, and if we change our government but our thinking remains the same, these new technologies and this new government will be just the same as the old ones as long as our consciousness stays the same. A change in consciousness towards greater mindfulness, grace, grit and detachment allows us to regroup and dissolve some of these ambiguities and generate a new paradigm, a new thinking and a new way of managing problems.

36. We are aware that the two mental modes (S1 and S2) and the two hemispheres (right and left). are not identical, but overlap to a large extent. However, each psychological property—such as thinking, feeling, perceiving, decision-making or motivation—always requires both separate hemispheres and ultimately both mental modes to be successful.

37. It should be noted that the following argument for a parallel currency system responds to basic findings in psychology which show that positive reinforcement seems to lead to better results than continuous punishment or aversive incentives. It is simply easier to steer behavior through positive than through negative reinforcement. With negative reinforcement, each time something has to be corrected the agent has to change course. By contrast, the reward mode is more attractive and motivational, meaning that we exert more effort to achieve a specific goal. Each time a green dollar or Euro is invested, each agent can be sure that he or she is contributing directly to a better future. Positive reinforcement therefore enhances the probability of a specific desired behavior, event or result. Historically, see Pavlov (1927) and Skinner (1990). For a more recent work, see Schultz (2015). The carrot is more effective than the stick—however, in the meantime we might need both.

38. Personal thanks to Daniel Kahneman for his personal feedback on this topic.

39. The more complex a challenge is—and living in the Anthropocene represents such a challenge—the more humans need to access both systems. In an era of paradigm shift, the most efficient way to deploy the two systems (and the two hemispheres respectively) is to first apply system 1, which is fast, fuzzy, non-linear, contextual and holistic, in order to evaluate the main strategies, risks and challenges ahead. Once they are identified, system 2 is more appropriate to re-evaluate, analyze, focus and dissect the next sequential and linear steps.

40. We are realizing that we have "oversold globalization" (Stiglitz 2017a). The process of further global integration increases the productivity and efficiency of resources, but does not necessarily create new jobs. In the standard model, any free trade will create cheaper imports (with losses of domestic jobs) and potentially create new jobs in the export sector. Empirically, however, globalization generates at least four imperfections: 1. imperfect risk management (e.g. loss of energy supply or loss of jobs), 2. an imperfect competitive advantage, which generates spillovers and externalities that are not priced in (e.g. cars, solar panels); 3. imperfect competition, where market power and monopolies distort price and regional supply; 4. imperfect distribution of income and wealth, where the winners take all. All four imperfections go hand in hand with a loss of domestic jobs, wealth and lifestyle. This all started with a change in market rules at least a decade (1970s) before the disruptive impact of digital technologies. A global corporate flat tax, trade unions, minimum income, and antitrust laws are conventional

measures to regain control over the process of globalization. A more extensive analysis of the issues addressed here is provided in Stiglitz (2017b).

41. Among the other effects causing this form of inequality (differences in taxing capital versus labor), corporates have been using up to 50% of their revenue to buy up their own shares. Another 40% are dividends for the shareholders (Lazonick 2014). Taken together, this means that 90% of the profits go to their owners. As most of the shareholders belong to the upper 10% of society (Wolff 2017), this mechanism increases the wealth gap rather than closing it and does not help us to solve the problems ahead.

42. This Jevons paradox (Jevons 1866) has been empirically verified and further specified. Over a dozen different forms of rebound effects have been found. For example, Santarius (2015) distinguishes financial, motivational, industrial, economic and structural forms of rebound effects, which in part reinforce themselves. See also Sorrell and Dimitropoulos (2008).

43. Four taboos dominate our modern society: sex, power, death and money. A taboo is something that is not discussed but always remains indirectly present. Overcoming a taboo requires a critical mind, an expanded consciousness and a corresponding social agenda. In this text, we are trying to overcome the taboo of the monetary system only.

44. For example, during the "green revolution" in India, hybrid seeds were able to strongly increase the crop yield of rice and wheat in the 1970s and therefore allowed India to feed its hungry growing population. Similar attempts to introduce a green revolution in Africa have been less successful due to a lack of infrastructure, corruption, and other failures of the existing system (Oladele et al. 2010). After all, the success of a green revolution to end poverty and hunger requires not only technological innovation, but also an adequate political, a social environment and a suitable infrastructure (Griffin 1979; Paarlberg 2009; Rosset et al. 2000).

45. Events for which we do not have words in consequence are not fully mentally available and semantically represented. Behavioral science classifies such states as "hypo-cognitive states". However, not having a proper word for an event does not mean that it does not exist. It will still affect us even if it is underrepresented in our mind. Market failures or policy failure are examples of such effects. See Lakoff (2004), Wu and Dunning (2018).

46. Complex is not complicated, is not contingent: *complex* simply means that a system has so many variables that we cannot fully grasp it. *Complicated* means that a procedure is manageable, but requires a lot of training—for example, a neurosurgical intervention or a complicated mathematical equation. But both are fully intellectually and practically accessible. *Contingent* by contrast means that an event happens randomly and was unforeseeable within a given scenario. Each setting—complex/complicated/contingent—requires a completely different mindset. In a complex situation, we need greater tolerance for uncertainty, in a complicated situation we require endurance, training, talent und discipline. And in a contingent state, we might require luck and serenity, because sometimes shit happens!

47. Bermejo Carbonell and Werner (2018).

48. Complementarity defines a relationship between two components that are incompatible yet mutually required, both necessary to describe one and the same thing. The opposites do not cancel each other out, but are both needed to describe an event, a thing or an item. Examples include location and momentum, energy and time, wave and particle, determinism and chance, physical and mental, structure and function, substance and process, autonomy and interconnectedness. In this sense, the two currency systems described in this text are intertwined; they lead to multiple positive feedback loops and operate in such a complementary manner. See Bohr (1966); Meyer-Abich (1965); Walach (2010).

49. See Fowler and Christakis (2010); the power of cooperation is not only true for humans, but also for flowers and animals, see with further examples Hare and Woods (2020).

50. We can take the topic one step further. In order to have a person change their behavior, they require contradictory information that builds up their tolerance for ambiguity. This is well known in clinical psychology, especially when it comes to lifestyle changes. Studies have shown that people need not just the motivation to change, but also information to evaluate the

difference between changing and not changing: this is called the *mental preparedness for change* (Miller and Rollnick 2012).

51. See Scott and Cogburn (2017).

52. To note: coordinated group behavior is universal throughout human history, in contrast to current neoliberal economics, which pretends that competitive, selfish behavior is what increases wealth. See Anshel and Kipper (1988), Cross et al. (2016), Rennung and Göritz (2016), Vicary et al. (2017).

53. Even if this number is a "fatal calculation", where we risk underestimating the costs of climate damage, the argument still holds: we don't know whether we will, but we *could* adapt to this new reality and one way to do this is changing our mindset and our monetary system. See: Spratt et al. (2020).

54. For data, see references and further empirical findings in Lomborg (2020), which includes UN MOSAICC modeling, Nordhaus' DICE models, EMF (Stanford's Energy Modeling Form), IAM (integrated assessment models) and SSPs (shared socioeconomic pathways) as well as latest IPCC recommendations. In fact there is a subtle, but significant trade-off between the costs of rising temperatures (which are real) and the costs of our climate policy. Both are relevant. The challenge is to strike the right balance between T (temperature rise) and GDP (economic activities), between avoiding temperature rise and adapting to temperature rise. Qualified economic growth—mainly the SDGs—, investment in research and development, a wise CO_2 tax, lifestyle changes, infrastructural investments, new forms of social security systems (collective health coverage, basic income), and an adaptation of our monetary system providing new incentives are such creative components.

55. For example: *Poverty and inequality* are increased through global warming, but the causal link is weak, there are other more important factors causing poverty and income inequality. Take *wildfire or pandemics:* Both are correlated to global warming, but up to four fifths of wildfires are human made and the loss of original habitat causing pandemics is causally linked to the expansive economic activities. Both are only indirectly linked to global warming. Expansive economic activities built upon renewables would cause the same loss of habitat. *Loss of biodiversity* is a severe challenge for humanity, but only 15% is causally linked to global warming, the rest again is due to expansive land grabbing. The same weak link is true for *urban air pollution*. Or take *rising sea levels*: The Netherlands has shown over the last century how to deal with high sea levels. Schiphol Airport is 3.4 meters under sea level and the income per capita in the Netherlands is one of the highest in the world. Another one is *water stress*, a severe life-threatening challenge for millions of people. Israelis are living in the desert and can, due to innovative water irrigations systems, export water. The point is: global warming is probably the most threatening challenge for humanity, but we as humans can get back into the driver's seat. Besides technology, lifestyle changes, R&D, taxations schema, we have to come up with wise, differentiated adaptation strategies for all these associated problems. A redesign of the monetary incentive is one of them.

Chapter 4
Unleashing the Sleeping Giant: Discovering New Ground and Starting the Dance of the TAO

In Chap. 2, we explored the conventional way of financing social and ecological challenges and introduced the notion of a "six-pack" of tools. This included regulatory efforts (transparency, taxation, taxonomy), impact funding, hybrid ex-swap strategies, and public-private partnership initiatives to tackle an unstable financial system. We also provided a rationale for why and how to redistribute money. In Chap. 3, we saw that systems theory offers a different perspective in which the optimum of any sustainable pathway lies in between efficiency and resilience, in the "anti-fragile zone" of a given system. Additionally, we elaborated upon the full mental capacity of the human brain and mind, distinguishing between linear and parallel thinking. Using this dual perspective, the present chapter analyzes the aspects of our current financial system that prevent us from creating the liquidity to finance our future. Using the SDGs as a benchmark plan, we estimate the required amount of additional liquidity needed to finance these goals. Lastly, we describe the alternative and complementary mechanism of parallel currencies to circumvent these limitations. However, our discovery of this new ground needs to begin with a better understanding of the global commons.

From an empirical perspective, the presence of high yield and revenue can promote societal cooperation. From a behavioral standpoint, however, high yields also lead to the challenges of the free-rider effect, moral hazard and the so-called "tragedy of the commons". To overcome this mismatch, a legally binding and reliable mechanism is required. This mechanism needs to be able to harmonize and reconcile two major challenges. The first challenge is the "social paradox" of game theory, which describes the tension between personal and individual interests on the one hand and collective and public interests on the other hand. In our scenario of a green, parallel currency, where the SDGs represent the collective perspective, any individual activity will automatically be in line with these public goods from the very beginning, 7 days a week and 24 hours a day for all participants.[1] The second

The original version of this chapter was revised. The correction to this chapter can be found at https://doi.org/10.1007/978-3-030-64826-8_7

challenge is the "moral dilemma" that exists between maximizing individual interests and adhering to greater moral and ethical standards. Here, the SDGs represent a kind of moral map of objectives that we, as a global human society, have agreed to implement. Individual interests can be maximized within this realm without violating ethical standards, as they are now one and the same. The mechanism we are describing here fulfills these criteria.

4.1   The Tragedy of the Global Commons

In 1968, Garret Hardin published a seminal paper on the tragedy of the commons.[2] He came to the conclusion that any good that cannot be sufficiently excluded from private use is a common good, and will eventually be either overused or neglected. This triggered several decades of debate, culminating in the Nobel Prize in Economics awarded to E. Ostrom.[3] This discussion is far from over today: the SDGs have raised the issue once again, as most, if not all of these goals fulfill the characteristics of a common. Here again, the question arises: when a good, a right or a service causing a free-rider effect is either overused or neglected, how can a sound and safe financial incentive to change this behavior be guaranteed?

This concept of commons is an established component in both economic literature and current social debate. Any good that cannot be sufficiently excluded and that leads to free-rider and moral hazard effects becomes a common good. Commons in this sense can be categorized in two major groups: firstly, ecological commons such as air, water, land, and biodiversity, and secondly, so-called social goods such as the right to education, access to health care and information. Such social commons then take on the character of human rights.[4] Hence, the taxonomy we choose becomes a political question. Once a community defines a common good as such, it is a common.

In both cases, humans should have access to these goods and services and each individual should enjoy equal access to them; therefore, they should be financed, by and large, through the community as a whole. Whereas there is a general consensus on the definition and the social impact of commons, the opinions on how to finance them differ.

There are several reasons why we generally take a favorable view of commons. They can ensure greater societal stability (like democracy, the civil sector), they help to pool private risks (like health care) and they can increase the given society's overall allocative performance (like national security, the sewage system, highways or health). Fresh air, access to basic health care, and the protection of biodiversity always stay the same, regardless of which type of economy we have. It is the economics and the financing of the commons that are different.

Three options traditionally have dominated the economic discussion on how to best manage our commons. The first is to privatize all commons, and thus remove any liabilities associated with them by turning them into private goods. The second is to manage common goods by restricting access to them to defined communities. They are thus turned into club or cooperative goods. This form of limited membership resolves one of the biases that commons are subject to, namely overuse. The third option is to allow public or state authorities to regulate the usage of commons through laws and entitlements. In this case, the commons are co-financed through taxes, fees, charity or philanthropy.[5] Below, we describe a fourth option, which uses new and different monetary channels to finance common goods. To be more specific: most of the SDGs are common goods such as clean air and water, universal access to health care, education (including preschool education), and maintaining biodiversity. None of the common goods referred to in the SDGs are exclusive. They should be accessible to and enjoyed by everyone during their lifetime on this planet. Additionally, none of these goals are separate from one another; they are all interconnected. In order to finance commons, we need to correct the misalignments of the financial system that prevent us from realizing the potential of the commons instead of privatizing them. Imagine a world in which air is private property: every human is allocated 15 breaths per minute, with the air coming from a tank on their back. Once they exceed these 15 breaths, they have to buy more of the fresh air, meaning that the individual's purchasing power determines the number of breaths they take. A first step towards a better understanding of our commons is to create a so-called total cost analysis (TCA).

Box 4.1   The Total Cost Analysis (TCA)

Just an intermediary step: the total cost analysis (TCA). Instead of searching for a quick fix, we can start to broaden our mind and look at the same economic process from the perspective of a total cost analysis (TCA). Such a TCA is a parallel form of risk assessment in which the whole context is taken into consideration rather than just pre/post linear benchmarks. In a fully connected world, the traditional form of herd behavior or lemming effect is costly and inefficient, even though the social and environmental costs are clearly identified. A TCA changes both the benchmark and the investment strategy and we start to look upstream and downstream along the value chain as far as we can. For example, at the gas station, gasoline costs around 1.50 USD. Up to two thirds of that price is made up of tax. However, from a TCA perspective, this price is not accurate, because private fossil-fuel-driven mobility leads to spillover costs in the form of accidents and climate change. These costs are covered by society at large, regardless of whether one drives a car or not, and are up to 150% higher than the initial price one pays at the gas station, namely 3.40 USD.[6] The same is true for farming, smoking, drinking alcohol, using plastic, heavy industry (steel, aluminum) among others. When we start looking at the entire value chain from a broader perspective, we will end up seeing more, evaluating more and considering more.[7]

We should take this argument one step further, and start differentiating between three different levels of risks: individual life risks (health, unemployment, poverty, security), wholesale risks (running a for-profit business) and systemic risks (loss of biodiversity, pandemics, global warming or air pollution). Societies themselves decide into which category each risk event falls. Once this has been decided, the risk profile requires a different financial approach each time. The cheapest way to organize individual life risks is to cover them through collective fees or taxes (e.g. collective health care insurance). Systemic risks require national and international institutions (e.g. WHO, World Bank), whereas wholesale risks should remain a private liability. The credit default swap (CDS) market, a highly volatile and liquid market of 25–65 trillion USD annually, can play a crucial role in private de-risking. Put options, futures, arbitrages, and short sell–long buyings among others provide a variety of financial tools and experiences to increase resilience to black swan events, uncertainties, and increased asymmetric shocks, and enable the transition towards a greener future. Governments are bigger than most corporates, have different interests and tasks, and are not better private managers able to bail out corporate responsibilities. In fact, increasing public debts that place an additional burden on future generations is less efficient than wholesale risk management for wholesale and business affairs. It is less the CDS itself and rather its unregulated form and size ("over the counter"—OTC) that can become weapons of mass destruction (Warren Buffett) (Fig. 4.1).[8]

4.2   Financing the Global Commons

The most commonly advocated form of financing our commons is so-called co-financing, which constitutes the core argument in most, if not all economic theories on financing social and ecological commons. This co-financing strategy is a form of end-of-pipe approach, well known in engineering science: we first implement a technology, lifestyle or economic activity that harms our environment (polluting fresh air, for example), then add a filter at the end of the process (i.e. at the end of the pipe) in order to avoid too much damage.[9] Co-financing has the following rationale: goods and services freely traded on the market are taxed and this revenue becomes the main source of finance for common goods. In this widely accepted view, commons are secondary and subordinate to the activities of the free market. Only when the market generates sufficient yields and liquidity and the political will is strong enough can common goods be financed.

To give an example: if a pig farmer wanted to set up a business with 1000 pigs in a rural area, providing jobs for 30 workers and supplying pork to the region, the communal authorities and the media would see this as an innovative investment that deserves to benefit from tax breaks and other state support. But if a nonprofit organization wanted to establish a nursing home for 100 children suffering from parental neglect and educational deficits, employing 80 co-workers and benefiting dozens of additional small and medium-sized firms and hundreds of additional families, and where the exactly same amount of money is invested as in the pig farm, the project would instead be considered a cost to and burden for society. This is surprising, given that we know that investing in early childhood has a return on investment (ROI) of 1:10 to 1:15 for society as a whole. Addressing domestic violence has an

Fig. 4.1 The dissociated world: the private world and the underutilized rest (Tuca Vieira (C))

even higher ROI (1:50).[10] The pork business model will never achieve this ROI and has several negative externalities besides, such as increased water consumption and a negative impact on human health.[11]

It becomes obvious that the gap between the funding required and the money available is so large that we need to discuss fundamentally new ways of financing this agenda and identify fundamentally new channels to support it. To phrase it as a rhetorical question: does it make sense to support a political and economic agenda that seeks to overcome gender inequality, educational biases, forced migration and universal health care if the core mechanism in place (expensive economic growth, redistributing money, end-of-pipe finance) means that it will take about a century to overcome gender inequality,[12] bridge the education gap between Brazil and South Korea or Finland in the PISA evaluation, equal out general access to basic medical care, and achieve basic water, sanitation and hygiene standards globally?[13]

In contrast to the pre-industrial era, when we lived in a large, slow, empty and transparent world, our world has become small, fast, full and complex. The more connected we are and the more we have to deal with planetary boundaries, the more we find ourselves confronted with global and common goods that cannot be privatized. In short: in our connected world, commons we all share become more important than private goods that belong exclusively to individuals. A private good is organized around private equity and property claims (like a car, a pool or a corporate share) with limited private liability. Private goods maximize yield and the gains are either reinvested, consumed or partly redistributed through taxes, fees, charities or pledges. In this understanding, private goods are so-called positional or luxury goods. The nature of a positional good is characterized by its relative value to a comparable good or service by someone else (like a bigger car, a larger pool or a greater corporate share). To note: this process is endless, as there will be always someone with a bigger car, larger pool or greater corporate share.[14]

By contrast, commons are different: common goods are not something that we redistribute, they are not a form of charity to be asked for or dispensed, they are something to which every human being has a (legal) entitlement. Once they have been achieved, the mission has been accomplished. For example, once the protection of biodiversity has been achieved, global warming has been challenged, and universal access to health care has been organized, these common goods will be complete. We will simply have to maintain the status quo. In this sense, common goods are circular and regenerative by their very nature. They are a means to an end and do not force a community to grow in order to maintain their status. By contrast, private goods are an accumulative process resulting from continuous linear, exponential and unlimited growth, yields and insatiable desires.[15] It gets even better: the willingness the pay for common goods, to invest in national and regional assets, and interpersonal trust (helpfulness, friendliness and hospitality) is astonishingly high on a global level. Measured in over 140 countries on a scale from 1 to 10, most citizens are prepared to pay for their commons, ranking their willingness 6–8 out of 10. These empirical findings prove that communities all over the world are more than prepared to value and pay for common goods. The question however remains: where is the money to come from?[16]

Common goods traditionally are characterized by their excludability, private versus public nature and/or by their mis- or overuse as a result of the free-rider effect. However, these characteristics can be misleading because they emphasize the economic use rather than the intrinsic value of commons. Removing this economic lens changes their value entirely. We then see that common goods have the capacity to stabilize society, as seen for example in democracies or in the nonprofit sector. They help to pool private risks, as seen in health care. And they can increase societies' overall allocative performance, as seen in national security, sewage systems and public highways. Seen through this lens, fresh air, basic access to health care, and the protection of biodiversity have an intrinsic value in themselves and transcend the type of economic system in which they exist. So the way we look at the world and the way we calculate and measure it depends on whether we take products' entire life cycle into account and consider their total costs, including the costs of common goods. In this book, a common, be it social or ecological, is defined as the sustainable use and universal access to a good, service, or right, regulated by a body of peers and operating partly through a different financial network than the conventional one. A common can be local, regional, national or global, depending on its nature.

4.3   The Private Purse Is Not the Public Purse

We can look at this topic from another perspective: private households and corporates require a stringent balance sheet so as not to go bankrupt. From a microeconomic perspective, private households and corporates cannot spend more than they earn in the first place. The public purse is different, however. When we have a sovereign nation state with the ability to issue money, the rationale for financing its public budget is fundamentally different than in the private sector: it follows the idea of reverse financial engineering. The public sector needs to identify those projects that potentially will generate the most ROI for the public entity and then generate the money to make them possible. The SDGs are the best example. In other words: the budget has to balance the economy, not the other way round. The motto is: invest and spend first and tax, regulate and expect revenues later.

In a larger context, the very nature of the creation of money is best described as a complementary relationship between debt and equity. Debts refer to what we have to do for the monetary system—mainly paying back the loans in question. Equity, by contrast, refers to what money does: it creates a better world. Traditionally, we emphasize the debt aspect. Emphasizing equity, however, reveals a completely different perspective on the same phenomena: if 95% of the money created is invested in default assets on which the monetary regulator sees no return, the central bank's balance sheet has to be adjusted and 95% of potential revenue for the commercial banking sector written off.[17] But 5% of real net gains still remain for society as a whole. And if this 5% has been invested in a common future, building hospitals, kindergartens, universities and public facilities, we will be better off than without it.

So we see that debt and equity are complementary to one another, just like many other components of our monetary system. And this why the private purse is not the public purse. And if the public purse is substantially different to the private one, what is the key indicator of its performance?

4.4   Waking the Sleeping Giant: The Return on Investment in the Commons

What is the ROI of a red sofa in your living room? Does it pay off to be green? In fact, it all depends on the way we look at the world and the way we calculate and measure it. It depends on whether we are prepared to look at the whole life cycle of products and consider their total costs. As mentioned above, a well-established method of evaluating future investment is to look at ROI.[18] In a very general way, ROI describes the economic performance of the profit or loss generated on an investment in order to compare different alternatives. In short: how much do we get per dollar invested?[19]

We have long known that all common goods benefit everybody and therefore have a significant impact on society as a whole: federal security, highways, sewage systems, public research and development, access to universal health care, or simply the provision of a place at kindergarten can make a huge difference to our lives. But only recently have we become able to measure the potential return on investments in such commons. Empirical economic analyses have found that the return on investment in common goods is higher by far than in most, if not all private business.

Historical data from the Federal Reserve database[20] on the arithmetical average of Standard & Poor's 500 index versus three-month and ten-year treasury bills demonstrate the differences in yield over differing time spans, expressed in the Table 4.1 below.

We thus see that over a time period of almost 100 hundred years, private and state bonds yielded a 5–10% return per year on average. These data can be compared to the ROI of common goods, such as the goods included in the SDGs. Indeed, the SDGs have an arithmetical average return of 1:15 per annum—up to 100 times larger than the S&P values or returns on treasury bills.[21] The Copenhagen Consensus,[22] a think tank including several Nobel laureates, has produced some stunning figures in this regard: the ROI of universal access to contraception is 1:120;

Table 4.1 Return on investment of the S&P 500, a three-month treasury bill and a ten-year treasury bill over differing time periods

Different time span	S&P 500 (%)	3-month treasury bill (%)	10-year treasury bill (%)
1928–2015	11	3	5
1966–2015	11	5	7
2006–2019	8	1	3

the ROI of making public information on the ownership of illicit financial flows is 1:49; that of allowing greater migration, 1:45; and that of reducing child malnutrition, 1:45.

Because common goods for the most are part non-excludable and cause inherent free-rider effects, society as a whole benefits once the commons are in place (Table 4.2).[23]

In order to get a sense of proportion and priority, we can take this argument one step further. If we prioritize the 17 SDGs and their 176 sub-targets according to ROI and feasibility, we end up with a portfolio of strategies that allows us to assume a return of 1:15. This means that investing 100 billion USD generates 1.5 trillion USD of social and ecological goods, creating a benefit 10 to 15 to 100 times more than the invested dollars—for all of us. This is like waking a sleeping giant.

If global commons have such a high proven ROI[24] and private and state investment does not, then two further questions arise. First: what is the estimated amount needed to fully cover all SDGs worldwide? And second: what is the mechanism required to implement their full potential? Could it be that the fault lies not with the commons themselves but with the chosen monetary system, which systematically prevents us from meeting unmet needs and unleashing the full potential that common goods can offer for humanity?

As mentioned earlier in the book, we are now living in a new era, the Anthropocene. In this world, humans determine the geo-ecological state of the planet. In this era, unlike in former times, we are fully interconnected and need to operate within planetary boundaries. Economically speaking, in such a world there are no more externalities, as every agent could be affected by potential negative feedback loops directly or indirectly at any time. This affects private property and its liabilities as well as common goods and their potential overuse or underutilization. As long as economic agents are isolated subjects and operate in an environment where losses can be externalized, it is rational to overuse or neglect common goods as a free rider, as others will have to pay the bill anyway. In a fully connected world, however, free-rider behavior is irrational, as ultimately we end up harming ourselves. In the Anthropocene, it is investing in the commons that is rational.

So how do we go about this investment and wake this sleeping giant? We know how to treat malaria, how to educate children at preschool level, how to set up sewage systems in order to avoid water-borne infectious diseases, how to build hospitals and schools, and how to train teachers and medical doctors. Rousing this sleeping giant from its slumber requires not technical skills, but rather sufficient liquidity and purchasing power. Anybody engaged and invested in unleashing this giant will benefit directly from its revenue. The selfish free rider benefits from the commons in a passive way as usual, but misses out on the additional gains that only come into play if an agent is actively committed to unleashing the full potential of the commons themselves. In short: in the era of the Anthropocene, the cooperative agent is better off, whereas the selfish, competitive free rider simply loses future opportunities and misses out on wins. What we are still missing is the right financial engineering and the right monetary incentives and design to guarantee that this sleeping giant is woken and its potential unleashed for the benefit of all.

Table 4.2 Waking the sleeping giant: ROI in global commons

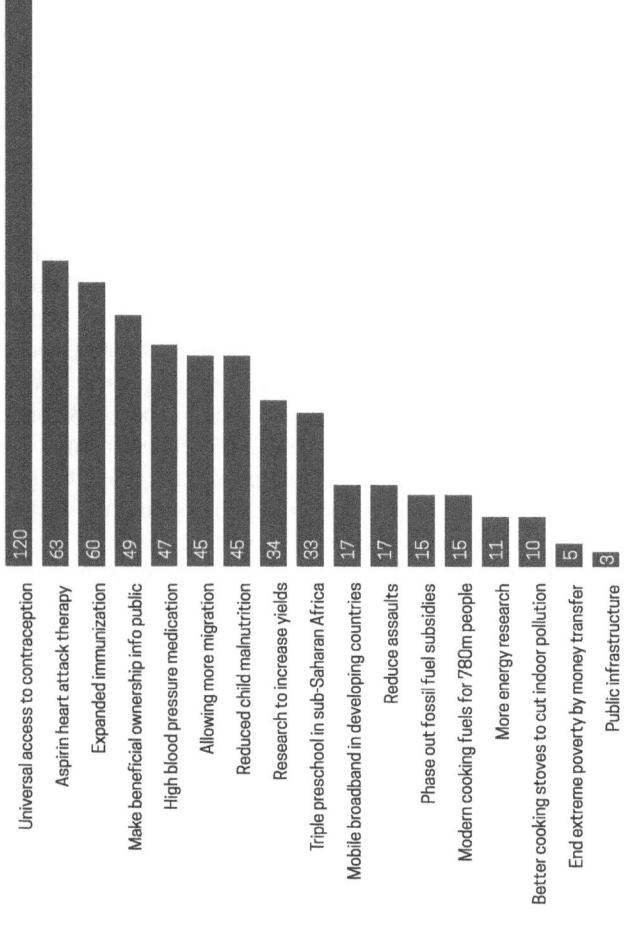

4.5   The Very Nature of the Global Commons: Overcoming Their Tragedy

A common is not a thing. It is a convention, an agreement or a rule of a given community that organizes a resource or an entitlement as a public matter instead of a private asset. As soon as a community has decided to consider something such as protecting biodiversity, challenging global warming, accessing health care, or providing pre-schooling a public good, the economic logic changes fundamentally. Therefore a global common (a social or natural common) is characterized by the sustainable use of or access to a good, service or right by and for all, regulated by the peers involved (locally, regionally, nationally or globally).

The misalignment between our current monetary system and the global commons has led to their erosion and partial destruction. It has prevented the achievement of their full economic potential for the good of humanity. Our task, then, is to adapt the economy to conform to the nature of the commons for purposes of sustainability. Traditionally, however, we have viewed sustainability as a triad of social, ecological and economic issues and left the monetary system out of the picture. This is misleading. Sustainability rather should be viewed as a funnel, as explained in the previous chapter, to better capture its complexity. The monetary system actually plays a central role in our concept of sustainability, and no discussion on the future can omit the new role that money will play in it. As money is not a thing or a commodity either, but something created by law (G.F. Knapp), we can change that law. What we need is a social mechanism or invention that allows us to dampen or fence in the destructive impact of negative externalities on our commons and our common future. Various solutions have been proposed. They include a simple "demographic fix",[25] where we stabilize and educate the world population; a "technology fix", where we invest in renewables; a "growth fix",[26] where we increase our expansive economic activities and redistribute assets; and a "governmental fix",[27] where we advocate for a global democratic parliament to regulate a global shift. While none of these "fixes" are wrong, they remain too fragmented and siloed in their approach to result in sustainable change towards a better future for the planet.[28]

A common is a common and remains a common as soon as we, as a world community, declare it as a common. A private equity is a private equity as soon as we, as the world community, declare and define it a private asset. Both cases—commons and private goods—are not a natural law, but a social convention, like a club rule or a marriage contract. However, the finance required to achieve them is different. Financing commons as commons requires an entirely different view than turning them into private equity. Instead of violating the nature of commons, we should adapt our financial architecture to the nature of the commons and not the other way round. This requires a shift both in our mindset and in the architecture of our monetary system. However, this is no easy task. There are multiple so-called lock-in effects that prevent us from unleashing this sleeping giant. They will be explained in the next chapter. To anticipate some of our argument: a dual monetary system is required to fully unleash the return on investment in commons for our society as a whole. And again: as Taoism tells us, parallelization and complementarity are key to better understanding the dynamics and the impact of the world around and within us; and this is true of the financial sector's involvement in a sustainable future, too.

Technically speaking, two further questions are being asked. First, how are common goods like clean air and water, health care, and education currently being funded, and can we do a better job at funding them? Second, is there a social optimum beyond the given equilibrium within the utility function and can we achieve a Pareto-superior optimum, including all spillovers and externalities? Currently, we are seeking to achieve this optimum using disruptive technology, moral imperatives, improved good governance, better demographic development and simple lifestyle changes. Yet we are failing to effect change. What is the missing link? Before we answer that question, we first need to identify several aspects associated with our current financial system that prevent us from creating the adequate amounts of liquidity and directing it to global common goods. These are so-called lock-in effects.

4.6   Multiple Lock-in Effects

Probably the single most important factor that explains why financing our global commons—expressed in the conversion rate consisting of co-financing and transferring money—has been so low is the so-called lock-in effect:[29] lock-in means we are compelled to follow a certain path, even when this pathway violates our values or is in some way unsustainable, unhealthy or unfair. The "lock-in" occurs because of ongoing costs within a particular sector of the economy, because of which funds then are not available to finance social and ecological projects.[30]

The most relevant examples of lock-in effects in our context include the inherent instability of the financial sector, where we are confronted with ongoing banking, currency, and sovereign debt crises, preventing us from creating a stable financial system operating in a sound, fair and green manner.[31] Every time another monetary or financial crisis occurs, it is social and ecological projects that fall off the cliff first and taxpayers' public money that has to carry the burden. The shadow economy and the huge number of illicit financial transactions, which include money laundering, trafficking, drugs, and illegal financial transactions, accounting for at least one third of our world GDP, represent another lock-in.[32] The shadow economy is widely deregulated but is interconnected with the conventional financial and real economic sector, and this informal sector is pulling our entire society in the wrong direction.[33] Yet another lock-in is the debt burden and the current volume of subsidies and taxation, which prevent us from a real transition into a green future. Our global debt burden measures over 240 trillion USD with a distribution pattern of one quarter public debt, one half corporate and household debt and one quarter financial sector debt. This debt load crowds out alternative investment possibilities,[34] creating a backlash and postponing real green investments. For example, in OECD countries between 2007 and 2009, the debt burden to GDP ratio doubled. At the same time, the amount of subsidies on the one hand and taxation on the other create push and pull effects that end up negating themselves, making a sound transition next to impossible. We are currently subsidizing the fossil industry directly with roughly

500 billion USD a year. To this sum, we need to add another 5 trillion USD (!) in indirect subsidies due to the increasing health care costs and environmental burden associated with fossil fuels.[35] Our dependency on fossil energy represents yet another lock-in: given that over 80% of our entire value chain depends directly or indirectly on oil, gas or coal, taxing this value chain without having any alternatives in place will cause multiple negative rebounds and spillovers with no real steering effect towards green business or a greener lifestyle. We are sitting on a carbon bubble equivalent to multiple trillions of USD in search of alternative investment. Our defense and military complex constitutes another such lock-in.[36] Every year, we spend several trillions of USD on protecting ourselves from one another. This involves millions of jobs and results in sustained warfare and asymmetric wars across the globe. Then there is a huge sector in our economy that represents damage control, the so-called "entropic sector". This sector reflects losses and costs that accumulate as the consequence of social disorder such as corruption, drugs, violence, terrorism, hacking, extreme inequality, irresponsible speculations, asymmetric wars, cyber wars, environmental destruction, and forced migration among others. This list is intentionally incomplete. Along our value chain, we are generating multiple such spillovers, externalities and side effects that nobody wanted to create in the first place but that still need to be managed, repaired and contained. Estimates calculate that the entropic sector represents up to 20% of our global GDP. Finally, there is the farming and agricultural sector itself:

Box 4.2 The Lock-in of Big Farming and the Relevance of Smallholders
As a rule of thumb for further discussion on Big Farming[37]: By 2050, we will require an additional two thirds of calories to feed over 9 billion people. 70–80% of the agricultural sector globally is decentralized and SME-based, requiring 20–30% of natural resources (water, energy, land). By contrast, 20–30% of agriculture is industrial, requiring 70–80% of resources and four fifths of the arable land. Smallholder farming generates 20 times more jobs than Big Farming. Regional and traditional agriculture require one to two calories to produce one calorie of a farming product. Industrial agriculture, by contrast, requires about 100 calories to generate one calorie of the same good. In addition, about one third of the entire food chain globally is wasted. Apart from some exceptions, domestic agriculture has no need to export its goods. We simply do not need subsidies to export pork from Europe to China and import strawberries vice versa. Under such conditions, 1 USD in food production generates 2 additional systemic USD in negative externalities (mainly health and environmental costs). If we further differentiate between yield per season versus yield over the long term, the situation is exacerbated further. At least two questions arise here: why should we subsidize industrial farming, which is highly inefficient from this perspective? How can we create a more regional value chain that reduces externalities? These and similar effects will be part of the global ex-swap described in Chap. 2. This ex-swap will create a market place with fewer negative spillovers that therefore is less expensive for all of us.

The following list summarizes some of the major lock-in effects preventing us from shifting towards a more sustainable future.

Some examples of so-called lock-in effects within the conventional view that prevent real transition

1. Unstable financial system
2. Massive illicit financial transactions
3. Debt burden, taxation and subsidies
4. Dependency on fossil energy and the carbon bubble
5. Defense and military complex
6. Entropic sector and social disorder

These "lock-in" effects show that any steering of our economy towards a more sustainable future is next to impossible without changing or adapting our current financial and monetary design. Under the current regime, we simply are unable to generate enough liquidity and purchasing power for large-scale projects to be carried out and instead trigger huge crowding-out effects that prevent the emergence of desperately needed future new markets.

We need to develop a social mechanism that has the magnitude, volume and power not only to meet the global challenges, but to transform our global economy towards more positive externalities and greater justice, peace and sustainability. Each attempt to manage and organize our economic transactions through a monopolistic money system is irrational in economic terms, as the costs of the inherent instability of the financial system,[38] the costs of the entropic sector, meaning the costs for damage control and the misalignments of the shadow markets cannot be corrected sufficiently, causing permanent negative spillovers. And none of these lock-in effects come cheap. In fact, the opposite is true: taxpayers, consumers, citizens in developing countries, future generations and our planet will pay the bill. It is not just a rhetorical question to ask: how long can we afford this traditional monetary monopoly? The effects of these multiple lock-ins prevent transformative change. Implementing the transformation from within the given system is like doing open-heart surgery on a marathon runner while he or she is running. The required societal shift towards sustainability will fail if we do not develop a secondary pathway to ensure it.

4.7 Purchasing Power Overrides Price Allocation

In order to better understand why the abovementioned additional liquidity is required and what its potential impact is on our common future, we need to take our argument one step further and acknowledge the difference between price and purchasing power. The former is a qualitative, the latter a more quantitative parameter. While we need both, currently the second one is overriding the first one. The price signal is the most powerful instrument available in any market economy to achieve a Pareto optimum in which goods and services are allocated in most efficient way. This is true for wages, bonuses, commodities, services and interest rates. However, the price mechanism is dysfunctional when it comes to future generations, to nature and to the majority of the current world population. Prices always follow the purchasing power. Ten percent of the world population own 90% of its wealth, and 20% of the world population earn 70% of the income and use two thirds of all global resources. This results in a situation where 80–90% of the world population cannot earn sufficient income and thereby lack the purchasing power to accumulate wealth and access resources.[39] For example, a pair of jeans at a discount store in the global North costs 100 USD. Only 5% of this price remains with those who produced the jeans in the global South. And as long as two full tanks of biodiesel in the global North cost the amount an African citizen needs to survive for a full year, the global South will never be able to create enough purchasing power to ensure a basic livelihood for its population. To remedy this asymmetry in purchasing power, additional liquidity is needed in the first place to give the majority of the world population a fair chance at economic participation, where real purchasing power enables proper market allocation and pricing, not the other way around. More importantly, this dysfunction of the price signal is not a market failure, as it is often called, but the lack of an existing market system itself.[40]

Let us be more explicit: why does the rate of starving Indian citizens increase as a result of the increased consumption of quinoa in Europe and North America? The increased popularity of the South American protein-rich grain quinoa in Europe and North America has resulted in a situation where South Americans no longer are able to purchase their own quinoa. Instead, it is exported because of the higher price it can generate and the local population then needs to rely on imported rice from India, which is less expensive. Consequently, the rate of malnourished Indian citizens increases, as does the global ecological footprint. Seen from this standpoint, this process does not make sense.[41] If there were enough purchasing power in South America, there would be fewer people starving in India. Again, price follows purchasing power and not the other way round. Accordingly, in situations where the volume of money is unevenly distributed, the price signal is not the only way to correct or balance out the overall system. Quantitative changes in the volume of money available can also balance out the system if we use different monetary channels in parallel—much like a bike with two wheels that creates greater balance and stability. In other words: there are over 7 billion people on this planet in over 200 nation states. They speak over 6000 languages, have hundreds of different cultural identities, and more than a dozen differing religious belief systems. However, there are only four main categories or levels describing income and purchasing power globally: approximately 1 billion people live on 1 USD a day, 3 billion people live on 4 USD a day, another 2 billion on 16 USD and approximately 1 billion live on over 32 USD a day. To note: each dollar has a different marginal utility function, depending on the level at which one is living.[42]

Increased purchasing power affects life expectancy, level of education, birth rates, health, gender sensitivity and democracy in a positive manner. It thus has a far greater influence on these variables than cultural context.[43] We will see below that introducing a parallel currency system can address the issue of insufficient purchasing power. It is not biased towards any specific culture or nation, religion, economic or political system. It simply advocates increasing the purchasing power available to billions of people who currently do not have access to it.

4.8   Conclusion: The Money, the Mechanism and the Measures

We need to start differentiating between three further aspects: first, where will the money for our common future come from? Will it be private, public, or additional parallel liquidity, as described in our "six-pack"? Second, what mechanism can guarantee that the money generated gets to where it is supposed to go? What does the technology and what do the monetary channels look like? Third, what are the potential positive measures to come out of this? Can we assume that the money collected and the mechanism installed will help us to steer our society towards a better future? What is the outcome? So the money, the mechanism and the measures are the three aspects we will build upon in the next chapters. Is there another mechanism beyond traditional finance without lock-in effects and sequential thinking that can finance the SDGs? And what would it look like? In other words: where can we get the money to make this huge global shift?[44] When designing a new financial system, taking this book's preliminary findings into account, we will need to accommodate findings from systems theory, like the correlations between efficiency versus resilience or the anti-fragile zone, so we can start to learn from failures to improve the system's integrity. We further need to acknowledge findings in psychology that show we have a dual brain, operating in two different but intertwined modes, and two major mindsets (system 1 and system 2), providing different frames to cope with our reality[45]; we always require both modes and systems to survive in a complex and competitive environment. We also need to take into account the fact that humans are most motivated to accept and pursue change if they can perceive a purpose in their activities, where self-efficacy and intermittent reinforcements outweigh punishment (like taxation or fees) and extrinsic motivations (like bonus programs or subsidies). Yet another fact we need to take into account is that in order to deal with uncertainty, we have to learn to dance with the system rather than regulating or controlling it. The following graph illustrates where the money should come from, the additional mechanism involved and the potential outcome measures (Fig. 4.2).

Any new financial design should be aware of the fact that the given monetary system is not neutral with regard to our behavior. It favors short-termism, forces us to grow, facilitates pro-cyclical tendencies, enhances inequality and in its current form is intrinsically unstable, as explained in previous chapters. We need to take even greater account of the fact that the given conventional tools, including regulatory efforts, taxation schemes, subsidies and private impact funding, represent an

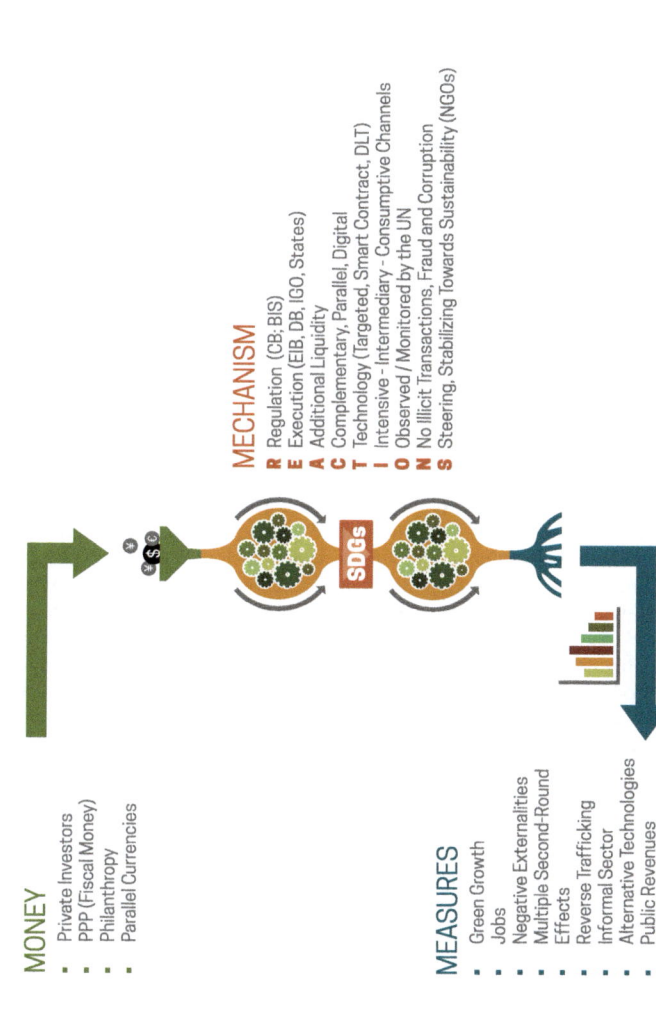

MONEY
- Private Investors
- PPP (Fiscal Money)
- Philanthropy
- Parallel Currencies

MECHANISM
- **R** Regulation (CB; BIS)
- **E** Execution (EIB, DB, IGO, States)
- **A** Additional Liquidity
- **C** Complementary, Parallel, Digital
- **T** Technology (Targeted, Smart Contract, DLT)
- **I** Intensive - Intermediary - Consumptive Channels
- **O** Observed / Monitored by the UN
- **N** No Illicit Transactions, Fraud and Corruption
- **S** Steering, Stabilizing Towards Sustainability (NGOs)

MEASURES
- Green Growth
- Jobs
- Negative Externalities
- Multiple Second-Round Effects
- Reverse Trafficking
- Informal Sector
- Alternative Technologies
- Public Revenues

Fig. 4.2 Money, the additional, parallel mechanism and the potential outcome measures. (To note: consider the required components of the mechanism R.E.A.C.T.I.O.N.S)

important contribution but remain altogether insufficient in scale, speed and capacity to steer and ensure change. Furthermore, we need to consider the multiple lock-in effects that currently crowd out future initiatives, preventing us from achieving a real shift. And we need to pay attention to the sleeping giant of our global commons that nobody talks about and we are unable to wake. Any future monetary design needs to allow agents to make economic decisions that operate in a relatively targeted, resilient, and anti-cyclical manner, where a critical mass can be attained within a short period of time.

And all of this needs to happening within 12–15 years, enabling 7.5 billion of people to steer towards a better future around the clock. And in light of the link we have claimed between the TAO and finance, all this finally needs to resonate with the overall philosophy of Taoism, in which duality, complementarity and the idea of integrating opposites play an indispensable key role. In short: any future monetary design needs to favor a collective, pre-distributive, parallel monetary mechanism, integrating all of this and reconciling the free market economy and state interventionism at the same time. This will form the topic of the next chapter.

Notes

1. To note for experts in systems theory: by treating evolution as a thermodynamic process, theorists are able to answer the question of why and how organisms have evolved to cooperate. Selfish behavior (called "defection") can undergo rapid transformation, with organisms shifting towards cooperative behavior through punishment. This change happens when the individual organism starts mimicking or adopting the behaviors of the neighboring individual organism. The researchers used the so-called Ising spin model, well known in physics. In such a prisoner dilemma situation each individual can act "defectively" or cooperatively towards proxy neighbors, with a reward offered for cooperation and nothing if they do not cooperate. While "defective" and cooperative behaviors balance one another over time, under certain circumstances cooperative behavior spreads like wildfire through the entire population. This is enhanced by introducing some sort of punishment or cost for those who are not cooperating. The mechanism we describe here as the TAO of Finance meets most of these criteria and can be applied to common goods. See Adami and Hintze (2018).
2. See Hardin (1968).
3. See Ostrom (1990); Ostrom was awarded the Nobel Prize in Economics in 2009.
4. What is often missing from this list of commons is the fact that the international trading and payment system is also considered a common good. Central banks and regulators have the function of providing tools that can create greater stability, safety, and sound regulation, providing liquidity and operating as a lender of last resort. These are all functions that the free market system cannot provide; also see McIntosh (2015).
5. See Heckman (2012). The conventional way of financing has been redistributing money through an "end-of-pipe" strategy. There are three reasons why traditionally we have redistributed money: first, it stabilizes our political system; second, personal life risks (such as unemployment, health, poverty) are better managed when pooled collectively; and third, regional and global common goods (security, highways, sewage systems, fresh air and biodiversity) are often better financed through the community. Could it be that we are using the wrong mechanism for our problems? Could it be that the mechanisms of distributing money work well in a stable environment with a high growth rate, strong governance, low externalities and less interconnectedness, but that now we are living in a different era that requires different measures?

6. Between 1900 and 2010, 20% of the world population increased their wealth, which was associated with an increase in global GDP by a factor of 26 and an increase in the use of energy, material and resources by a factor of 10–12. But this is history. Emerging markets now represent 60% of the world population. Given a use of materials of 70 billion tons in 2010, we should expect an increase to 125 billion tons by 2030 and 180 billion tons by 2050. When talking about a socio-ecological transformation, we should take such data into account. Considering that we have to operate within planetary boundaries, TCA can demonstrate two aspects: first, it will help us to decouple the global economy, as regional value chains might be cheaper. Second, there will be regions on this planet where less of material throughput is necessary, mainly OECD countries.

7. The Kuznets Curve, an inverse U-curve that describes the relation between the income/wealth of a society and its negative impact (environmental burden) is only valid as long as we do not consider international trade flows. As soon as we consider the import of goods with a high resource (fossil) burden, high-income countries do have high environmental burdens. From a global perspective, OECD countries would only be allowed to have an income/wealth level of countries such as Jamaica or Morocco, because their environmental footprint can be globalized. We need to differentiate between more territorial (production-based) emissions and consumption-based (trade-adjusted) emissions. There is evidence for a decoupling of production-based CO_2 emissions and growth, but none for a decoupling of consumption-based CO_2 emissions, which increases with per capita GDP, using the Kaya sum rule. See Kaya and Yokobori (1997), Obama (2017), Storm and Schroeder (2018), and Kuznets (1955).

8. To note: CDSs (Credit default swaps) do not eliminate risks but rather shift them from one private agent to another. Once the counterpart risk and associated moral hazard are cleared and the agents can take into account whether the CDS is associated to a physical delivery or remains a nominal delivery, a regulated and tailored CDS market can play a key role in shifting, diversifying and hedging the transformation described in this book.

9. Any co-financing scenario faces a twofold dilemma: in a market equilibrium, where allocation is already Pareto-optimal, any intervention or redistribution generates suboptimal results. Alternatively, if the market is not yet allocated fully optimally, then every intervention leads to an even greater deterioration of the given equilibrium. In both scenarios, distributing liquidity towards commons means that benefits for the private sector will be disproportionally low. However, the more the commons are financed, the more both the private and the state sector can benefit from their positive externalities. How this would work and how the twofold dilemma can be overcome will be explained in the following sections.

10. See Heckman, Moon, Pinto, Savelyev, and Yavitz (2010).

11. When it comes to eradicating poverty, redistribution does not work on a global level. Out of 118 countries, studied over 40 years, the vast majority of the increase of income (77%) is due to general economic growth only (Dollar, Kleineberg, & Kraay, 2013).

12. See World Bank (2016). Calculations have shown that it would take about 100 years to level out education, health care, and gender issues among others between the global North and the South by redistributing money the way we have in the past, where 95% of any given global growth goes to the North and 5% to the South. There are other ways than redistributing money that can achieve these goals much faster. One of these instruments is explained in this text (see Woodward, 2015).

13. See Winthrop and McGivney (2015); World Economic Forum (WEF) (2018).

14. For the historical debate, see Veblen (1899); Hirsch (1977) and Schneider (2007).

15. In this sense, commons are hybrids. They are public goods with a private or individual liability, like accessing a public park or a collective health care system. In contrast, most private goods are luxury or so-called positional goods, like owning a car or a pool. They are characterized by their relative property value in comparison to others. See Veblen (1899).

16. A. Dill (2019): https://trustyourplace.com; world social capital monitor 2019, https://sustainabledevelopment.un.org/content/documents/commitments/6686_11706_commitment_World%20Social%20Capital%20Monitor%202019.pdf

17. All QE programs (OMT; SMP; ELA etc.) imply some sort of liability, which increases the assets of the donor. Indirectly the taxpayers have become richer, their balance sheets increased. Once the liability has been defaulted upon, however, the balance sheets shrink again. If the donor has to write off 90%, the taxpayer would still have a gain of 10% (Sinn & Wollmershäuser, 2012).
18. The methodological background to the comparison of the ROI of global commons with the S&P 500 or state bonds can be found in D. Kahneman's so-called "reference class forecasting" effect: humans have the tendency to be over-optimistic with regard to the future and to misevaluate risks, certainties and probabilities. Costs, risks and time effort are chronically underestimated, whereas positive gains are overestimated. External evaluations and "outside-the-box" perspectives can broaden the spectrum and reset and objectify overall risk and investment strategies. See Flyvbjerg (2008); Kahneman and Tversky (1982).
19. The ROI of the red sofa is probably zero, showing that in a private setting we have no problem buying something with no ROI.
20. See Damodaran (2019).
21. For example: in a complex world where there are no single isolated causal links, the ROIs will benefit as many people as possible: high blood pressure medication (1:47); halving malaria infection (1:36); research on increasing yields in agriculture (1:34); tripling pre-schooling in sub-Saharan Africa (1:33); mobile broadband for developing countries (1:17); reducing domestic violence (1:17); phasing out subsidies for fossil fuels (1:15); modern cooking devices for 750 million people (1:15); increased skilled worker migration (1:15); cutting down indoor air pollution through better stoves (1:10); or eliminating open defecation (1:6): see Copenhagen Consensus (2019b); none of these strategies can be singled out for each individual, but in a world where everything is connected, the community as a whole will benefit hugely. As seen from a labor market perspective, unemployment is not only a waste of human capital, but far more expensive (if we consider all direct and indirect costs) than creating (public/ subsidized) jobs. The point is: the payment system has to adapt to the commons and not the other way around. For general information, see Copenhagen Consensus (2019a).
22. See Lomborg (2017); Bourguignon and Morrisson (2002).
23. Preston (1975) evaluated the difference between market-based private initiatives and public interventions across countries over several decades with regard to increase in life expectancy and economic growth. He concluded that only one quarter of the increase in life expectancy is due to general improvement of living standards, whereas three quarters are due to education, vaccination, antibiotics and vector controls, including hygiene measures. This means that public health and scientific innovation are more important than individual improvements in living standards. Also see: The Lancet August 5, 1978, 300–301, "Water with sugar and salt", where oral rehydration therapy (ORT) is considered the most significant progress in medicine of the twentieth century.
24. Here, there is a link to the Minsky argument: it is cheaper, economically more efficient and more sustainable for society as a whole to purposefully create jobs than to finance the increasing costs of health care, crime, social exclusion, inequality, and additional negative spillovers of increasing unemployment (Minsky, 1965).
25. However, the absolute number of humans living on this planet is not a geospatial challenge. If we take the density of population of San Francisco as a benchmark, with 6500 people per square meter, this density would be enough to house over 60 billion humans on the territory of the US alone. It is less the absolute number than the lifestyle we have chosen and the pattern of distribution of the given resources that is critical for our planet and our species (Lammar, 2013).
26. The original sin of the ecological growth theory is the illusion of the decoupling of resources, consumption and production from energy and material input and throughput. Empirically, however, there is no absolute decoupling of input and output globally, only a relative decoupling: for each USD or Euro spent, we have increased resource efficiency by 1% annually over the last 30 years (Flachenecker & Rentschler, 2018). As all relevant modelings show the world

economy growing exponentially up to 2050 (see e.g. Economist Intelligence Unit, 2015), the absolute amount of resource consumption (energy, material, steel, land use, rare materials etc.) will increase further in absolute terms.

27. This is a kind of prisoner's dilemma in global governance: on a global level, we find ourselves in a prisoner's dilemma. We are only prepared to make a change if the others make changes. As we have no institutional incentive that all agents cooperate in, meaning we do not have a global governance structure but nations only, there will be no cooperation. In order to overcome this prisoner's dilemma, we require a mechanism that allows everybody to act in a potentially beneficial manner for everybody involved, regardless of whether all agents cooperate or not. See e.g. Lempert and Nguyen (2011) or Soroos (1994). Snidal (1985) provides a more theoretical explanation of how the prisoner's dilemma and coordination modeling can help us to understand the cooperative behavior of global political institutions.

28. Most natural and human-based commons require forms of economic activities and legal requirements between the conventional dichotomy of state and market regulation. Simple state regulations or free market solutions are second best. It depends on the very nature of the commons themselves. There are rival and non-rival commons. Wikipedia, solar energy or the CO_2 concentration in the atmosphere are non-rival and require a different set of rules than rival commons like biodiversity, access to health care or preschooling. See Helfrich and Heinrich-Böll-Stiftung (2012); Ostrom (1990).

29. For example: achieving the 2DS only requires investments of 2–3% of global GDP, which is comparable to military expenditure worldwide. The subsidies for the carbon economy, including direct and indirect costs (mainly health care costs), are estimated to lie in a similar range of trillions of USD. Such figures demonstrate how our world economy is locked in to its current trajectory, preventing change towards a low-carbon future. Costs and additional investments sterilize each other and prevent us from achieving real change.

30. The Nash equilibrium describes a situation where opposing players reach a position in which they are no longer able to collaborate without harming their position due to the given rules. In order to overcome this lock-in, the players have to change the rules of the game. Globally, due to the multiple lock-in effects, we currently find ourselves in such a Nash equilibrium where the commons are concerned. In order to transcend or unlock it, we need to introduce a dual currency system that fundamentally changes the rules of the game and further maximizes the outcome for all agents involved. For the original text, see Nash (1950).

31. Four monetary tools are available to deal with a debt crisis from a public perspective (the so-called TRAP): first, Transferring money from one sector to another via taxation or fees; second, Restructuring the loans according to different forms of maturity or debt defaults; third, implementing an Austerity policy in some sectors in order to pay back the loans; fourth, Printing or creating additional money via easing, interest rates or direct spending. This approach to deleveraging a debt trap requires us to find the right balance between the four tools. See Dalio (2018).

32. The losses for the least developed countries (LDC) due to illicit financial flows (IFF) between 2004 and 2013 is recorded as 7.8 trillion USD, with a growth rate double to global output. Every 1 USD in formal inflow—measured in ODA, foreign direct investment, remittance payments or philanthropy—equaled an outflow of more than 10 USD in IFF leaving developing countries over the same time period. See Kar and Spanjers (2015).

33. On the shadow economy, see Mai and Schneider (2016). On shadow banking, see Adrian and Jones (2018). On the informal sector, see Neuwirth (2011).

34. See Tiftik and Mahmood (2019); International Monetary Fund (IMF, 2016).

35. See Edenhofer (2015).

36. See Shah (2013).

37. See Knapp and Van der Heijden (2018).

38. See Laeven and Valencia (2013); Lietaer, Arnsberger, Goerner, and Brunnhuber (2012).

39. ILO, Department of Statistics (2019); Shorrocks, Davies, and Lluberas (2018).

40. See Shorrocks et al. (2018), and ILO, Department of Statistics (2019). The income in OECD countries falls into the upper one fifth of the world's income bracket. The poorest one tenth of Norwegians still fall into the richest one tenth income bracket. By comparison, "dogland" (expenses for dogs) represents a middle-income country (richer than 40% of the world) measured in purchasing power parity (PPP). We have to admit that there is not much to redistribute globally. Korzeniewicz and Moran (2009); Lessenich (2019).

41. Another example serves to illustrate this: empirically, forced migration from Africa to Europe for economic reasons would cease at an average GDP per capita of 7000–9000 USD per year. At the current level of 3500 USD per head, assuming a growth rate of 3% annually it would take around 25–30 years to level this out. 39 of the 47 sub-Saharan countries with available data have an annual income per head below 7000 USD. In 2030, 35 countries will be still below that benchmark (cf. Dadush, Demertzis, & Wolff, 2017). We need a completely different mechanism to avoid forced migration and all the problems it entails.

42. Gapminder (2018).

43. Take health care for all: any collective health care system will always transfer resources from the healthy to the sick, from the young to the old and the very young, from the rich to the poor, from those who have a job to those who are jobless, from those who are trained to those who are not—always (!). However, the gap between the knowledge about medical cures, prevention and diagnosis and its realization in society has never been greater. As a society, we have never known so much about diabetes, hypertension, cancer, COPD, mental disorders, and infectious disease, or about lab findings, surgery, nursing and internal medicine. Despite this, our generation is unable to unleash their potential for the whole of humanity, not because of a lack of knowledge in medicine or education, but because of the monetary system. 50% of the global population do not have access to basic primary care; 9 out of 10 citizens in developing countries do not have access to basic surgical care; 85% of patients with severe mental disorders do not receive treatment; and we still we lose about 20,000 humans to diseases associated with WASH (water/sanitary/hygiene) every day. About one fifth of the health-related SDGs have been achieved, which means four fifths have not. We should be aware that out-of-pocket payment (500 billion USD annually) is a huge waste of money. (Forty percent is directly wasted.) If the system pooled risks, it could cut down costs, and the situation would be much better for everybody. For the 100 most relevant medical/health priorities we require an additional 25 USD annually per capita for the bottom billion. 1 billion humans are spending over 10% of their income on health and about 100 million are forced into poverty because of this. Furthermore, if we take into account a strong bilateral correlation between health and economic growth, we require more targeted liquidity to ensure health for all. A parallel currency system can provide just that. See The Economist (2018).

44. There are different ways to look at the same phenomena: from a pure market perspective, there are 1.45 billion people suffering from multidimensional poverty (UNDP, 2019), 1.9 billion have to manage on less than 3.20 USD per day for food, shelter and housing (World Bank, 2018a), 170 million are unemployed (ILO, 2019) and an additional 140 million are underemployed. 4.5 billion people lack access to safely managed sanitation services, and 50% do not have access to basic primary care. These stark figures reveal huge underserved, unmet potential and needs. Seen from this perspective, the world is vastly deflationary, requiring adequate liquidity to create additional wealth.

45. The central findings of experimental and clinical psychology certainly include the findings about so-called "frames" (Lakoff & Johnson, 1980). Frames function like maps in the brain and are always selective and context-driven. We speak about what we see, but we see only what we can think and speak about. All frames have a physiological component where the mental property is linked to sensory, tactile, emotional or gustatory experiences. When we speak of "comprehending", "handling" or "rejecting", our premotor cortex is actively coded for exactly those physical processes, and when we speak of a "garlicky smell" or a foul-smelling poisoned cesspool, then the corresponding areas of the olfactory brain also become active. This is referred to technically as "embodied cognition" or "embodied thinking"

(Niedenthal, Barsalou, Winkielman, Krauth-Gruber, & Ric, 2005). There is no thinking without somatic reference. But this goes even further: when we talk about the future, we tend to lean forward in our posture, when we talk about the past, we tend to lean backward, because we have learned to provide time perception and its conceptual version with a spatial component that is directly expressed in body perception (Miles, Nind, & Macrae, 2010). It is already enough to manipulate chairs in a meeting room in such a way that they are either slightly inclined to the left or to the right in order for a significant political positioning in favor of a rather conservative (right) or rather progressive (left) attitude to be adopted (Oppenheimer & Trail, 2010). If we had different frames, we would have a different language and consequently different actions. Over 200 such frames have been described, most of which are irrational (Wehling, 2016). These mental frames have the purpose of aligning the inner picture with the outer reality. The better the match, the better we are able to cope with reality. Currently our inner pictures do not match outer reality.

Chapter 5
The Tao of Finance: A Social Invention That Can Change the World

5.1 Not Like a Fish in Water

Humans' perception of money often is like a fish's perception of water. Fish see water as neutral, unchangeable, like a natural law. Similarly, many of us consider money a neutral element that enables our individual desires and societal goals. Money is seen to be like a thermometer: we insert it into water and it simply measures the temperature. But money is not neutral.[1] If we want to understand the nature of water, we need first to step out of the it, then examine it. The same is true of the monetary system. Only by distancing ourselves from it do we become able to see that the monetary system in its current unbalanced form forces us onto a non-sustainable path: it enhances income and wealth disparity, pushes us onto a forced growth trajectory, and is intrinsically unstable, favoring short-term private yields. This system acts in a mainly pro-cyclical manner and exacerbates anxiety, greed, and competition while reducing social capital such as trust and solidarity. And despite advanced new technologies and well-intended individual lifestyle changes, the monetary system prevents us from achieving a more sound, stable and sustainable future. In consequence, more of the same simply will generate more of these unwanted, one-sided and unbalanced results—over and over again.

If we want to develop a financial order adapted to the social and ecological needs of the planet, we need to balance out the system: this means long-termism, the freedom to decide whether or not to grow, an anti-cyclical stabilizer mechanism, and less income inequality. From a behavioral standpoint, it means gaining more trust, solidarity, cooperation and responsibility. We always need to bear in mind that any decision within the financial sector occurs within a complex system where uncertainty prevails. And we need to bear in mind that the window of viability we called the "anti-fragile zone" is a corridor expressed by the inner balance between two variables only: the amount of efficiency, measured in throughput per time, versus the value of resilience, measured in the amount of interconnectedness. Anything

---

The original version of this chapter was revised. The correction to this chapter can be found at https://doi.org/10.1007/978-3-030-64826-8_7

© The Author(s), under exclusive license to Springer Nature Switzerland AG 2021, corrected publication 2021
S. Brunnhuber, *Financing Our Future*, https://doi.org/10.1007/978-3-030-64826-8_5

outside this zone is either too sluggish or too brittle, and certainly not sustainable. Any monetary system with a different design needs to meet these criteria. If we start zooming in on the inner circle of the monetary system, it reveals a non-linear system with multiple feedback loops, visualized in the graph below (Graph 5.1).

This chapter delves deeper into this bold, unconventional and often overlooked "sixth" step of our "six-pack" ladder introducing a parallel currency system as an additional tool to enact the agreed-upon SDGs within a 15-year time frame. We describe what a parallel currency looks like, the technology involved, and some further figures, mathematics and new monetary channels associated with it. We elaborate upon its potential impact on the economy and on society as whole, as well as the need for a multi-stakeholder approach to our common future. We will emphasize

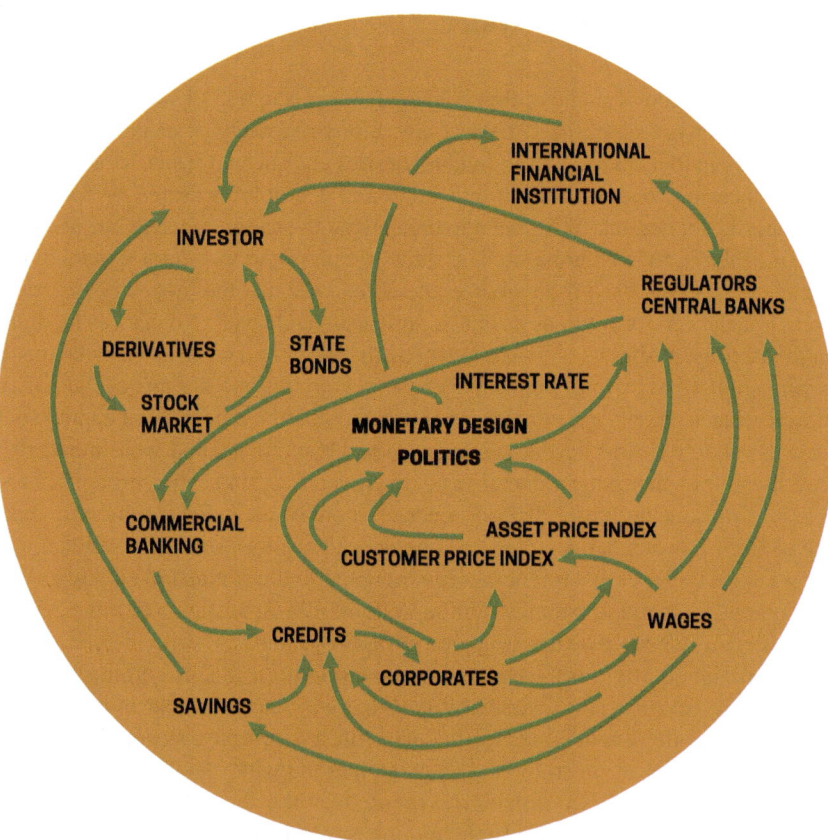

Graph 5.1 Zooming in on the Inner Circle—The monetary domain and its multiple feedback loops simplified. To note: The monetary design follows a specific political agenda, which can be changed. As long as multiple self-reinforcing feedback loops prevail asymmetric wars, forced migrations, failed states, global warming, resource supply shocks among others will cause further instability, short termism, pro-cyclical enhancement, and inequality and a further decline in social capital will dominate the system dynamic

why such a parallel currency is important to balance out both our overall economy and our life on this planet and will explain the fundamental and often neglected shift that is required to achieve it. It is no exaggeration to state that the monetary design is probably the single most important variable in achieving a common future, but despite this it is vastly neglected. In short: we will emphasize the missing link of a so-called monetary ecosystem. And once again, Taoism will lead the way.

> Fish are unable to understand the nature of water. If we want to understand what water is, we need to step out of it first and then examine it. The same is true of the monetary system.

5.2   The Next Step in the Evolution of Money

All living or evolving systems undergo change via processes of either development or decay. Genuine developments mainly follow steps of differentiation and integration in which the later steps or levels both honor and criticize the former ones, transcending them on a higher level, increasing their internal complexity and hierarchy. This involves a process in which the previous units become parts of a bigger or more encompassing system. For instance, atoms, cells, organs, organisms, societies constitute one such a sequence. Letters, words, sentences, paragraphs, chapters, books, libraries are another.

A vast literature originating in the fields of ethnology, anthropology and developmental psychology shows that consciousness enhancements and personal development occur in clearly identifiable steps or levels. The capacity to perceive, to feel, to think and to communicate therefore is conditioned by the gravity of consciousness at which one operates. Different authors use different numbers of levels and different labels to describe each level. And each level of consciousness involves different worldviews and notions of the self. So whenever there is a change in the level of consciousness, the given inner and outer reality is re-interpreted differently. But these changes in perception are only half of the story. It is not enough to "see and interpret reality differently"; one also needs to "act differently" on the basis of that new perception. For example, at the pre-modern level, people ritually worshiped the sun, while at the modern level the sun's astronomical movements were measured with a scientific apparatus, making it possible to predict its course. But that is not the end of it. With the change to a post-modern worldview, we could, for instance, use solar energy as a way to reduce global ecological stress. Another example is the shift from primitive agriculture to chemical-based agro-business and finally to ecological permaculture. In each of these cases, a change in the perception of reality is a necessary first step, but this move needs to be completed by the second step of a different praxis and technology. Concrete, real-life changes in bringing up one's children, in political activities, in economic and scientific initiatives, in the way one deals with day-to-day choices, will end up fundamentally changing the relationship between the individual, his or her community, and the environment.

Self and world are not just interpreted differently; they are also fundamentally changed by what one does.[2]

If these general assumptions on evolving systems are true, they should also hold for the evolution of money, with its economic activities and institutional frameworks exhibiting an evolutionary pattern directly related to the level of consciousness and the people involved. This should not come as a surprise, because the value system corresponding to a specific psychological level of development affects the nature of all interactions, including economic exchanges.

Historically, money as simple unregulated barter has only existed in exceptional circumstances such as in cases of war. As a rule, money has been created through a legislative and administrative process involving some type of regulation. So while the basic functions of money—to store value and serve as a medium of exchange—remain the same over time, their forms evolve. If this historical pattern holds true, then any further step in the evolution of money will be associated with a fundamental shift in legislation and regulation.

As financial systems evolve too, what is then the next step in the evolution of money? From commodity-based money to coins, to paper-based money and checks, from different forms of bank deposits, to fiat money, to electronic money, to private commercial or community currencies, each evolutionary step implies a greater reach or deepening complexity in finance. The single most important factor in the evolution of the financial system has been the increase of financial inclusion, along with the inception of consumer protection and privacy. One next step could be the creation of e-funds for specially earmarked purposes, to target poverty or reduce global warming, for example.[3] Evolutionary steps normally have a vertical and a horizontal component. Horizontal components involve a translational aspect where a given legislation or regulation is spread within one level (B). The vertical component involves a transformational aspect (A), where the focus is not on spreading the given rules, but on creating new rules that enhance financialization, financial inclusion, consumer protection and wealth in a society. The mechanism of a parallel currency system described here represents such a vertical transformative process. The following graph illustrates this in the form of an inverse cone (Graph 5.2).

The parallel currency system we are going to describe in greater detail below has the following characteristics: it provides additional, optional, targeted liquidity and thus additional purchasing power; it runs in parallel to the given system and is designed differently to the established monetary system; it uses distributive ledger technology and is earmarked to finance global common goods; and lastly, it operates through complementary monetary channels.

Such parallel currency systems do not operate as substitutes for, but rather as complements to the existing system, making market allocation more efficient and more resilient at the same time. They transcend the downsides of neoclassical and Keynesian economics. They do not represent a form of interventionism, nor do they pretend to have better information or knowledge than market allocation. A parallel currency system completes free market allocation, reducing instability and negative externalities. We need to learn to upgrade our financial system and not replace or destroy it. A dual-currency system would represent such an upgrade from mere free

Graph 5.2 A reverse cone—the next step in monetary evolution embraces, honors and transcends the previous one

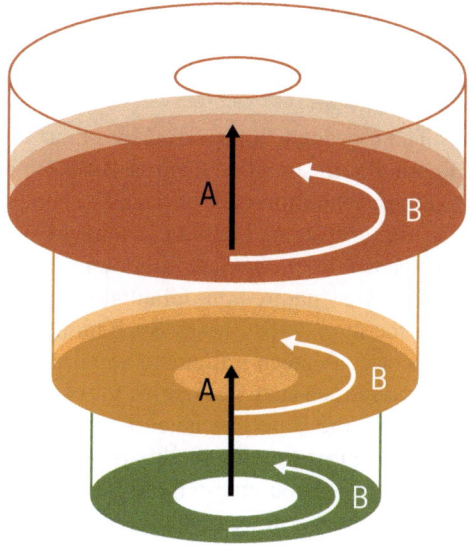

market to a regulated market to a parallel enhanced targeted market. And, as mentioned above, this dual-currency system—the later step of the staircase—not only honors and criticizes, but also integrates and transcends the previous steps.

5.3   Towards a Monetary Ecosystem: Central Bank Digital Currencies, Community Currencies and Cryptocurrencies

From a systems perspective, parallel currencies can take either a bottom-up or a top-down approach. The underlying mechanism remains similar, regardless of whether a top-down or a bottom-up approach is chosen. The goal is to stabilize the overall system, render it more resilient, and provide tools to solve large-scale problems.

Above, we defined a parallel currency as an agreement of a given society to accept something other than the conventional currency as means of payment. Such a parallel system should be designed in such a way that the society enables its members to match underutilized resources and unmet needs. And as such parallel currencies are not considered to be a substitute, an alternative, or a competitor but rather a complement to the given financial system, the parallel system should literally complete and balance out the negative side effects, weaknesses and constraints of the given system in one way or another. In this vein, we should focus on its capacity to move us towards a longer-term perspective, increasing social capital and trust, operating in an anti-cyclical manner, favoring public, common goods and basic needs and creating positive externalities. Such a monetary ecosystem would also then serve as a necessary back-up system, which while prevalent in the information technology sector is as yet inexistent in the financial realm. Increasing empirical evidence suggests that developments towards a parallel system are happening already.

The top-down approach: More than a dozen central banks are currently experimenting with so-called Central Bank Digital Currencies (CBDCs).[4] The purpose is to expand the monetary base and to better control and regulate the entire monetary and fiscal system. Unlike conventional credits and loans, which are sterilized or written off when they are either paid back or become non-performing, CBDCs are by their very nature non-defaultable loans.[5] A central bank never goes bankrupt, nor does the money they issue. Such monetary features increase safety, reduce transaction costs, enhance settlement and transmission, generate an additional seigniorage fee and reduce state warranties for bank loans. The larger the volume of the CBDC, the lower the state guarantee has to be. Full convertibility to conventional money and an interest-bearing facility provide additional properties through which the state can steer the economy in the right direction.[6] CBDCs exist only in digital form and also fulfill the criteria of lender of last resort. In this setting, money remains a public good. CBDCs can exist in parallel to cash, reserves and bank deposits. While CBDCs do not settle wholesale inter-banking payments, nor provide the anonymity of cash-based transactions, they have a larger functionality for retail markets by virtue of their targeted liquidity. In sum, they can provide a significant welfare effect through targeted and earmarked output.[7]

The bottom-up approach:[8] We can observe two major trends that adopt a bottom-up approach: community currencies (CoC) and cryptocurrencies (CyC).

5.3.1   The First Type of Bottom-Up Approach: Community Currencies (CoC)

Community currencies do not necessarily replicate the general purpose of conventional money as a medium of exchange or as a storage of value, but often target a "special" purpose. Examples include creating a community currency for specific social or environmental projects, or having local businesses provide additional liquidity to a sector or region experiencing a liquidity shortage.[9] There are currently over 3400 such local and regional forms of community currencies in 23 countries spread across six continents. Despite their diversity, they can be grouped into four categories. These include (1) time-based currencies such as the Time Dollar system, where the unit of account is the person-hour or some other time unit; (2) mutual exchange schemes such as the Local Exchange Trading System (LETS); (3) local or regional currency schemes such as the Bristol Pound in the United Kingdom or RegioMoney in Bavaria, Germany, where money can only be used for defined local goods and services; and (4) the barter system, such as trueque in Venezuela. While the capitalization of community currencies is low and their macroeconomic impact is often irrelevant, in some cases they have a 75-year history and are growing in importance. These thousands of real-time community currency experiments all over the world simply demonstrate as a proof of concept or as case-to-case evidence that a parallel system works and fills a local need. They obviously facilitate transactions that otherwise might not happen, and they have grown to the point where they cannot be dismissed as insignificant.[10]

5.3.2 The Second Type of Bottom-Up Approach: Cryptocurrencies

A cryptocurrency (CyC) is a digital asset designed to work as a medium of exchange that uses cryptography to secure financial transactions, control the creation of additional units, and verify the transfer of assets. There are approximately 2300 different types of cryptocurrencies currently in use, including Etherium, Bitcoin, Ripple, Cardano, Skycoin, and Libra. These currencies exist exclusively in electronic form and use digital ledger technology in the form of a blockchain. They are issued mainly through the private initiative of private "miners" and follow the underlying purpose of speculation and investment. Cryptocurrencies are both highly capitalized—in 2020, they amounted to over 350 billion USD—and highly volatile. This form of currency primarily is seen as a private good and favors denationalizing the monetary domain. Most cryptocurrencies have a built-in smart social contract—a digital algorithm that permits or prevents certain transactions and therefore restricts and channels economic activities. The following table provides a general overview of different parallel currencies (Graph 5.3):

Parallel currencies, once they have reached a sufficient volume, can operate as lifeboats. When properly established, they remain a constant optional medium of exchange and value storage. In monetary crises or transition phases they thus provide a buffer or act as a safety net, eventually becoming a "normal" tool for transactions. CBDCs, community currencies and cryptocurrencies can all be understood as a systemic response to the general shortage of liquidity or purchasing power needed to solve real-time problems.

Are risks associated with these currencies? The risk involved with bottom-up parallel currencies is the privatization of monetary systems and the ensuing impact on regional or national wealth. When a society leaves the money-creating process up to the private sector, it risks private monopolies dominating the market, thereby controlling consumer behavior through Big Data algorithms, underinvesting in the security and resilience of the system and under-regulating potential illicit transactions through these private monetary channels. Additionally, if there is no political involvement or any participation by the monetary regulators, the costs of propagating a bottom-up complementary currency approach for each region or village can become prohibitively high.

Several rhetorical questions relate to such complementary currencies: do we want private companies to have access to this data, with the potential risk of manipulating citizens and customer behavior via hidden algorithms? Do we want private companies to earn profits in boom times and transfer risks to the public sector in bust times? Do we want global commons to be privatized? Do we want private firms

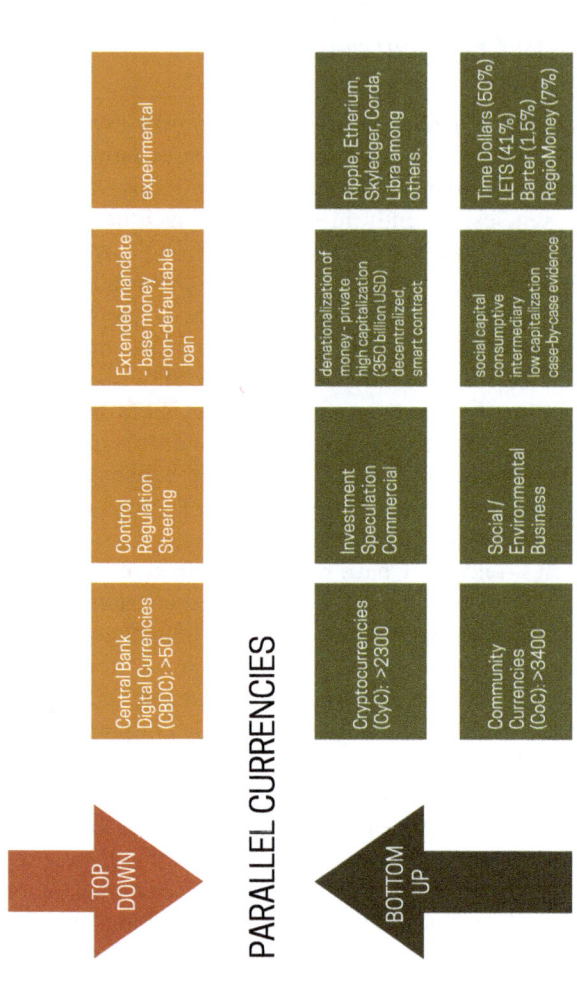

Graph 5.3 Parallel currencies top-down and bottom-up: empirical evidence for additional targeted liquidity to solve real-time problems

with limited liabilities to gather data and information on individuals' schooling, health care use, eating habits, mobility and energy supply in order to sell targeted products based on Big Data correlations? Or, when individuals go bankrupt, to sell this information to any company abroad? The answer should be no, we don't. Private companies may not invest enough in the security of their customers and in the resilience of the pay chain in the event of a crisis.[11] Any kind of bottom-up approach therefore needs to be regulated to guarantee large-scale societal transformation with the aim of eventually allowing the payment of taxes using these local, regional or private currencies. On the other hand, any kind of top-down approach by virtue of its public nature can help to regulate private or locally issued complementary currencies.[12] Whether we as a society prefer the top-down or bottom-up approach when organizing this social mechanism depends on the political will and mandate and the power play between and interests of the different stakeholders involved. This is why we need the monetary regulators to have skin in the game in order for all of us to move successfully towards a brighter future. We can describe the whole field of evolving parallel currencies today as roughly at the stage aeronautics was when the Wright brothers took off in their first plane. When an innovation of this type appears, it is most likely to be muddled, incomplete, confusing, and insignificant in scale. The miracle is less that the Wrights' contraption flew at all. Their real achievement lay in proving that flying was possible. The same is true of the development of complementary currencies.

5.4   The New Game in Town: The New Role of the Regulators

The purpose of monetary regulators all over the world is to facilitate and meet human needs. While the tools to do so may change over time, the institutional bodies themselves do not. Monetary regulators have a unique role to play in the creation of parallel currencies, both in creating CBDC and in regulating bottom-up parallel currencies.[13] This unique role is associated with their capacity to create money: so-called "fiat money", which creates money out of nothing.[14] Fiat money represents an agreement of a given society that allows this society to organize exchange and trading more efficiently than without this agreement. Whether this agreement and this fiat money is wrong or right depends on how we organize it—to facilitate short-term interests involving negative externalities, or for the good of people and the planet as a whole. Fiat money does not have an intrinsic value; we as a community provide our money with the value required in order to perform as desired. Monetary regulators and central bankers can help to compensate for the disadvantages of local private and communal complementary currencies by regulating privacy, risk management, and misuse of data, and operate as a lenders of last resort.[15] Traditionally Central Banks are using open market policy, Base Money and /or Citizens' Money to provide liquidity to the economy.[16] We will see that we might have to further differentiate this schema. We will call it a monetary ecosystem, like a river delta, running in parallel to the given traditional system (Graph 5.4).

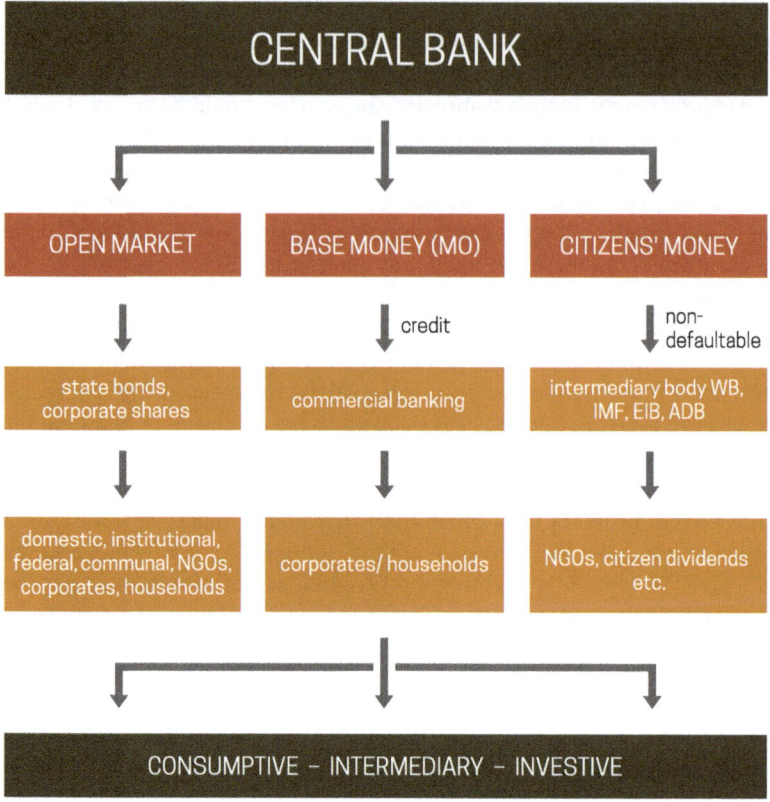

Graph 5.4 Providing liquidity to the economy

Traditionally most central bankers pursue a dual mandate of price stability and a high employment rate. Over the past 25 years, monetary regulators have become more independent when it comes to national governmental or international policy worldwide. This guarantees legislative accountability and a kind of "sector neutrality" in relation to individual political decisions. This independence and neutrality mean they are ideally set up to regulate on global concerns such as the SDGs. Because a significant part of the SDGs are global commons, monetary regulators could actually be given an additional mandate to "do whatever it takes to save humanity and the planet".[17] They would then have a third tool to create additional, electronic liquidity, issued against government bonds, exclusively earmarked[18] to fund SDGs, and with this liquidity also create the ability to steer our economy for the better. No other institution in our modern society besides the central banks has the capacity, the knowledge, the tools, and the leverage to do this once a mandate is in place.[19] And it should come as no surprise that the current treaty of the European Union, for example, supports this agenda in its third article, which includes not only price stability, but also a "high level of protection and improvement of the quality of

Table 5.1 The role of the regulators: advantages of implementing a dual-currency system from a regulatory perspective

Impact of a dual system	Explanation
Anti-cyclical stabilizer	A dual currency system enhances regulatory efforts to stabilize the overall economy in the case of a crisis, providing additional channels to ensure price stability, purchasing power, employment and trading.
Steering	Imperfect substitute can operate through pricing (interest rate) or volume (easing); the elasticity of the imperfect substitute determines the steering effect.
Anti-inflationary	State bonds and interest rates are two tools that can inject / withdraw liquidity from and to the market.
Costs of cash	Managing costs of cash of up to 0.7% of gross domestic product (GDP).
Financial inclusion	Reaching out to unbanked segments of the population (e.g. Paypal, WeChat or M-Pesa); narrow banking, where private money is backed up by central bank reserve liabilities.
Financial stability	Additional earmarked seigniorage, safe, cheap, semi-anonymous, less risk of a bank run and preventing a negative interest rate; zero loan bonds (ZLB), non-defaultable loans reduce risk premiums and interest rates.
Financial integrity	Protection against illicit transactions, featuring semi-anonymous channels, combatting finance for terrorism (CFT) and anti-monetary law (AML) rules; finding the tradeoff between illicit transactions and private anonymity.
Improved monetary policy	Reduced settlement risks, transaction costs, scalability and online data are available in a fully connected world; incomplete substitute, increasing steering capacity, with a dual currency in place, the target regions require fewer foreign currencies to run their regional and local business.
Political mandate	Increased mandate: price stability, unemployment and sustainability.
Transaction costs	In a corporate setting, transactions costs are considered to be 1–2% of each transaction. Globally we are nominally witnessing 180 trillion USD in transactions. These costs are significantly reduced with a digital currency.
Credit card fees	Up to 50% reduced costs (3% instead of 6%) of credit card transactions

the environment".[20] The following table summarizes some major aspects of the impact regulators can have on our common future (Table 5.1).[21]

In fact, the fractional reserve system as a standalone mechanism providing liquidity for the market is a pretty expensive procedure. 97% of money creation is carried out by the private for-profit banking system, where the private bank creates the money and loans it to the government and to citizens. This business model can generate substantial income. For the US or the EU, the bill amounts to almost 500 billion USD annually in public and private interest payments and nearly doubles federal income tax.[24]

Growth and redistribution revised: Redistributing money through taxes or fees remains sensitive to economic booms and busts. In presence of a recession, payments for schooling, health care or basic food supplies dwindle or cease. Taxation is thus sensitive to and linked with economic growth.[25] However, if the mandate for monetary regulation were to be enlarged to include funding the SDGs, financing our future would become less dependent on the overall economic growth process. Regulators would be in a position to generate the necessary liquidity to target the three goals: inflation, jobs and sustainability. As a reminder, money is created when a monetary institution buys financial assets such as state bonds or corporate shares. The sellers of these assets consequently have a deposit at the institution that bought the financial assets. This money, deposit, liquidity or purchasing power in turn can be used as a reserve base to extend loans to households or companies or to directly finance projects. For a monetary regulator, there is no limit to the amount of financial assets that can be bought. Theoretically, all financial assets on the planet could be bought up without any restrictions as to the types of assets they are. If the regulators were to be given a mandate that removes their neutrality and makes them partisan to ensuring our common future, they would target inflation, address unemployment and deal with the SDGs. Intermediary institutions such as the European Investment Bank or the Asian Development Bank could guarantee that any additional money was channeled based on the political agenda. It is these institutional bodies that could create the additional trillions of dollars required, using an electronic and digital format such as blockchain technology. We would then have a supplementary currency running in parallel to the existing conventional system, able to generate what is required to match the 5 trillion USD needed over the next 12–15 years. This is the indispensable missing link (Box 5.1).[26]

Box 5.1 Where is the money coming from? A discussion between fellows of the World Academy of Art and Science and the Club of Rome and international financial experts in developmental economics

A story about a simple question: where is the money coming from?[22] A group of eminent financial experts in developmental and financial economics with over 2 decades of hands-on experience of the topic and world-renowned academic records had a conversation with representatives of the TAO of Finance Group of the World Academy of Art and Science (WAAS). When confronting all the global challenges, the experts' question was: "Where is the money coming from?" The representatives of the TAO of Finance group at first did not fully understand the question and responded with a counter-question: "Do you mean that there is not enough technological know-how to drill holes for fresh water and set up a sewage systems that prevents people dying from toxic water?" Oh no, said the experts, we know all that. "So you mean there is not enough expertise to build kindergartens, schools, hospitals and roads?" One of the WAAS fellows refined the question: "Or is it about how to treat malaria, diarrhea and tuberculosis or how to train nurses, teachers or medical doctors?" Neither, they said, we have 317 million unemployed people and over 1 billion underemployed globally and we know how to train nurses, teachers and medical doctors. The world is indeed vastly deflationary. On top of that, we lack millions of kindergartens, schools, hospitals and universities. On this,

---

(continued)

Box 5.1 (continued)

both parties were agreed. Then the WAAS fellows said: "Could it be about the energy system, meaning we need more technological support to set up solar panels on roofs? So you need more engineers?" The discussion went on and on for a while until the topic got onto the financial and taxation system. "Is it," the academy fellow asked, "that you have a far to small tax base in your country, and in net value lose more of it through illicit financial flows than you gain through FDI,[23] philanthropy and ODA?" Yes, they said, this is one aspect of it, but there is yet another: we simply need more money, purchasing power, liquidity, name it what you will, in order to do the job ahead: from pre-schooling, health care, the energy supply, and public infrastructure to building up good governance. Oh, the fellows said, we understand. What you need is another monetary system, one that is designed in precisely such a way to provide you with all the tools necessary so you can do your jobs. If this is the requirement, the fellows said, we have such a mechanism and such technology available now. We call it the TAO of Finance. It is a parallel currency system, using different technology to the given system and operating through different channels than the traditional system. And we can settle taxes, debts and wages in it, as it is accepted as general medium of exchange and payment. It can be implemented in less than 18 months with fewer than 200 staff. Some of the experts are still in disbelief, but will become fully convinced of the opposite in the near future.

5.5 Patterns of Change: The Right Figures and the Right Channels

The SDGs provide the world with a map that charts a course for the coming years. The 17 targets formulated in this map have replaced the previous Millennium Goals.[27] The SDGs represent a consensus reached through the UN's largest consultation and review process in history. Hundreds of surveys, expert groups, panels and hearings took place, and millions of citizens were involved through population-based questionnaires contributing to this agenda.

We know what we want and where to go, but we still lack answers to the questions of where the money for this is going to come from and how we can guarantee that the funds are actually correctly allocated. The SDGs have provided us with empirical evidence and the political will on the questions of how to overcome poverty and hunger, which kind of health care system should be implemented, and how to educate our children. We further have set the approved agenda on moving away from fossil fuels towards more renewable energy sources to run our businesses and supply our lifestyle, and we have identified the urgency of how and why we need to protect biodiversity. We basically know how to do all this, but we are lacking the financial preconditions to make it possible. If we fail to discuss where the funds are coming from, the SDGs basically will be stillborn. The need to come up with adequate funding is great.[28] If we consider the most optimistic scenario, in which the world economy grows at a rate of 2% per annum over the next few years and we dedicate (through a political process) 1% of world GDP to SDGs, we end up with roughly 750–800 billion USD a year.[29] However, this is well below the estimated 5 trillion required. Another option would be to withdraw 5–7% (4–5 trillion USD) from the global GDP (85 trillion USD) every year.[30] However, even if withdrawn from the market economy at a gradual scale, funding the SDGs in this manner would create the largest economic recession in modern times and be economically irrational. Thus, neither conventional option is feasible.

Putting it into perspective: To better assess the cost of funding SDGs holistically, we need to use the right proportions. On the one hand, there are impact funds dealing with green investments, remittance payments providing additional funding for families back home, and Official Development Assistance (ODA),[31] which consists primarily of public taxpayers' money and private philanthropy and charity.[32] While these financial mechanisms are implemented with the best intentions, they provide insufficient purchasing power for infrastructure development, investment and adequate consumption for the majority of the twenty-first-century global population. Furthermore, the costs of financial crises, disaster management and the financial volume of the shadow market are pulling our global economy in the opposite direction to where we want to be going. In combination with the so-called lock-in effects, and a general growth trajectory of 2–3% globally,[33] statistically we would only be able to meet the targets of the SDGs in three generations. This means that under "business as usual" conditions, we would take at least 100 years to accomplish the SDGs. In addition, because of the accelerated path of climate change and the systems dynamic of the Anthropocene, where interconnectedness and planetary boundaries prevail, causing multiple non-linear tipping points and feedback loops, these goals need to be achieved much faster than we assume.[34] In comparison to the magnitude of other financial sectors or activities, the amount of money required to finance the SDGs is smaller than we are led to believe (Graph 5.5).[35]

From a geographic perspective, the money required differs from region to region. The following table summarizes the outlay required to finance our common future, depending on the level of income. The graph illustrates that for low- to middle-income countries (LMI) and low-income countries (LIC), financing the SDGs is a next to impossible mission, as it would require liquidity far beyond the current national budget (Table 5.2).

A further consideration: On a global level, 5–7% of any given gross domestic product is required additionally every year on average. This does not include infrastructure and associated costs (such as additional administration, logistics, etc.). As a rule of thumb, we can say that two thirds of the expenditure are required for health care (22%), education (26%), and infrastructure (21%). Further investments include the protection of biodiversity (1%), humanitarian emergency projects (2%), agriculture (2%), social security measures (10%), as well as necessary non-SDG public expenditure (6–13%), which refers to courts, policing, tax offices, land registry offices, sewage systems, transportation and roads. To further clarify the figures, we need to distinguish between targets that are consumptive (such as overcoming

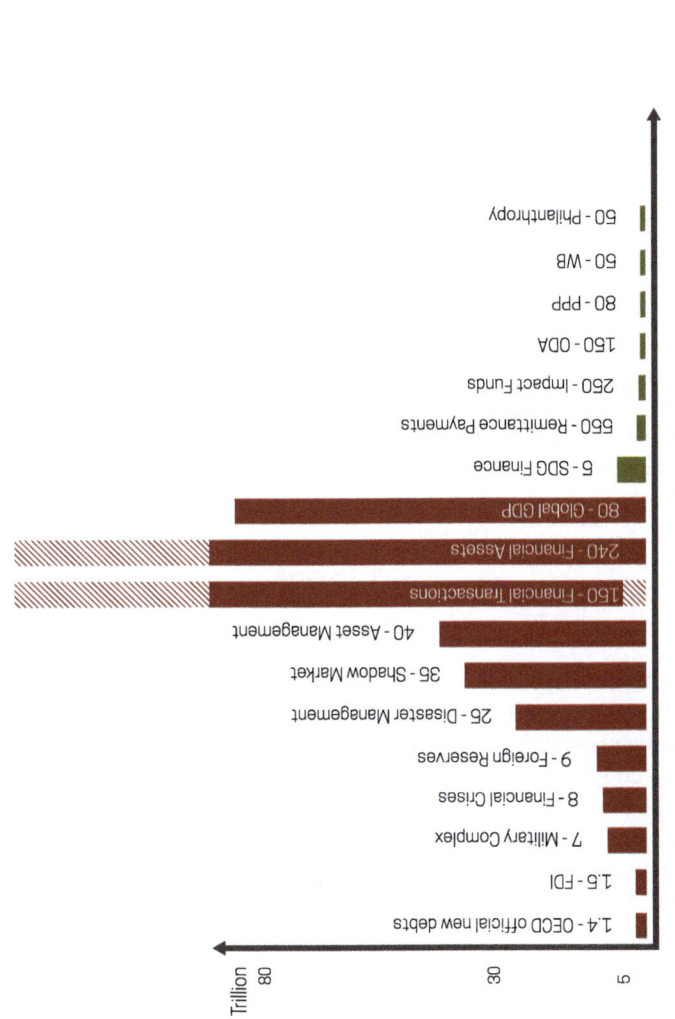

Graph 5.5 A sense of proportion: putting the figures into perspective: the scale of various finance-related events/areas per year in relation to what would be necessary to adequately fund the SDGs

Table 5.2 Geographic distribution of the required volume

	Region of different income	Required outlay in % of gross domestic product (GDP) and absolute numbers to finance Sustainable Development Goals (SDGs)	
A	High-income countries (HIC)		
	>12,000 USD/capita/y 52 countries GDP 55 trillion USD 1.25 billion people	1.5–2% GDP	1 trillion USD
B	Middle-income countries (MIC)		
	Upper middle-income countries (UMIC) 53 countries 4000–12,000 USD/capita/y GDP 25 trillion USD 2.6 billion people	6–7% GDP	2.5 trillion USD
	Lower middle-income countries (LMIC) 1000–4000 USD/capita/y 52 countries GDP 7 trillion USD 3 billion people	36% GDP	2.0 trillion USD
C	Low-income countries (LIC)		
	<1000 USD/capita/y 30 countries GDP 700 billion USD 600 billion people	>60% GDP	500 billion USD
	Global	7–8% GDP	5–7 trillion USD

poverty and hunger), those that are intermediary (pre-schooling, health care), and those that are investive (infrastructure programs). The practical reason for this distinction is that the respective targets have a different impact on the consumer price index. So far no country is on track. 5–7% of GDP is in fact a conservative figure; including population growth might increase the absolute volume by 25% to one third of the budget. This would mean that instead of 5–7% of GDP, we would be talking about 8–9%.

The 5 trillion USD bill for the SDGs in more detail: The cost for all SDGs is estimated at around 4–5 trillion USD per year in public spending, investments and direct aid. General estimates, however, vary remarkably from 2 trillion USD to over 10 trillion USD, depending on the extent to which public infrastructure is considered.[36] This is a big, abstract and terrifying number, and so we need to dismantle it and get the right sense of proportion. The main message is that we are talking about additional trillions of dollars annually. Taking 5 trillion USD annually as a rough benchmark, some distinctions need to be specified. The equation is as follows: within the spectrum of the SDGs, one third of investments, approximately 1.5 trillion USD, are eligible to be financed through some sort of private sector investment and private-public partnership (PPP). This is true especially in the field of agriculture and electromobility. The remaining two thirds of the SDGs, approximately 3.5 trillion USD in investments, are unsuitable for private financing as they are non-excludable common goods. Looking at these 3.5 trillion USD in more concrete terms, it is here that the monetary regulators could lean in. Traditionally, M0 refers to base money or "hot money", issued exclusively by central banks. There is a relation between the amount of M0 issued and GDP—their proportion usually is around 1:10. At present, M0 amounts to 7 trillion USD globally,[37] which accounts for the annual global GDP of 70–80 trillion USD. Applying this same logic and process to the 3.5 trillion USD required to fund global commons, central banks would need to create one tenth of that sum as M0, amounting to an extra 350 billion USD annually.

However, the 350 billion USD calculated above would only suffice if the funds were directed through traditional channels, where the multiplication effect of the banking system causes money to amplify. If alternative channels were used where this amplification process does not occur, the 350 billion USD sum would be too low in volume. Because some projects would run through channels other than the traditional ones, additional liquidity of approximately 500 billion to 1.5 trillion USD per year represents a more realistic estimate of the sum required to finance SDGs. Just to note: this would be fiat money. But fiat money is not a bad thing. It depends on what we do with it. In sum, if we had 1.5 trillion USD of additional liquidity or purchasing power in the form of an optional, blockchain-enabled parallel currency, we would have the potential to steer the world economy towards a Pareto-superior equilibrium. In other words: a dual currency system, as described here, does not prevent market allocation and a Pareto optimum, but rather enables them.

It is simple as that: money is what money does. However, in order to ensure that money does what we as a community decide it should do, we need to pay attention to the channels through which that additional money is directed.

Finding the right monetary channels: A monetary channel is like a water pipeline, which when constructed properly directs money where it is most needed. However, most conventional monetary channels no longer meet this criterion. The majority of money currently channeled remains in the so-called FIRE sector (Finance, Insurance, and Real Estate).[38] So despite the fact that lots of money is in circulation, it does not gravitate towards the most pressing needs of society. Injecting money into the real economy largely depends on the transmission belts or "channels" through which the money is sent to meet the requirements of the real economy of goods and services.

Recent history has shown that the conventional quantitative easing (QE) mechanism has limited leverage to ensure real investment in the real world.[39] Traditionally, central banks and monetary regulators have used various channels in an attempt to ensure that the liquidity generated reaches the real economy effectively. Such channels include the "banking credit channel": commercial banks can lend cheap money and offer cheap credit that households and firms can use to build houses, pay for a college education or set up construction sites. Then there is the "portfolio channel": this channel explains the effect of money creation through central banks buying state bonds. These bonds increase in value and decrease the cost of the interest rate, which in consequence encourages rational investors to choose alternative strategies to state bonds. There is also the "signal channel": conventional QE signals to the real economy that interest rates will stay low, which should encourage investors to consume or reinvest in productive assets. Another channel is the "wealth channel": QE measures lead to increased stock-exchange and real-estate values. As 40% of stocks belong to the upper 5% of society (as in the UK, for example), this cohort will consider itself wealthier and consequently consume more, which will then stimulate the economy through "trickle-down effects". A "fiscal channel" follows the argument that buying state bonds increases their value and decreases the cost of interest. These reduced costs for the interest rate leave the public sector with greater leverage for additional public investments in education, healthcare and so on. Finally, there is the "interest-rate channel": low interest is a general incentive to invest in the economy with cheap money.[40] None of these channels central bankers are using are wrong. Empirical evidence proves that each of them has worked historically in some cases. But none of these channels provide empirical evidence of a causal link between the amount of money created and the amount that finally reaches the real sector.

The conventional monetary tools of recent times have therefore limited evidence to ensure that the money created enters the real economy.[41] As both central banks and governments are public bodies, wins and losses equal out on both sides. To illustrate this concretely: over the course of the post-2008 crisis in the UK, the Bank of England generated 435 billion pounds. This additional liquidity stimulated the real economy with 10–15 pennies per pound—meaning that 90 pennies remained in the so-called FIRE sector and the "trickle down" into the real economy was a mere 10 pennies.[42] Using a citizen dividend, civil society or public sector pathway as described below, each pound would have generated 2.8 times as much revenue. The difference between the conventional and the alternative scenario is a factor of 35. With same amount of liquidity, simply changing the pathways through which money is processed can create 35 times more wealth! In light of these figures, it makes sense to take a closer look at the channels available. In theory, 10 billion pounds distributed through one of the alternative channels by now could have created an additional 300,000 jobs in the UK. Our approach builds on these findings, yet differs substantially from the existing conventional and alternative parallel currency systems.[43]

While a number of proposals have developed these traditional mechanisms further, they all remain within a monetary monoculture. New and additional channels therefore are required to ensure that liquidity reaches the sectors that most benefit society. When it comes to global commons, it is important to bear in mind that we are dealing with a different kind of economics. In order to avoid the mistakes of the traditional Quantitative Easing of the 2008 crisis, where the additional liquidity mainly went into the financial sector or the real estate market, we need to identify new monetary channels, operating in parallel to the conventional ones, like a river delta. Here, we can identify at least three major tracks (Graph 5.6):[44]

These new channels would be consumptive in order to stimulate the local market economy directly, to overcome poverty and hunger for example; they could shift consumer behavior towards a more sustainable lifestyle and encourage regional agriculture and public transportation, for example; they could be an investment strategy to strengthen the political system, targeting public finance, land registry

Graph 5.6 The river delta: a monetary ecosystem with several major trajectories to inject additional liquidity into the market

offices, public affairs, or national security, for example; and lastly, these new channels could target intermediaries such as education, renewables, ecological agriculture, or health care. The core argument with complementary currencies is that the proposed mechanism should itself stimulate the real economy via a democratic mandate. This can happen through several alternative pathways (Table 5.3):

In addition to generating new employment and tax revenues, these additional pathways would also have the effect of reducing expenditure on social security and pensions, as well as creating wealth. These examples differ from the academic literature and public discussion in that the additional liquidity provided runs in parallel to the conventional system and operates using digital ledger technology. They thus provide complete transparency, immediacy and scalability.

An important intermediary step—the nonprofit and development banking sector: gaining a deeper collective consciousness will make us more aware of the fact that money is simply one of many fictitious narratives we commonly believe. The underlying design of the monetary system has remained unquestioned and untouched for centuries, despite clashes between civilizations, cultures, values, religions and political systems. Even terrorists abide by the rules of the established monetary system. But now is the time to start questioning this narrative of the traditional monetary monoculture and to start telling ourselves a better story about money and sustainability. Regardless of the form it takes, money is built upon trust. This should also

Table 5.3 Examples for complementary monetary channeling

Complementary channels	Explanation
Citizen dividend	Citizens benefit from a tax reduction in the conventional monetary fields. This reduction is replaced by green USD or green Euros, enabling citizens to target their consumption towards a greener future.
Advance market commitment (AMC)	Binding contract by public authorities offering guarantees for a product for a future market once successful/ developed (e.g. vaccines).
Private-public partnership (PPP)	Most SDGs operate at the interface between private and public interests, for example upstream financing with mezzanine products (output oriented).
Small and medium-sized enterprises (SMEs), NGOs, communal public authorities	Instead of leading staff being in charge first and foremost of raising funds, the expertise of 1 million NGOs worldwide can be put to use directly by offering them green dollars.
Institutional building channels (IBC)	Building governance is key for all Sustainable Development Goals (SDGs) and global commons. Additional liquidity can target civil society (universities, the press and healthcare) as well as administration (communal tax authorities, land registries and sewerage).
Remittance channel	Remittance, which already reflects double the volume of official development assistance (ODA) globally, could benefit from additional green liquidity. The money goes directly to the poor and the places on the planet that need it most.

hold true for any future fiat money that is developed. And the more reciprocal trust we generate, the higher the currency value will be.

One essential component of such a future narrative is the banking sector itself. Big banks tend to lend to big firms and a substantial part of these loans remain unproductive. For example, the UK has a highly monopolized banking sector where about five banks account for 92% of the lending transactions. However, only 22–25% of these credit lines are made available to the real economic sector. The rest of the credit remains in the so-called FIRE sector of Finance, Insurance and Real Estate. In this case, the financial transactions simply shift ownership but are not necessarily invested in the GDP. By contrast, Germany has a communal, co-operative non-profit banking sector with over 1700 communal co-operative non-profit banks. In this case, over 70% of the lending process goes to small and medium enterprises or private clients. The beauty of a decentralized communal, co-operative non-profit banking sector is that it is more resilient to financial shocks. It also provides a more targeted lending strategy, thus maximizing economic productivity and wealth. Because banks generate and add additional purchasing power to the economy rather than being intermediaries between savings and lending, co-operative banking and the developing banking sector have the potential to be easily capitalized by domestic central banks using a parallel, digital currency, as explained in this text.[45]

Let's take the so-called Sovereign Wealth funds. They are state funds, where budget surpluses, mainly through fossil resource extractions are channeled to stabilize the domestic economy, to serve as a source for intergenerational pension funds and / or to provide money in order to finance the socio-economic transition. The SWF market reflects an 8 trillion USD market, where only about 0.15–0.7% are invested in green assets. The revenues and volume of such funds are mainly determined by the so-called fiscal breakeven oil price. This benchmark reflects the price of oil, where the state budget is balanced out and reserves start to accumulate. The lower this breakeven is, the higher the potential revenues are. SWFs are increasingly confronted with stranded assets, oil price volatility and/or a low oil price itself. The "One planet sovereign wealth fund working group" is currently addressing this issue.

As SWFs are a substantial player in the global market, it is in their self-interest to consider out of the box approaches in financial engineering to catalyze and enable the change required.[46] To note: The big advantage of SWFs is that they represent a public fund, and therefore public interests, public goods and public ownership. The following graph illustrates a potential shift from their traditional strategy towards a more resilient and greener strategy (Graph 5.7).[47]

5.6 The Bigger Picture: Riding a Bike with Two Wheels or a Mechanism That Can Change the World

What would happen if such a new social mechanism were in place?[48] Any form of parallel liquidity such as CBDCs or CoCs issued against government bonds, earmarked exclusively for SDG-related projects, represents a whole-system approach. For any public co-signer, investing in such projects would have a potential ROI 10–100 times higher than for private investments. Investing in common goods through this mechanism thus increases the overall welfare effect in the form of millions of "green" jobs, additional "green" growth and an enlarged tax base for SDG-related projects. But besides these positive effects, it also decreases the negative effects, reducing illicit transactions and lowering costs for negative externalities and disaster management. In short, this mechanism has the potential to redirect the overall economy towards a Pareto-superior equilibrium.[49] This is the indispensable link we have been missing thus far and describes the specific future role of monetary regulators in a sustainable future. The following graphs provide an overview of the traditional way (a) and the complementary, parallel way (b) in financing our future (Graph 5.8).

In more detail: The above graph describes the bigger picture of this mechanism from the viewpoint of systems theory. The global GDP (represented by the large orange arrow) contains the carbon bubble and increased damage control costs generated because of the way we run our economy (e.g. global warming, unwanted migration, air pollution). The dark box represents the shadow economy and the informal sector, which feed and stabilize the GDP. Without the shadow economy, a large proportion of the GDP would be missing and the global economy would collapse. The thin green arrow flowing from the GDP reflects the redistributive

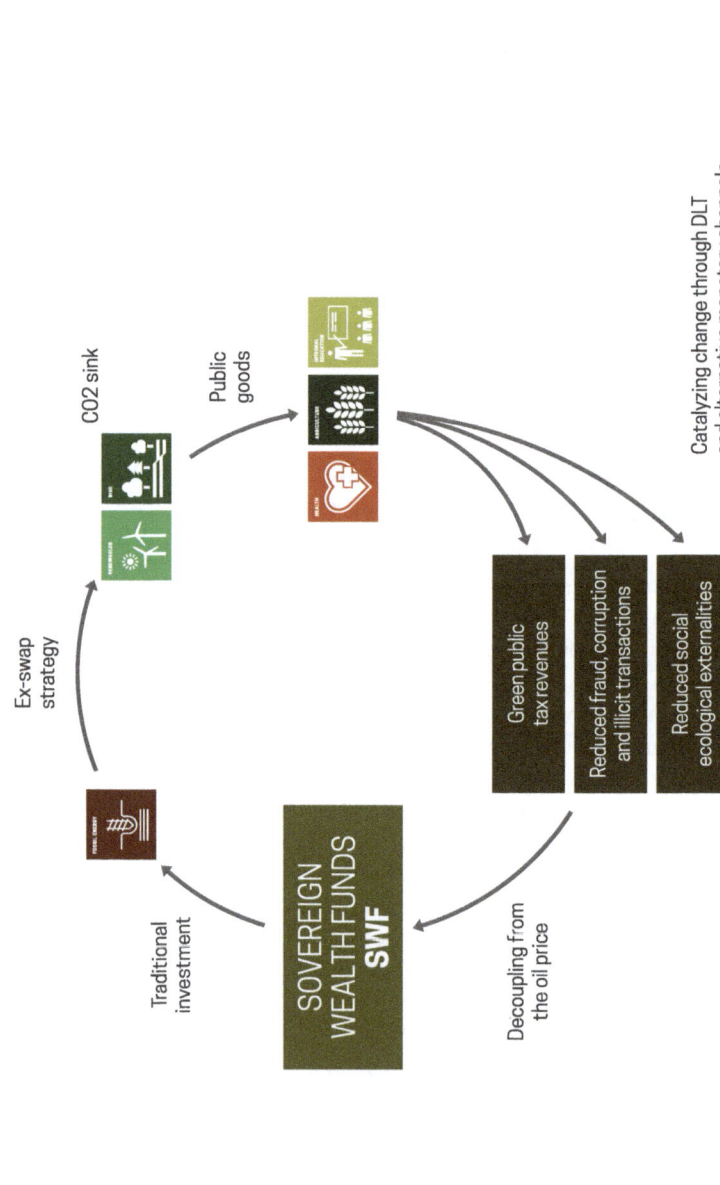

Graph 5.7 Sovereign wealth funds—Catalyzing change and enabling public goods through distributive ledger technology (DLT) and alternative monetary channels (explained in the text)

a

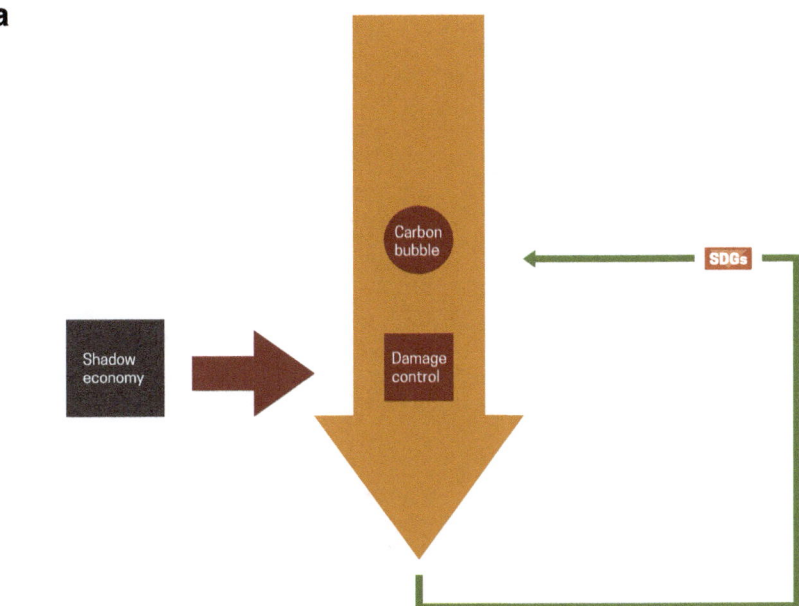

Graph 5.8 (a) The traditional way of financing our future is characterized by end of pipe financing through taxation, fees and philanthropy. (b) Green, parallel, optional liquidity would create new green jobs, allowing people from the shadow economy to shift over into the green domain (inverse trafficking). It would reduce negative externalities and downsize costs within the entropic sector (inverse pricing). It would reduce the pro-cyclical tendencies of a monetary monoculture in money creation, inter-banking, credit lines and real investment (anti-cyclical); it would stimulate qualitative growth pathways, generating positive externalities through different channels. It should be noted that this mechanism does not disregard or reject conventional regulatory efforts or redistributive schema, but broadens the perspective

co-financing of global commons (SDGs) through taxes, fees, subsidies and reinvestments. While it accounts for 0.5 to 2% of GDP, this sum is 8–10 times too low to properly finance the SDGs. The big green arrow at the top represents additional liquidity created to finance the SDGs, which is injected into the system through a pre-distributive mechanism. It could be top down, as in CBDCs, or bottom up, as in community currencies (CoC) or cryptocurrencies (CyC). Either way, additional liquidity—properly regulated, pegged to central bank money, eligible for wages and taxes—will flow through an additional, parallel mechanism and multiple alternative channels and will allow us to generate sufficient liquidity that is decoupled from the traditiona l capital market and its interest rates, from the general growth trajectory and its lock-ins, and from tax revenue and its potential evasion. This social mechanism would allow us to fence in negative externalities, bypass the multiple lock-in effects, unleash the power of the global commons for the good of humanity, and meet the requirements of millions of future green jobs.[50]

b

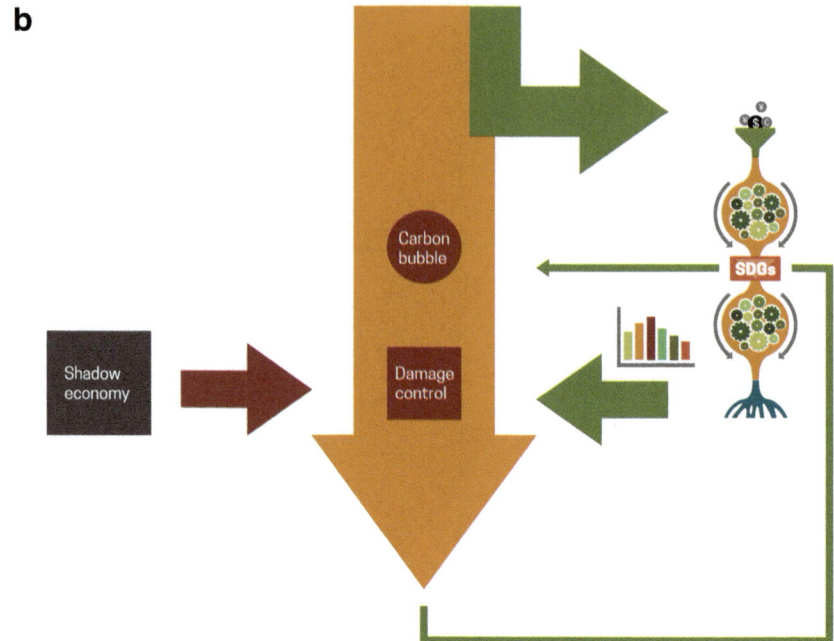

Graph 5.8 continued

Economists define a currency as something that can be used at once as a medium of exchange, a storage of value and a unit of account. The parallel currency system explained in this text meets all these requirements. Having properly financed common goods will have a positive effect on the conventional global GDP, represented by the green arrow pointing left. These positive effects include inverse pricing (anti-inflationary) and reverse trafficking (employment will migrate from the shadow to the conventional to the common goods economic sector). The increased activity in the common goods sector will thus reduce the size of the shadow economy.

Because this parallel mechanism is 100% electronic, there is no cash involved.[51] Transactions are thus traceable and involvement in the shadow economy for purposes of money laundering and tax fraud remains limited and will fade out over time. Governments decide whether to accept this form of liquidity as official tender, including for the payment of taxes and wages. This additional liquidity is bounded: in contrast to traditional quantitative easing (QE), the purpose of this mechanism is investments in SDG-related projects only. This limited investment portfolio by and large avoids falling into a liquidity trap because bounded liquidity is injected directly into the real economy. Additionally, a "banned list" guarantees that funds are only spent on goods and services that are healthy, fair and sustainable. While it is difficult to identify a list of positives, reaching a consensus on a negative list is easier. It could, for example, exclude drugs, guns, and human trafficking, but would allow firms, governments and households to cash in their wages for anything else.[52] In practical terms, additional liquidity in the form described here would create not only a windfall profit, but multiple secondary positive effects by self-reinforcing the trajectory towards sustainable goods and services and ensuring that the money steers society in a sustainable direction.

5.7   The Immediate Impact Towards a Better World

What would happen if such a complementary currency were available? As soon as this parallel currency becomes an eligible means of payment for taxes and wages, communal offices would acquire additional earmarked liquidity to rebuild public infrastructure, including kindergartens, public parks and pools, communal hospitals and libraries. Likewise, the millions of NGOs across the world would receive proper funding to do their jobs. This targeted added liquidity would provide education and access to universal health care that would otherwise never happen. We could target funds to reduce resource depletion and clean up the air, thus avoiding all the negative effects on our common health. We would eventually tap into the untapped potential of millions of human beings without jobs, and unleash the creativity of billions of people. And we would ensure new and healthier, more ecological and fairer forms of economic activities, requiring the circulation of alternative goods and services that in part are independent of the traditional economy. The public sector needs to ensure that these "green dollars" can be spent on wages and used to pay taxes according to the ratio the "green dollar" is spent and used on a corporate and private level. For example: if a local grocery accepts 15% of its sales in green money, it would be allowed to pay 15% of its taxes and wages in green dollars. This ensures that the loop between the private and the public sector will close and will increase trust in the parallel green economy. Monitoring this process remains less of a challenge, as the currency runs in digital form only. International investors and corporates can demonstrate and prove their sincere interest in the region in question by paying their wages in this parallel currency. Phantom foreign investments in offshore locations, which currently represent over 40% of all FDI, will be eliminated little by little.[53]

Let's take the agro-food sector as another case study: This sector reflects an around 6–7 trillion USD market and 40% of the global labor force. The direct and indirect costs for damage control, loss of biodiversity, land use, water stress, including the impact on the nitrate and phosphate cycle, antibiotics resistance and pandemic zoonoses are huge. On top of this, the sector with 25–33% represents the single most important contributor to greenhouse gas emissions (GHGE) and contributes to additional mortality (including cancer, diabetes, Alzheimer's). The current agro-food sector is simply too big to feed the word sustainably. Empirical evidence has shown, however, that the transition to more organic, decentralized farming   would   require   a   three-year   period.   This   includes   mainly   the implementation of crop rotation, new equipment and training. There is increasing data showing that organic farming is up to 3–4 times more profitable due to premium pricing, larger harvest quality (higher resilience), decoupling from the volatile oil price and increased natural capital (mainly biodiversity and soil enrichment). If we admit that protecting fertile land is of highest value for future generations, new financial engineering, beyond conventional funds and bonds are necessary. This could include harvest default facilities, selected plant-based investments (non-meat proteins), alternative protein technologies (clean meat), new agro-food technologies (drones) and alternative collective bonds that finance the transition, all part of a so-called organic farming transition facility (OFTF). Such an OFTF could be issued rather quickly, using alternative monetary channels with targeted distributive ledger technology, using additional green electronic money and issued by developing banks (WB, EIB) that can catalyze that change.[54]

Take a rare vaccine for a subtype of Ebola or Zika virus. Investing in research and development (R&D) for rare diseases does not always make economic sense for for-profit enterprises because the incidence of the disease is too low or unstable for a marketable amount of the expected vaccine to be produced, and the costs are then too high. Nevertheless, a public interest in vaccine development exists, on a local level on the part of the health care ministry on behalf of its citizens and on a global level on the part of the WHO.[55] However, both of these players are chronically underfunded.[56] The mechanism described has the potential to overcome this dichotomy. Central banks could receive a political mandate not driven by short-term cash flow to issue funds for the R&D and production of rare vaccines via this new mechanism, thus creating a win-win for all agents over the long term. Such public investments turn into private wealth. The health status of the target population is ensured, they become more productive, corporations benefit from healthy workers and consumers and society from having engaged citizens. Public health and preventive health care programs in general create a ROI of up to 14 USD benefit for each dollar spent.[57]

Take poverty and hunger. To date, there are no private business models that demonstrate any reasonable ROI for a private investor. At the same time, the public sector in impoverished regions is generally overindebted. The financial mechanism of a parallel currency targeted to address starvation combined with a so-called advance commitment strategy (ACS) can overcome these constraints in less than 18 months: local and international businesses are contracted by the public sector, which guarantees the sale of goods to meet the expected increased demand for food.

Take preschool education. Similarly to poverty and hunger, there is little private incentive to invest in a three-year-old girl living in a suburban slum of a sub-Saharan metropolis. The combination between private-public partnership contracting, including additional green liquidity designed as a parallel currency, is a perfect investment in the future of the next 100 years. The child has a life expectancy of 100 years, and the higher her level of education, the higher her productivity, the lower the birth rate, the lower her health costs, and so on. Early childhood educational programs have demonstrated a ROI of 10–15% annualized in the form of cost savings and revenues for the public sector. Thus, the lifetime earnings of a college graduate student can easily outperform those of a high school dropout by a 1 million USD.[58] The ROI of infrastructure investments has demonstrated a 10–20% yield for the public and the private sector.[59] Each of these examples needs to take into account some sort of default. The local ACS does not work 100%, the R&D for the vaccine is prolonged, the girl can be kidnapped by a fundamentalist religious group, thus preventing her from attending school. In all these cases, we as a world community will grapple with sunk costs; however, it will still have been worth trying to create a better world. Even if only one or two thirds of the projects are successfully realized, this will be a win for all. And if we start to calculate the stranded assets of the fossil fuel industry, or the costs of keeping our Western wealth model alive, we see that the money lost in the abovementioned examples is very low in comparison. A similar rationale is true of other projects as well. For example, because of a lack of tax revenue or ODA, the public sector is unable to drill millions of wells, create thousands of kindergartens, set up first-aid medical centers, establish hundreds of universities and colleges in sub-Saharan Africa or subsidize several hundreds of dual vocational training centers in Northern Africa. With the introduction of earmarked targeted liquidity in an electronic parallel format to enable additional "green" purchasing power, such projects suddenly become rational. The additional jobs created in the region have the effect of increasing local wealth and reducing negative externalities. Conversely, the lack of such investments will lead to forced migration to Europe, reduced educational standards and social instability, and consequently losses in future productivity.

Such a green parallel system is not about "eating the rich", but about transforming the world into a better place for all. A parallel system is a pre-distributive, proxy mechanism, guaranteeing that human behavior and decision-making are steered directly towards greater sustainability. It is a mechanism from which both the rich and the poor benefit directly and indirectly, reducing negative externalities.

Importantly, contrary to our current conventional system of transfer payments, which is redistributive, this system is pre-distributive. So rather than being like an "end-of-pipe" filter trying to clean up polluted air, it addresses the issue at its source. In the conventional system, we generate unspecific, expansive growth as a first step, and then battle with regulatory efforts and transfer payment systems through fees and taxation to generate the liquidity to finance ecological and social projects as a second step. Never, be it historically, mathematically or politically, have we achieved the volume required to fully invest in our commons. This financial mechanism does not solve all our problems, but all problems are affected by this mechanism. It is probably the single most effective, the fastest and the best mechanism we know of, beyond what is currently being discussed in the media, in science and in politics.

What would the effects on the conventional economy be? The additionally created 5 trillion USD equivalent would not hurt or harm the conventional economy. Precisely the opposite is true. Corporate and state planning, production and price levels such as the Consumer Price Index (CPI) and the Asset Price Index (API) would become more robust and reliable and less speculative, embracing a longer-term vision. Furthermore, the 5 trillion USD would stabilize the cyclical economy of booms and busts. It is this pre-distributive design rather than a redistributive mechanism (end-of-pipe financing) that has the potential to shift and transform our entire society, moving it in the right direction. The following table lists some of the immediate impacts the introduction of this mechanism would lead to (Table 5.4).

Table 5.4 Examples of the immediate impact of a parallel currency system on regional and sectoral transformation

Green parallel complementary liquidity	Impact/explanation
Liquidity trap	In a globally deflationary situation in which we lack 4–5 trillion USD for Sustainable Development Goals (SDGs) annually, a parallel currency system offers additional liquidity in an intelligent design. Instead of providing liquidity through the standard protocol, which failed to provide credit to the public sector, bounded direct investments in green and social projects can ensure that the liquidity reaches the real market.
Debt trap	Most countries are over-indebted, with little to no leverage for funding additional ecological or social projects. The additional liquidity will trigger the green and social investments most countries lack.
Inverse trafficking	There is less need for people to earn an income through drugs, crime and human trafficking. Regional resource wars and forced immigration will be reduced and employment in the 'green sector' will reduce the attractiveness of terrorist movements for unemployed young people. A Green Quantitative Easing (QE) can create over 300 million new jobs globally.
Shadow banking	The earmarked electronic procedure ensures that shadow banking (offsheet and offshore) will dry out in the long run, stabilizing the world economy, regulatory efforts, transparency and monetary policy in general.
Positive externalities	Generally speaking, with each transaction green QE produces positive externalities, creating a win-win situation for both private business and public interests.
Market allocation and efficiency	Additional bounded liquidity will reduce the efficiency of any economic transaction, as there are two pathways for processing economic activities instead of one. However, these forms of parallel processing will render systems more resilient and shock-proof, despite the loss of efficiency. In short: a net gain can be derived from a parallel system that stabilizes the overall system.
Green growth	Our conventional growth process, measured in units per gross domestic product (GDP), will change. Long-term investments in socio-ecological projects and an increase in labor intensity are two of the most prominent impacts, shifting our growth paths towards a more green, balanced and healthy planet.
Employment	A parallel currency system can create additional jobs, meeting unmet needs and unleashing human potential in society, and decreasing collateral or defensive costs (lost output, crime, reduced physical and mental health, family breakdown, social exclusion).
Anti-cyclical	Whereas traditional QE has a pro-cyclical impact upon money creation, the interbanking sector and credit lines to the real economy, a green dual system can operate anti-cyclically as such investments are optional. Any time a bust or deflationary pressure looms, the green channel can provide safe and sound liquidity.

(continued)

Table 5.4 (continued)

Green parallel complementary liquidity	Impact/explanation
Anti-inflationary	A 4–5 trillion USD additional stimulus will create an inflationary pressure on price levels. However, any dollar spent through this 'green' mechanism will reduce costs in the conventional economy in the so-called entropic sector. This 'inverse pricing' effect will reduce the price level (wages) in sectors nobody really wants: crime, forced migration, human trafficking, ecological disaster management, unemployment, poverty are just some examples, as human activity is invested in a greener and more socially just world.
Corruption/illicit transactions	Drying out shadow economy activities: there are unregulated markets in which firms/investors provide bank-like services and maturity transformation through alternative tools (Special Purpose Vehicles (SPV), Systematic Investment Plans (SIP), hedge funds, repos, etc. equal to 60–70 trillion USD). An electronic-based green dual system can make a substantial contribution to avoiding corruption (e-government).
Currency stability	A currency created through a parallel system would be backed up by long-term sustainable tangible assets, making such a currency less volatile.
Bank runs and market panic	Both banking and the market become more trustworthy without the need for additional regulatory efforts, as green investment provides sustainable and tangible assets.
Distribution	Socioeconomic distribution through taxes, fees or philanthropy is politically volatile. Once a new political party is in power, or the donor changes his or her mind, needed socioeconomic projects are abandoned, A parallel system remains a stable source for financing our future.

And there is one aspect missing in our argument: New distributive ledger technology (DLT), properly designed can finally enable a parallel currency system, new monetary channels and a new mandate for the regulators. All this will be explained in the next subchapter.

5.8 The Wealth Effects: Some Math, Distributive Ledger Technology and the Multi-stakeholder Approach

All technology is ambivalent. This is true of the Haber-Bosch process and DNA coding as well as of new technologies such as Artificial Intelligence (AI), Big Data, nanotechnology, robotronics, cryptocurrencies and blockchain.[60] We as humans decide which technology we want to implement and to which extent in order to create the type of society we want to live in. Accordingly, the question of the type of society we want to live in needs to come first and the technology to achieve this second. If we want to have a more sustainable future, in which the financial sector and its underlying monetary design play a prominent role, the technology required to achieve this becomes key.[61] Distributive ledger technologies such as blockchain are general purpose in nature, much like the printing press, the internet or the steam engine. Privatizing such a general-purpose technology transforms its associated activities into a private good. This will lead to the well-known effect of wealth concentration and issues of unclear liability. The opposite also holds true. Using a general-purpose technology as a public good makes associated activities a common good, leading to greater decentralization and different forms of liabilities.[62] This digital process creates a kind of second world around us that consequently feeds back into the analog world. In this sense, blockchain "doubles" the world through an alphabet of 0 and 1, and generates complex algorithms to reveal features, patterns and regularities that the untrained eye cannot grasp. The advent of this process is akin to Galileo looking through the telescope, or to identifying microbes using a microscope. In each case, humans are forced to apply assistive technology to better understand the world. The information obtained through digitization is part of the answer in an increasingly complex world. For example, blockchain can optimize and allocate resources more efficiently by avoiding waste and anticipating potential risks. It can also provide additional information on the complexity of the financial system and help to better target financial flows.[63]

Distributive ledger technology (DLT): fast, efficient, resilient and transformative: third- or fourth-generation blockchain technology would be used for the complementary parallel optional electronic currency system described in this text.[64] In combination with public-private key pairs, hash functions, elliptical curve cryptographs and a smart social contract algorithm—a built-in algorithm that allows certain transactions and prohibits others—DLT increases traceability, trust and transparency.[65] Because this technology does not require intermediaries, traditional transaction costs, which normally amount to 2–3% per transaction, are reduced. The ability to track transactions can facilitate business automation and cross-organizational harmonization. Furthermore, this technology enhances authentication by proving a person is who they claim to be; provides authorization by proving that a person has the permission to do what they are doing; and increases accountability by showing who did what and when, much like a patient record or a drug safety protocol. Public calls, contracting and procurement, fraud, illicit financial transactions and corruption would also be positively affected. Implementing a second monetary system requires bridging incentives that increase trust, reliability and efficiency at the same time.[66]

A parallel economy needs to have relatively autonomous forms of consumption and production in order not to be absorbed by the conventional system. DLT can ensure this separateness. Such a parallel optional currency mechanism would provide targeted, programmable, identifiable, recordable financial transactions and earmarked and dedicated funds, avoiding fraud and corruption. The ID block chain would ensure that the additional liquidity is spent only on SDGs from the outset. This would create a new parallel marketplace for the 75% of the world population who have not benefited from the existing operating model. The new mechanism would eventually become intertwined with the traditional sector. From central banks to governments, to local state authorities, to IGOs, to NGOs, to SMEs, to large international corporations, this mechanism enables the creation of additional liquidity to empower humanity and overcome the shortfall in financing our future.

It should be noted that the wealth effects created by this mechanism are potentially several times larger than the traditional Keynesian multiplier. This is mainly due to the different technology in place (blockchain), making it possible to target and awaken the sleeping giant of the global commons, using different monetary channels.[67] Further, this mechanism systemically reduces negative externalities in the entropic sector, generating multiple second-round effects: unlike the conventional approach, where we invest in green assets and benefit from a single windfall profit, but produce multiple rebound effects and unwanted spillovers, this new DLT allows us to generate ongoing positive, sustainable feedback loops over and over again. Each time we use this green currency, we generate some sort of good for humanity of which we can be sure. This will further help to reduce the negative impact of the shadow economy, which we will address in the next chapter. Accordingly, this mechanism would provide a more stable and resilient framework for the global economy as a whole. Both large-scale investment strategies of institutional agencies and small-scale business will start operating within a more stable and reliable framework, allowing the development of long-term perspectives. The same holds true for local and global policy: political leaders, regardless of whether they have a democratic mandate or run their country in an autocratic manner, will be able to agree on this mechanism as it will enable them to generate additional green revenue and stabilize the economy.[68]

It is no overstatement to say that a complementary optional currency system would be Pareto superior to a monetary monopoly. The wealth equation represents a proxy estimation of the additional wealth created by implementing a parallel currency system and is summarized below. This mechanism creates a wealth effect that is larger than the well-known Keynesian stimulus (Graph 5.9).[69]

$$WE = \frac{L \times ROI \times M \times C \times i}{y} (df)$$

WE	Wealth effect generated by a parallel currency
L	Additional liquidity created by the central bank
ROI	Return on Investment per project realized
M	Keynes's demand multiplier
c	velocity of money
y	Annual adjustment
df	% default of failed projects
▲i	Interest differential

Graph 5.9 Keynes 2.0—the green leverage towards the future

5.9   Conclusion: The Missing Link

We could look at this matter from a different angle. The average citizen is not interested in spending his or her whole day thinking about ecological and social issues; the average citizen simply wants to live his or her life and make sure that he or she is doing the right thing. We need a mechanism that ensures 24/7 for 8 billion humans that all of us are doing the right thing with every single step we take.[70] Currently, we are demanding economic growth first in order to redistribute parts of it to co-finance the commons second. This is not wrong, but it is relatively inefficient, leading a suboptimal allocation of goods and services, as this approach does not take the entropic sector, negative social and environmental externalities, or the shadow economy into account. In this sense, markets are efficient, as they represent the best-known mechanism to allocate goods and services. But they are not effective, in the sense that they do not have a built-in target or purpose. If we take 4–5 trillion USD annually as the rough figure required to "make the world a better place", we might have to consider doing things differently. Because approximately 1.7 billion people do not have a bank account, and cannot create wealth through savings or trading, greater financialization—meaning a larger financial sector/GDP—is required to cover their needs.[71] Generally speaking, we need far, far greater financialization to cover the needs of over two thirds of the global population, not less.[72] If the major monetary players and regulators (IMF, World Bank, central banks, United Nations, development banks, governments) were to create an additional 4–5 trillion USD annually, and this sum were linked primarily to funding projects pertaining to common goods, the entire situation would change. As everything is connected to everything and affects all of us, the mechanism described here should at least have a positive impact on those who are engaged in building a shared, more just and greener future. This is why we need a multi-stakeholder approach, honoring all the different agendas involved and providing benefit for most of them. The following table summarizes the impact for the different agents involved (Table 5.5).

On a more operational and executive level, additional liquidity adequately regulated by the central banks would lead to an expansion of the central banks' balance sheets while purchasing international or national SDG bonds, facilitating SDGs on a domestic level. We would then also use the parallel digital distributive ledger currency track to channel donations, charity and philanthropy towards SDGs in a similar manner. We could then further use the same parallel digital distributive ledger currency track for national or international taxation and official developmental aid (ODA). Impact investors and institutional investors could swap their fossil-based assets for green ones at high volume. Considering the volume, speed and scope of the challenge, we probably will end up with a blend of all these factors.[73] The lower taxation, ODA, donations and private investment are, the higher the amount of additional liquidity needed to meet the 5 trillion USD will be. Either way, the money is channeled through domestic bonds and monitored by the UN and development banks. This means that the state level, including the third sector, is responsible for the liquidity being spent properly, and that the

Table 5.5 Integral view of a multi-stakeholder perspective

Investor	Reducing costs, increasing efficiency, especially impact funds, reduced volatility
Politics	Tax revenues, political stability, improving democracy, political self-efficacy
Regulator	Improved regulatory efforts: anti-cyclical, riding a bike with two wheels, reduced volatility, law of money supply: plenty—paucity—proportionally
Security-military complex	Stabilizes any given political system (democracy to autocracy), reduces or dries out black/shadow market
NGOs/Non-profit organizations (NPOs)	Enabling future life: green growth, green jobs, health, education, peace, planet
Citizen	Remittance, which already reflects double the volume of official development assistance (ODA) globally, could benefit from additional green liquidity. The money goes directly to the poor and the places on the planet that need it most.
Corporate world	The world is vastly deflationary; dealing with corruption, fraud, illicit transactions; reduced transaction costs
Intergovernmental organizations (IGOs)	Beyond global governance, overcoming the impossible trade: globalization—democracy—free market (D. Rodrik)
Least developed countries (LDCs)	Enabling leapfrogging, regional wealth, meeting basic social needs and decarbonization
Religion	Inter-religious dialogue, poverty, hunger, nature, earth, 'Laudato si'' (Pope Francis)
Science	Enacting empirical evidence; from knowledge and wisdom to transformation
Nature	Harmonizing/reconciling our life within the Anthropocene
Future	Future becomes a capability, not a curse; progressive, not repressive; and a leverage towards greater freedom, not a sanction.

UN will monitor that process. This exercise shows us once again that money is not a thing, but a social invention whose design we need to tailor for the good of humanity.

In this sense, a parallel currency system operates as an upfront stabilizer, independent of any growth stimulus and guaranteeing basic needs. Such an approach is also in line with findings in neuroscience and behavioral science which indicate that our brain and our mind have the intrinsic capacity to operate in parallel manner. Indeed, this provides a much higher selection advantage to humans than merely relying on single, linear or sequential processing. And it is this same procedure that will provide the background for a real transformation beyond any personal behavioral changes, a transformation with the potential to involve 7.5 billion people around the clock.[74]

In summary, this new financial mechanism differs from the current academic literature and public discussion in that the additionally created "green" liquidity runs parallel to existing channels.[75] Furthermore, it is designed to be a pre-distributive mechanism, where money is created based on need, rather than a

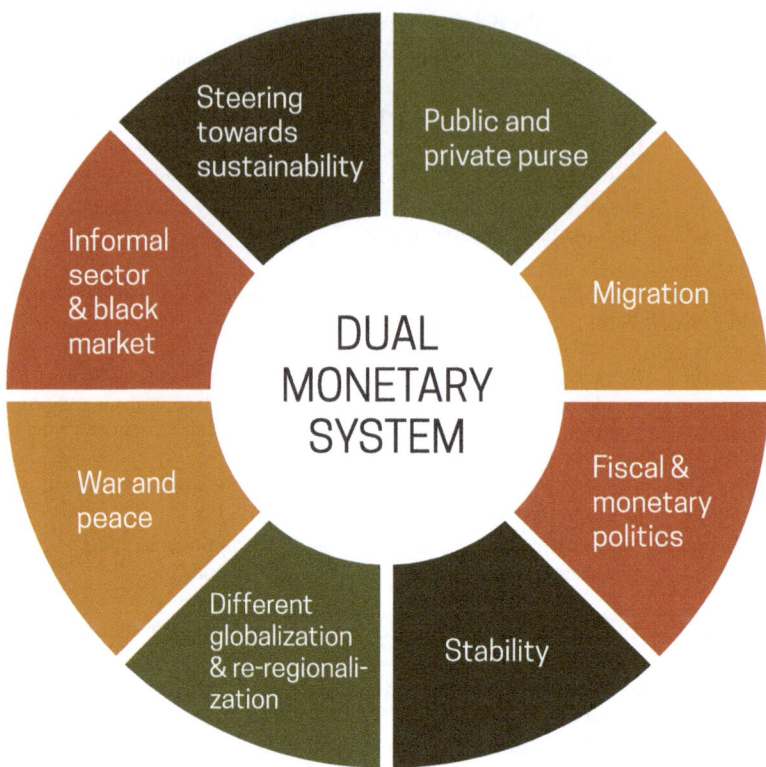

Graph 5.10 An integral view—The impact of a dual monetary system on the society

redistributive mechanism based on scarcity; it is a mechanism that honors market allocation and state regulation at the same time. And because of its multiple positive externalities, it has the potential to generate a Pareto-superior equilibrium. Once such a parallel currency system is in place, its numerous impacts will help to bring our society as a whole and our economic activities in particular back into balance. These new symmetries will be explained in the next and final chapter (Graph 5.10).

Notes

1. The real economic sector and the monetary sector follow different rationales. In the real economic sector, savings and investment ought to be identical (DSGE model). In the monetary domain, banks can create money, exceeding the savings rate. Savings in the monetary world simply reflect a shift between households and corporates (ISLM model). This aspect is widely used by monetary experts in the loanable funds model (e.g. Bernanke; Draghi; Krugmann). However, there is no causal link between the monetary base of the central bank and the credit expansion of the commercial banking sector. As the commercial banking system is profit-maximizing, the causal link leads from the expanded credit line to the monetary base (Werner 2014). A parallel currency system would change this.

2. For more details, see Lietaer and Brunnhuber (2005) or Lietaer and Dunne (2013).
3. 2 degrees of global warming has the potential to decrease economic growth by up to 0.5% with a time lag of seven years (harvesting, infrastructure and adaptation costs) in the global North, but to cause a decrease of 0.5–1% in the global South. This means that climate change will lead not to an economic bust, but rather accelerate the inequality between North and South (IMF 2017).
4. Barrdear and Kumhof (2016) define a CBDC as "a universally accessible and interest-bearing central bank liability, implemented via distributive ledgers, that competes with bank deposits as mediums of exchange"; also see Huber (2020a, b) with an update of the relevant literature.
5. One of the major concerns are default investments. The balance sheet of a central bank is different to that of a firm, household or state. On the one hand, it can sterilize lost investments, causing reduced seigniorage; on the other hand, however, the reduced seigniorage that decreases the state budget needs to be compared with reduced costs in the entropic sector (Ryan-Collins et al. 2012; Sinn 2016; Huber 2020c).
6. In a very long-term view (over several centuries), interest rates have been falling by 0.006–0.016 per year with a high volatility. This is due either to wars, which reduce the capital stock, to periods of peace with reduced risk premiums, or to plagues, where the population has been diminished substantially. Technically speaking, central bankers and regulators can control the interest rate in the short term, but we overestimate their control long term. See Schmelzing (2019).
7. Neoclassical economics usually defines three different types of quantities of money:
   M1 = money issued by central banks, also called "high-powered money" or base money;
   > M2 = M1 + checking accounts and short-term deposits (up to one year);
   > M3 = M2 + savings accounts and longer-term deposits.
   > To note: Since the introduction of the Euro, M1 increased by factor 10, M3 by factor 3.
   In the US dollar zone data exceed the Euro. But there is a third factor which is relevant: human behavior, which effectively leads to more qualified consumption, real private and public investment.
   We could define M4 = M3 + parallel currencies as defined in this text.
8. The origins of money can be traced back to the sixth century BCE in Syria, where the first coins appeared. According to anthropologists, the money economy was not preceded by a barter economy. It was rather a gift economy that preceded the money economy among small groups, families and neighborhoods. Money was used with enemies and foreigners, in long-distance trading, and always involved regulatory efforts by the respective political system (Graeber 2011).
9. For example, the M-pesa in Kenya is a widely used cryptocurrency covering almost half the Kenyan GDP, enabling people to trade and do business. The provider is an international private telecommunications firm which charges fees of up to 20% on each transaction (McGath 2018; Safaricom 2019).
10. All these sand-box approaches and grassroots activities are extremely helpful for learning how to steer the system in the right direction. For further systematics of all these activities, see Kennedy and Lietaer (2004) or Kennedy et al. (2012).
11. The history of money follows a history of reduced costs for transactions: from barter to coins, to the gold standard, to credit money, to distributive ledger-associated cryptocurrencies. On the history of money, see Davies (2010) and Ali et al. (2014).
12. There is a strong argument that any form of electronic money with the option of cashing in, whether issued by a central bank or by a private company, runs the risk of becoming totalitarian and controlling its users and consumers. We have to bear this risk in mind and apply adequate regulatory efforts to avoid such a development.
13. See Lagarde (2018); Mancini-Griffoli et al. (2018); McKibbin et al. (2017).
14. "Fiat Lux" were the first words that God pronounced, according to Genesis: "Let there be light." The next sentence is, "And God saw the light, that it was good." We are dealing with the truly godlike power of creating something out of nothing ("ex nihilo") by the power of the word.

15. For the experts in the field: the idea of green quantitative easing corresponds to a number of the ECB's monetary policies in different ways: OMT (Outright Monetary Policy), where the CB buys up state bonds; open market policy, where central banks buy up currencies, gold, private and public assets; ECT (Enlarged Credit Support), FAP (Full Allotment Policy), implying unlimited refinancing loans; LTRO (Long Term Refinancing operations), SMP (Security Market Policy), which is similar to the OMT; STEP (Short Term European Program) and ELA (Emergency Liquidity Assistance), which reflect emergency credit lines without any liability or rating requirements; and finally, simple bank loans have become eligible for central bank deposits. Draghi's "whatever it takes" strategy (2012) has caused a huge misallocation of risks and liabilities. In sum: low interest and low rating led to a credit bubble with a misallocation of goods and services from the North of Europe to the South of Europe—most of it without any democratic mandate. In each case the traditional money policy supports concrete investment strategies in member states. And this is exactly what is proposed in this text. However, we propose using different channels and a different monetary design.

16. *Open market policy (OMO)* is an essential tool to provide and withdraw liquidity to and from the market while buying or selling government bonds; *Base money* or high-powered money refers to the total amount of central bank money issued. After the 2008 crisis *quantitative easing (QE)*—buying different forms of financial assets including corporate bonds—became a major source of that figure; the *Citizens dividend (CD)* refers to the concept of creating direct cash transfers for all of us. There is an overlap between these three monetary instruments (OMO; QE and CD). Either way it inflates or deflates the balance sheet of the central bank involved. To note: the vast majority of the money in circulation is not created by the central banks, but by the for-profit commercial banking system (97%). However designed in the right way, introducing a parallel currency system increases the steering capacity of the (public, not for profit) regulators, benefiting from multiple so-called "second-round effects", navigating our society towards our global commons and the SDGs.

17. Said verbatim by Mario Draghi—ECB, July 26, 2012.

18. To note: additional earmarked liquidity has the potential to reduced foreign currency reserves at a state level, which currently stand at 11 trillion USD globally, offering further political leverage for resilience in case of monetary shocks (IMF 2019).

19. There is a more comprehensive argument to the "new normal": we are experiencing zero to negative interest rates as the "new normal". In such a world, the price signal for money (which is expressed in the interest rate) loses its signaling power, creating zombie-like corporates (estimates range from 1.5–2% in the EU), buybacks on the stock market and unproductive asset price inflation. This distorts efficient market allocation. 80% of the revenue of the banking sector depends on these interest-based revenues. Over 15 trillion USD of state bonds and over 40% of corporate bonds already have a negative yield. Besides demographic changes (aging population with higher savings) and new disruptive technologies (platform economies requiring less capital), the blame traditionally goes to the regulators for having printed too much money to stabilize the economy. However, in a complex, non-linear world, the "chicken-and-egg" argument no longer holds. The interest rate is one of the few instruments central banks have at their disposal to regulate the real economy. A dual currency creating a second, green market place would overcome the constraints immediately and put an adequate price on our green future. Once this price is higher than the new normal in the traditional economy, business will shift gradually but consistently towards a green future. In technical terms, we are talking about a carry-trade effect.

20. NGFS (2019); Lagarde and Gaspar (2019); Coeure (2018).

21. To be more specific for experts in the field: the classical regulator rule *"one needle in the compass"* (price stability) policy is complemented by an additional non-financial purchasing program, which reaches out through new monetary tools and is implemented through national or international development banks. This *"going direct"* policy identifies projects (SDGs) whose financing could act as bonds, grants and/or loans with virtually perpetual or very, very long maturities. In fact, this would increase the balance sheet of the operating central banks and their partnering developing banks. In case of a partial default, where the bank accumulates stranded assets, the initial seigniorage for exactly that additional amount of *"hot money"* has

to be written off, and the amount of M0 has to be sterilized. From a macroeconomic perspective, however, the monetary aggregate M3 is more relevant. If we start investing in projects with the highest ROI (return on investment) for society as a whole (mainly commons), using block-chain technology, we can ensure that the overall wealth generated for the society reaches a Pareto-superior equilibrium where price stability eventually is achieved, which was the policy in the first place.

22. Adapted from a dialogue referred to by J.M. Keynes in which an eminent architect who wanted to rebuild London asks: "Where is the money coming from?" (Keynes 1980, p. 308).

23. The World Bank, IMF and regional development banks have advised nations to borrow savings from abroad, via portfolio investment, FDI or loans in order to augment domestic savings and achieve a higher growth rate. Most literature, however, has chronically ignored the domestic banking sector. Money in foreign denominations (which is simply commercial bank-created money) never enters the receiving economy, but results in a credit expansion in the domestic bank. This can be achieved without foreign investment. There is increasing empirical evidence that foreign direct investment (FDI) does not trigger growth, but rather crowds out the domestic market. FDI simply competes with domestic investment for funding. Policy makers would do better not to waste taxpayers' money on attracting FDI and instead spend more on domestic education and SME. There is a significant increase in inequality in developing countries with high FDI, with a clear causal link between FDI and inequality. In addition, most figures on FDI are misleading. They become a kind of black hole. Large companies simply reroute their money through offshore locations. Empirical data demonstrate that 30–50% of FDI in the UK and USA and up to 80% in Russia uses this investment loop. In short: who is the largest investor in the UK, in the USA and in Russia? It is the UK, USA and Russia themselves. See De Haldevang (2017) or Bermejo Carbonell and Werner (2018).

24. See Dixon (2017).

25. Especially as social projects (unemployment) and ecological projects (global warming or biodiversity) require more than the average increase in GDP can cover in both absolute and relative terms. This forces the overall economy to grow. Empirically, a growth of about 1.8% is required so that the economy does not collapse (Binswanger 2006, 2009). Further aspects have been identified that force our economy to grow: from disruptive technologies, to changes within the human capital (like education), to different forms of output elasticity of the production factors (energy and labor), to planned obsolescence, to the compound interest rate. Each time, our economic activities are forced to grow in order to stabilize the system (Brunnhuber 2018). A parallel currency system, as explained here in the text, has the potential to reduce or even eliminate the need for expansive growth. Instead of redistributing money, it generates targeted and proportional liquidity and purchasing power to match the social and ecological projects identified in the region in question.

26. In its extreme form, redistribution is called the "Robin Hood effect" (Atkinson et al. 1992). If we consider the wealth of 2000 billionaires (each owning 1 billion USD), the fact that they have generated this wealth over one generation (30 years), and the fact that there are 7 billion people on the planet, we arrive at the following equation: 2000/7/30=10 USD per capita per year over 30 years. This means that in a world where wealth is equally distributed, each human could go and get him- or herself one extra fast food meal per year for 30 years. Or, to put the argument the other way around: a premium of 10 USD per capita per year is the cost of each human being living in the world of Bill Gates instead of a socialist dictatorship. Asymmetries are not always bad, especially when they occur above the minimum wage and basic living requirements. The SDGs need to meet basic needs; as long as this is the case, we can be tolerant of asymmetries in wealth.

27. See UN (2015).

28. Ellen MacArthur Foundation, Growth Within: A Circular Economy Vision for a Competitive Europe, 2015; Stahel (2019).

29. See World Bank Indicators (2018b). Agenda 21 cost around 600 billion USD annually worldwide, and the industrialized countries were supposed to contribute 100 billion USD annually,

which is equivalent to 0.7% of the GDP of the rich nations at that time. The idea was to extract this amount of money from the "Peace Dividend" of disarmament after the end of the Cold War and redirect it into ecological and social projects. In reality, most of those dividends went into tax reductions within the rich countries. See United Nations Conference of Environment and Development (UNCED 1992).

30. UNCTAD (2014); World Bank Indicators (2018b).
31. Historically, development financing started with UNCTAD III in 1972, involving a debt relief campaign and a more multilateral framework to examine debt problems; in 1977 there was a call for explicit debt restructuring (TD/AC 2/9); 1980/1986 saw further details for sovereign debt restructuring based on Chapter 11 of the US bankruptcy reform act of 1978; 1996 brought the HIPC initiative. All these proposals were ignored until the Russian and Asian crises in the late 1990s and the global liquidity crunch of 1997/98 (Kregel 2004; Ricupero 2004; UNCTAD 2019).
32. Charity, philanthropy and private pledges are good things, but from a systems perspective they represent something like a hobby, an amusement that appeases the conscience rather than changes the world. It would have been better to use this knowledge and money to improve the value chain up- and downstream along the given business model and to abandon or write off parts of the revenues instead. The money would have been invested better.
33. World Bank (2019).
34. See European Central Bank (ECB 2015).
35. For example, to meet long-term sustainability goals in the Sustainable Development Scenarios on a global level, low-carbon investment would need to grow two-and-a-half times by 2030, with its share rising to 65%; annual average investment required for 2025–30 in IEA scenarios is 2 trillion on a European level. On a global level, an additional global investment of 260 billion USD to 370 billion USD a year is needed to reach a 450-ppm climate pathway over the coming 15 years. An estimate of 53 trillion USD in cumulative investment in energy supply and in energy efficiency is required over the period up to 2035 in order to move the world onto a 2°C emissions path. The transition towards a more cyclical economy would cost Europe some 100 billion USD over the same period. According to International Energy Agency forecasts, decarbonizing our power grid would require 20 trillion USD up to 2035. The overall costs for all SDGs are estimated at around 4–5 trillion USD per year in public spending, investments and direct aid. According to the United Nations Conference on Trade and Development (UNCTAD), there is an annual investment gap of at least 2.5 to 4 trillion USD. See Ellen McArthur Foundation (2015); UNCTAD (2014).
36. UNCTAD (2014); World Bank Indicators (2018b). Throughout the last decades, there have been numerous proposals for so-called innovative finance: these included the Brown report in IFF, the LULA/CHIRAC working group proposal of air ticket taxation, the Tobin tax on currency transactions; THE WIDER report and §44 and §45 for development banks (AAAA 2015; Atkinson 2005; Brown 2004; Tobin 1978; Working Group on New International Contributions to Finance Development 2004). See additionally Club of Rome (2019) and Schroeder (2006).
37. Desjardins (2017); Van der Knaap and De Vries (2018).
38. See Grubb et al. (2019); United Nations Conference of Environment and Development (UNCED) (1992).
39. This so-called "liquidity trap" describes the phenomena that occur when monetary regulators fail to stimulate or influence price levels with an interest rate at or close to zero; Sumner, Scott. "The other money illusion". The Money Illusion. Retrieved 3 June 2011.
40. J. Ryan-Collins, T. Greenham, G. Bernardo, and R. Werner (2013). "Strategic Quantitative Easing". Published by the New Economics Foundation (NEF). Available at: http://www.neweconomics.org/publications/entry/strategic-quantitative-easing.
41. See Ryan-Collins et al. (2013).
42. Jackson (2013); Bank of England (2016); Van Lerven (2016); Positive Money (2014); El-Erian (2016), where the author concludes: "It is better to plan to fail than to fail to plan."

43. Empirically, none of the conventional monetary channels helped to provide adequate liquidity to the real economy. One of the reasons for this failure is that all these channels offer their own narrative on how it could work, but the conventional quantitative easing (QE) mechanism does not offer any empirical evidence of causality. This so-called "liquidity trap" describes the phenomena that occur when monetary regulators fail to stimulate or influence price levels with an interest rate at or close to zero (Ryan-Collins, Werner, Greenham, and Bernardo 2013; Sumner 2010; Benes and Kumhof 2012).

44. Traditionally *consumption* on the one hand refers to human capital, wages and day-to-day short-term requirements (food, transportation, rent, clothing), whereas *investment* on the other hand reflects economic activities, such as building a bridge, a sewage system, a hospital or simply buying land. However, this differentiation between investment and consumption strategies is arbitrary and outdated. Any investment strategy triggers consumption right away and any consumption implies additional investments. When the quality of human capital (education and health status) is key for any future successful business and politics, the only relevant economic performance indicator is return on investment. And as investing in humans has the highest ROI, we should simply abandon the traditional difference between consumption and investment. And at the end of the value chain, hopefully there always will be someone who will buy a veggie burger!

45. Werner (2003); Harari (2016); for a revised Chicago Plan see Benes and Kumhof (2012).

46. Despite defaults, restructuring and haircuts sovereign bonds have been a history of investor profits for a long period of time. A 200-year period on emerging markets reveals, despite wars, default episodes, global crisis and despite an average haircut below 50%, a compensating excess return over the risk-free rate of 7% annually, which outperforms corporate bonds. See Meyer et al. (2019).

47. Buteică and Huidumac-Petrescu (2018); Engerer (2019) or oneplanetswfs.org.

48. The Austrian School of economics (Hayek, e.g. 1976; Schumpeter, e.g. 1912) is one historical source for the TAO of Finance. Economic development should not be limited or constrained by domestic savings, external borrowing or taxation. Financial transfers are not necessarily required. Money can be "created out of nothing" as long as the financial sector has a monopoly on it. Bankers create additional purchasing power for entrepreneurs by generating credit lines. For Schumpeter, the banker is the "ephor", the "mastermind" of any successful development. Hayek even went one step further, advocating the de-nationalization of the monetary system, allowing everybody to create their own money. The free market system then would select the most powerful currency. The TAO of Finance represents a position in between a monetary monopoly and a fully decentralized and privatized monetary system, advocating a dual system only.

49. Technically there are three ways to get liquidity into the market: firstly, open-market policy by purchasing government bonds; secondly, lending money to the commercial banking system; and thirdly, injecting liquidity directly into the economy.

50. A further technical detail: if the green parallel currency were backed up by 100 kg of CO_2e, it would generate an upstream incentive to hold on to and invest in this currency for at least 15–20 years from now, as we can expect the price of CO_2 to increase over that time period due to regulation and carbon taxation. This would operate like a "new gold standard" for a new green age. This is the time span within which such a currency would rise in value as the price of CO_2 per ton would rise, until all investments have been cleared and we enter a low-carbon age. Then, 20 years from now, we would have to de-risk and deleverage this back-up. Details for this argument come from Chen (2018), or Chen et al. (2018); Chen, van der Beek and Cloud (2017).

51. Critics of digital transactions may argue that the state exercises excessive control over citizens' freedom to use cash. The argument goes so far as to say that central banks and governments have every control over all financial transactions, leaving individual companies and citizens completely exposed to potential state abuse. This argument cannot be dismissed entirely. However, it is important to bear in mind that over 97% of transactions today already

are conducted digitally. A possible interim solution would be for local transactions to continue to have the option of cash, although these transactions also would be marked as "green" (via a barcode). The main argument of a parallelization of the monetary system thus remains valid. For the debate on surveillance capitalism see Zuboff (2019).

52. A further technical detail: in the first phase, a limited convertibility with the conventional monetary system with, for example, a 10–15% exchange rate might be useful. This would encourage clients, companies and states to reinvest in the SDGs or to convert money with a loss. Long term, this mechanism would achieve a higher stability as it would be pegged to real, sustainable long-term investments.

53. According to IMF 2019, 40% of FDI is phantom capital, where the liquidity is transferred through Special Purpose Vehicles (SPV) to offshore places without any real economic activity. This amounts to 15 trillion USD in corporate money. Luxembourg and the Netherlands hold 50% of that capital. In total, 85% of the entire sum globally is located in 10 countries only (see: IMF 2019, Damgaard, Elkjaer, Johannesen).

54. Batini (2019); Crowder and Reganold (2015); Network for Greening the Financial System (2019); Willett et al. (2019).

55. See Masters et al. (2017).

56. The implicit public debt load in OECD countries is between 2–5 times higher than the explicit debt. Aging (pension claims, health care costs), increasing poverty and income inequality will increase this sum in the near future. The conventional calculation is that an increase of 5% in taxes or fees is required to finance this sustainability gap. Alternatively we could withdraw this amount from the current economic process, reduce the public payments for social security and pensions and/or increase the number of years before people can claim their pensions. The mechanism described in this text represents a better answer to these challenges, however.

57. See Masters et al. (2017).

58. See Ernst and Young LLP (2016); see also literature on the so-called "Heckman equation" (Elango et al. 2015; Heckman et al. 2010).

59. See Bivens (2017).

60. Blockchain technology and its derivatives involve several tradeoffs: trust and transparency on the one hand and control and lack of privacy on the other; or the well-known "garbage in, garbage out" effect: any smart contract can deliver bad, illegal or unwanted transactions, such as illicit financial transactions; or the tradeoff between security and energy consumption. Another tradeoff is the disruptive power of the loss of any intermediary for the mass aggregate demand. Each time, it is we as humans who decide which part of the tradeoff we are better off with.

61. Much as email is one of the first basic applications of the internet, Bitcoin is one of the first applications of blockchain technology. Much more is still to come.

62. We should note that often it is not the democratic mandate or the public discourse, but an AI algorithm that provides us with knowledge. Autocratic systems choose this same technology to control their people. The corporate world is also using AI to identify new business models. And this in consequence forces us to clarify several things: who creates the algorithms, for which purposes are they being used and who owns, monitors and controls the data?

63. Nassehi (2019).

64. Operating within market solutions, of this sort of technology has two substantial impacts: first, platforms replace middle men (law of the excluded middle), which impacts on mass demand. Second, the network effect produces monopolies which normally generate higher prices and lower quality. As corporate tax rates are lower than personal taxation, they further reduce fiscal yields and put pressure on governmental budgets, leading to further austerity and decline of social expenditures.

65. See the UN World Food program as a first proof of concept. A smartphone interface with a biometric identification system prevents misuse and fraud. There is greater security and privacy for the clients enrolled, as sensitive data are not shared with third private parties, like social media firms or banks.

66. In the information age, private versus public ownership affects not only tangible goods but also the way we organize the flow of data. We should differentiate between private and personal data ownership. Personal data are the information each of us generates on a day-to-day basis in any digital form. Private data ownership means that these data become the property of a private actor, like a corporation. A private actor can then monopolize, limit or distort personal data in order to generate profit. In order to guarantee a maximum flow of information, personal data should be distributed in a decentralized way. If we take the laws of sustainability as a given, where the "anti-fragile zone" between efficiency and resilience determines the degree to which a system remains on a long-term, sustainable path, we must request that personal information remains within an individual's personal network and not be privatized. See Sir Tim Berners Lee's project Solid (https://solid.inrupt.com) or Threefold (https://threefold.io).

67. As mentioned above, the most widely discussed alternative channels are the citizen dividend, the public channel, the channel for small and medium-sized enterprises (SMEs), and the NGO and IGO channels to directly fund these bodies and private-public partnerships, including so-called advance market commitments (AMCs). For an example of advance market commitment, see Barder et al. (2005), or Light (2005).

68. As each economic and policy intervention should have human labor as its final purpose, we can make the following equation: 52 weeks makes 2080 hours, 12 USD/h (gross salary) equals 24,960 USD annually. Assuming 350 million people are unemployed across the globe, 8.7 trillion USD are needed to provide them with jobs. Considering a Keynesian multiplier of two, 4–6 trillions are necessary to provide full global employment. This equates to the amount discussed above that is required to finance the SDGs. The parallel currency mechanism can therefore roughly meet unmet needs, creating purposeful jobs for our common future. The human being is the ultimate resource for wealth, creativity and labor (Simon 1983).

69. As a default scenario: even if only 70–80% of the projects targeted are accomplished and we have to write off the rest of the generated additional liquidity, two things will have happened. First, we will have achieved 70–80% that would not have been accomplished in the first place. For example, 70–80% of people below the poverty line will have been lifted out of poverty. Second, the sovereign central bank will have an enlarged balance sheet with an additional 20–30% of liabilities with unlimited maturity, which decreases the seigniorage for the sovereign state respectively.

70. One way to ensure this is synchronizing human behavior in large cohorts (like singing, dancing, running or walking together). Once such a synchronizing mechanism is in place, prosocial behavior is favored and free-rider effects reduced. The mechanisms we describe in this text support these empirical findings. Within the given atomistic, individualized, singular, competitive and deregulated free market, individual utility-maximizing behavior rather favors the opposite: free-rider effects, negative externalities and reduced prosocial behavior (see Spitzer 2018).

71. World Bank (2018b).

72. There is undoubtedly an overlap with Modern Money Theory (MMT): at its core, MMT states that the creation of money to solve real societal challenges is not dependent on tax revenue or achieving the same rate of saving and investment, but on the inflation rate and full employment in each economy. Banks are not intermediaries and saving is not the only source of public investment. This means that every nation with the sovereign right to generate a currency can print that currency to finance their budget without any corresponding liabilities. States do not have a tight budget belt, but there are political limitations to where they can invest their money. Any time when governments run a budget deficit, they create a central bank reserve at the same time. *So why not generate the liquidity necessary to finance our future?* Once full employment is achieved, taxation and issuing bonds can be adapted to the economy, removing excess money from circulation. From a private-investor perspective, jobs and public commons are considered to be costs that have to be minimized. In contrast, from a public perspective, public debts create private wealth. Once a deflationary scenario is iden-

tified, the sovereign state has a *free lunch* to finance these assets. In this sense, direct public investment in the intermediary creation of jobs is far more efficient than a general unspecific fiscal stimulus.

The difference between the TAO of Finance (ToF) and MMT is that we (a) advocate a dual currency from the first, (b) which can operate as a permanent automatic stabilizer for the overall economy, (c) steers the economy towards a certain target, (d) guarantees that funds will be directed towards these targets through distributive ledger technology, (e) operates through different monetary channels to the credit market and open market policy and (f) allows society to aim for greater sustainability through multiple second-round effects. To note: the dual-currency approach explained in greater detail in this text goes beyond job creation and targets the SDGs. For further literature on MMT, see Coy et al. (2019); Mitchell et al. (2019); Mosler (2010); Wray (2015).

73. *An important detail for investors:* an initial interest rate modestly higher than the domestic growth rate and higher than the interest rate of the given international currencies (USD, Euro) will attract international donors/corporates/institutional investors trapped in the "new normal" of "secular stagnation", encouraging them to swap their low- to negative-yield investments for higher-yield investments via green bonds. A *state guarantee* issued in this new green sovereign currency (we can call it a "green dollar") will create a *carry-trade effect:* a *debt to equity* swap will be converted into a so-called *equity to green equity swap*. This financial engineering avoids additional international debts and payments. To note: there is a *tradeoff* for the investor, who can achieve higher yields in the sustainability sector—with the exception of a digital ban list that prohibits the trading and buying of certain goods (e.g. child labor, land mines, alcohol, cigarettes and guns).

74. According to our calculation, a Global Sustainability Fund to manage the additional green parallel liquidity would require 200 staff (lawyers with experts in international trading and payment systems, investment bankers experienced in sustainability and development aid, IT and administration) and would take less than a year to get started.

75. For example, the concept of a Green QE (Anderson 2015), People's QE (Murphy and Hines 2010) or Helicopter Drops (Bernanke 2000), Overt Monetary Financing (OMF) (Turner 2013), or Sovereign Monetary Creation (SMC). As an overview, also see Van Lerven (2016). To our knowledge, despite their intellectual rigor, none of the proposals offer a dual-currency approach of the kind addressed in this text. All the proposals so far remain embedded within a monetary monoculture.

Chapter 6
New Symmetries: The Future Has a History or a Path with a Heart

We started this book by introducing the concept of TAO to illustrate a new way of thinking, perceiving and acting in this world, and have tried to apply this to the financial sector and in particular to the problem of financing global common goods as embodied by the UN SDGs. The incentive for this new thinking derives from the fact that we now are living in the Anthropocene. Humanity is in the driver's seat, determining both our own future and that of the planet. A paradigm shift is taking place. The philosopher Thomas Kuhn describes a paradigm shift as a situation in which irregularities and anomalies that cannot explained be within a given paradigm occur with increasing frequency. Responding to such a situation requires two major changes: a change in mindset and a change in the modus operandi. In this text, the old paradigm is the monetary monoculture, with its pervasively linear and sequential thinking. The new paradigm is a complementary monetary system that involves both linear and parallel thought processes. Operating with this new paradigm will allow us to manage anomalies and irregularities such as the widening of the income and wealth gap, increased ecological damage, and large-scale economic migration through different monetary pathways.

Nature teaches us that life tends to optimize efficiency and resilience within a window of opportunity and does not maximize its output. We have called this window an anti-fragile zone. The anti-fragile zone gives any living system the opportunity to maintain its integrity through learning from failure. The life sciences teach us that the human mind adapts to nature most successfully when we have access to two ways of thinking, perceiving and problem-solving. We have identified the scope, speed, scale and symmetry of the challenges ahead, estimated plausible figures to finance common goods, and exposed the multiple lock-in effects in our current economic system that prevent us from changing. We have gone through different traditional approaches, from economic growth first and redistributing money second to deregulating the system, to impact funding, to public contracting among others. This "six-pack" is required to navigate towards a more sustainable future within an

---

The original version of this chapter was revised. The correction to this chapter can be found at https://doi.org/10.1007/978-3-030-64826-8_7

anti-fragile zone, where resilience and efficiency represent the guardrails of our endeavor. If we follow this path, monetary regulators will become indispensable. As a last step, we need to explore the further challenges and consequences of such a TAO of Finance and its potential effects on the conventional economic system.

> When a system is highly unbalanced, small pockets of coherent thinking and acting can shift the entire system towards a new equilibrium.

6.1 The Impact and Challenges of a Parallel Monetary System

Several effects of implementing a parallel currency system require discussion: the impact on illicit financial transactions and the so-called informal sector; then, whether or not such a parallel currency system represents a Ponzi scheme; further, whether injecting parallel liquidity will lead to inflation or rather maintain price stability; and how a parallel currency system addresses the fundamental difference between a war and a peace economy. Each of these effects will be addressed in turn. The following list lists some major impacts and challenges we will need to face when we parallelize our monetary system.

Impact and challenges of a green, parallel, optional currency

1. Illicit transactions
2. Informal sector activities
3. Hazard of a Ponzi system
4. Impact on inflation
5. From a war to a peace economy

6.2 A Complex Basket: Illicit Financial Transactions and the Shadow Economy

Illegal, unlicensed and unregulated economic activities play a major role in the global economy.[1] Despite some overlap, this sector accounts for over one third of the conventional, regulated and taxed economy operating alongside it.[2] If we were suddenly to abolish this complex basket of activities, the formal sector would collapse immediately. The informal sector thus acts as an important stabilizer of the world economy. However, all these illegal and informal transactions increase inequality, reduce economic growth and social capital,[3] erode tax revenue,[4] prevent access to the credit market, and pull our entire global economy in the wrong direction.[5] What is more, this basket reinforces its own rules. For example, trading and working in a corrupt environment prevents the proper enforcement of legal systems, even on a small scale. If a police officer in a corrupt environment tries to fine someone for speeding, he may not enforce the fine because the person in question might be a member of the government or some other elite.

Illicit financial flows (IFF) have a different impact on the economy: IFF inflow generates income and jobs, but IFF outflow does not. Comparing the volumes of different illicit transaction flows to the formal sector from 2004 to 2014, the losses for the Least Developed Countries (LDC) due to IFF amounted to 7.8 trillion USD, with a growth rate double that of the conventional GDP. For example, in the Middle East, for every 1 USD of formal inflow from ODA, FDI, remittance payments and philanthropy, an equivalent outflow of 2.8 USD in IFF leaves the country. The reasons for this are multiple, and misinvoicing is the most significant cause. Generally speaking, the volume of IFF, redirection of ODA and expenses related to military conflicts outweighs the sum of ODA + FDI; FDI outflow, remittance, and external debt payments[6] together make it next to impossible to generate enough "green" and "sustainable" purchasing power in the region. Globally, tax losses due to the use of offshore tax havens and tax avoidance measure between 200 and 500 billion USD annually.[7] In particular, the relation to ODA reveals the dilemma: of the 0.7% of world GDP dedicated to supporting the global South,[8] three quarters are either indirect subsidies for prestige investments such as the military, are directed to middle-income countries (where the money is less needed) or support the domestic industry of the donor country. Only one quarter is thus considered to be "real" ODA. These figures show that not enough stable purchasing power remains in the countries that need it most and the world is being pulled in the wrong direction. Regulating the system has not worked for the last 75 years. Why should it work now? It will not. Instead, we need to come up with a mechanism that slowly but surely pulls trade and commerce out of this basket and towards a green and sustainable future, without disrupting the overall built-in economic capacity.

For decades, we have been trying to re-adjust, prosecute and harmonize regulatory efforts to formalize and legalize the illicit sector. However, these efforts have been like trying to put toothpaste back into the tube. Instead of focusing all diplomatic and political efforts on re-regulating and consolidating the given system, the proposed parallel currency mechanism using DLT can dry out illegal transactions, formalize how we conduct business and eradicate human trafficking. The fact that a parallel currency system has the ability to overcome the negative economic impact of the illegal and informal sector is a stand-alone argument in itself.

6.3   Informal-Sector Activities: From System D to System C

It is always symptomatic of a systemic deficit when the non-criminal informal sector grows even though the basic needs of citizens remain unmet. The informal sector consists of all non-formal sector activities in our economy, excluding drugs, weapons and human trafficking and excluding home-based services. This sector is sometimes also called System D. D stands for the French term "debroulliard", which means resourcefulness.[9] Resourcefulness is the capacity to achieve something purposefully and successfully in a complex and challenging situation. The main characteristics of System D are that it is self-organizing, is not formally regulated or monitored, has no liability and is not taxed. In this system, there are no claims to social security or health care, no part-time jobs or trade unions, no holidays and no differentiation between weekday and weekend work.

This informal sector largely operates in parallel to the official economy and accounts for up to 10 trillion USD annually on a global scale. In relative terms, it is the second largest economy in the world, employing approximately 1.8 billion people or up to 50% of the global labor force. Within the next five to eight years, as millions of young people reach working age, this ratio most likely will increase to two thirds of the global labor force. In this sense, System D represents the largest field experiment in a fully liberalized, atomized, singularized market system that the world has ever seen.

Economies with a large System D have been more resilient in the face of financial crises, as seen in the southern European states with their large informal sectors during the 2008 crisis, providing empirical confirmation that the presence of a parallel economy acts as a buffer in the case of a crisis. From a systems perspective, the informal sector serves an inclusive, anti-cyclical and reparative function in conventional economies that have one market and one monetary system to allocate goods and services. Any time this monopoly becomes unstable, there is a shift towards the second, parallel system that is not subject to the same conditions.

The economic power of property rights. Looking at the informal sector from the perspective of property rights, it probably represents one of the largest sleeping giants in the world economy. The Peruvian economist Hernando de Soto estimated the total value of undocumented and untitled property rights at over 13 trillion USD.10 This represents over 50 times more than any global aid or foreign direct investment (FDI) in less developed countries. In fact, only about one third of the world's population have access to jurisdiction on property rights and only up to 10% of Africa represents registered and formally documented land. This means that 90% remains terra nullius. This has tremendous negative consequences for regional wealth creation. Up to 3 billion people globally live on communal, unregistered land and over 1 billion people live in fear of being evicted from this land because of the lack of clarity on land ownership.11 Done the right way, land titling can substantially increase the productivity of agricultural activities. In fact, only clear, legally bounded property rights entitle humans to trade, subdivide, collateralize, sell and buy such claims, allowing the poor to participate in the world economy and generate wealth on their own.

One major reason why this registration of land is hard to achieve is local corruption and the abuse by national elites. In addition, the Western tradition of individualized property rights does not correspond fully to the more collective, family- or community-bound understanding of property rights that predominates in many Asian and African countries. The financial mechanism we describe in this text is for the many, not for the few, and it provides the tools to accomplish one of the largest, cheapest and fastest stimulus programs for the entire SDG program itself: investing in land registration and securing legally binding property rights, enabling people to live their own lives.

If we use the iceberg as a metaphor to understand the link between the formal and informal economies, we see that the 10% of the iceberg that is visible represents the official economy, expressed as wages, revenues and prices. The remaining 90% of the iceberg, invisible underwater, represents unpaid domestic work, the informal sector, child labor and common goods.[12] Traditionally, these two parts are looked at in a binary way, as excluding one another, the formal sector on one side and the informal sector on the other. However, the important link between the two is that the smaller formal sector in fact cannot exist without the large informal sector that acts as its base. The 90% can exist without the 10%, but not the other way round (Graph 6.1). More generally speaking, commons do not need revenue, but revenue and wages require commons. Instead of favoring a binary approach, we advocate a complementary approach. The pearl of wisdom here is that if we want to properly finance and regulate the 90%, we need much, much more financialization than today, but we need it to be designed in a different manner. The TAO of Finance is an approach that provides a complementary perspective and an enlarged, but different financial sector.

What would System D look like in the presence of a dual monetary system with a parallel currency? If we had a regulated, transparent, secure and fair parallel economy in place, System D would turn into a System C, where C stands for complementary optional monetary system. In System C, human activities would be regulated, supported, taxed, insured and so on. If this System C were to be backed up electronically, the expected two thirds of the future global labor force would become legal and integrated into the formal sector. In the long run, such a system represents huge cost savings for society because the tax base would increase, the crime rate and costs of social exclusion would decrease, and income lost due to lack of health care or disaster management would be lower. If System C were to have the additional selective incentive of job creation in the areas of SDGs, a growth impulse targeted towards a green growth scenario would be generated.

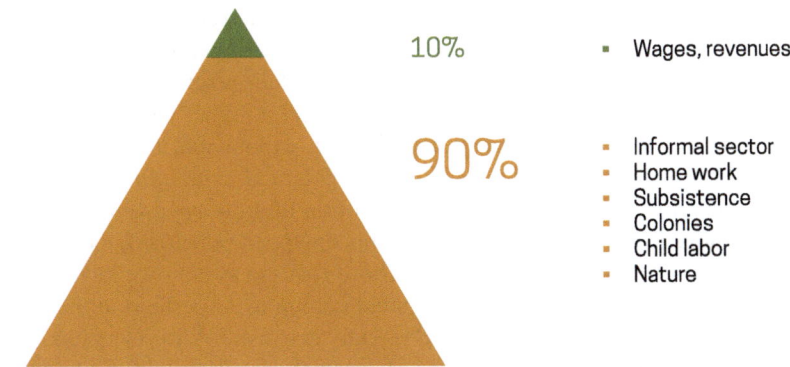

Graph 6.1 The asymmetric iceberg paradox

Implementing such a system is relatively inexpensive, fast, and does not disrupt the existing ongoing business activities worldwide. In fact, such a System C would stabilize and integrate a large portion of the world labor force into the global value chain. We would go so far as to say that we are now entering a phase in which we simply cannot afford to run our whole economy through the sole given traditional mono-system of taxation, regulation and distribution any longer. This will simply become too disruptive and too expensive in the long run.

6.4   Not a Ponzi Scheme—Liabilities and Collaterals

A Ponzi scheme is a type of fraud where "profits" are simply paid to recent investors by those who join the scheme after them. As long as new investors contribute to this scheme, the players can maintain the illusion of a sustainable and productive business. Well-known speculative economic bubbles represent a sort of Ponzi scheme, as the profit is the result of subsequent purchases of the asset where the price exceeds the intrinsic value—until the whole bubble bursts (tulips, housing, cryptocurrencies).

Is a parallel currency a form of Ponzi scheme? 95% of the money currently in circulation is backed up by the promise and the value of the given GDP. Because monetary assets are at least three to five times higher than real economic assets, the real collateral value of the existing conventional money system is only worth one third to one fifth of the entire value chain. This means that most of the money currently in circulation has no actual value attached to it, other than the worth we as a society agree upon.[13] We simply trust in this medium of exchange. The conventional collateral of central bank money consists of either liabilities of the commercial banking system or of so-called defaultable state bonds.[14] If the state were to go bankrupt, the central bank would need to write off their dues.[15]

In the new complementary system, by contrast, regional and global common goods would be one hundred percent backed by the collateral of this new financial mechanism. This is because money creation in the parallel system would be pre-distributive. Money would be created based on the requirements of the project at hand, where physical or tacit assets or defined commons would serve as tangible collateral. For example, if Austrian natural water and lake reservoirs were to be measured according to the market price, they would have a higher value than the country's GDP. Using this lens for the countries with exponential birth rates such as Nigeria or the Congo, we would see vast human potential, with millions of people in search of education, jobs, health care, and a trillion lifetime opportunities just waiting to be achieved. The capacity to unleash this untapped potential depends on having the proper system in place—and we believe that the system we have described would enable it. The high ROI of most global commons, described in the previous chapters, proves this. In other words: who owns that fish? Who owns biodiversity, and who owns the temperature of our climate or fresh air? We all do. And thus parallel currencies are not Ponzi schemes, but act as stabilizers of the monetary system.

6.5   Why Is This Mechanism Not Inflationary? The CPI (Consumer Price Index) Under a Parallel Monetary Regime

Generally speaking, while high consumer prices were a challenge in the 1970s and 80s, for the last two decades inflation has fallen globally. Despite some exceptions in some emerging markets—like Argentina and Turkey, where there was a transitory increase—the CPI has fallen, too. The main reasons for this deflationary trend are technology (IT) and the cross-border trading of goods, services and capital.

Any created money entering the real economy will eventually generate income or wages and increase consumption on some level. This is true whether one designs a helicopter, builds a house, plans a hospital or eats a hamburger. Under normal circumstances, increasing the money supply by for example 7% would increase the consumer price and prevent wealth creation because it would lead to inflation.[16] However, this parallel system, by the very nature of its sectoral and local steering mechanism, as well as the new pathways through which the created money flows, would prevent an increase in the CPI. It would even act to stabilize price levels.

How would it do so? First, the link between the CPI, which is composed of labor costs in the form of wages and capital as measured by interest and risk premium, and the volume of money created is weak in empirical terms. The money creation process requires a transmission belt or "pathway", as described in chapter 5, to effectively influence the price level. Most of the money created in the last decade has been channeled through the transmission belt of the so-called FIRE sector.[17] This means that the actual money created did not enter the real economy of goods and services, but rather was "parked" in the FIRE sector, increasing the API instead of the CPI.[18] We do not believe that collecting additional liquidity through additional taxation, regulating offshore havens, private pledges, ODA, blended finance or debt relief would be less inflationary than simply generating the amount of liquidity targeted at SDGs through a dual system. Collecting money through conventional channels simply activates unproductive liquidity to finance our future. The same is true of a parallel system. We simply will be creating the money rather than collecting und redistributing it to finance our future.

If we adopt a more systemic perspective, we can identify multiple different variables that have the potential to balance each other. While simply injecting money, a reduced tax base, subjective inflation expectations, a cost push (energy price) or a demand pull including a devaluation of the currency can increase the price level, wise monetary policy traditionally has been able to cope with these challenges. For example, an adjustable interest rate can avoid inflation due to money supply, a wider tax base likewise reduces the risk of inflation; and the higher the trust in a currency, the lower the inflation expectation; the smaller the dependency on foreign fossil-based energy, FDI and foreign currency credits, the lower the exposure to inflation. Several additional components further stabilize the overall price level, rather than causing inflation (Graph 6.2).

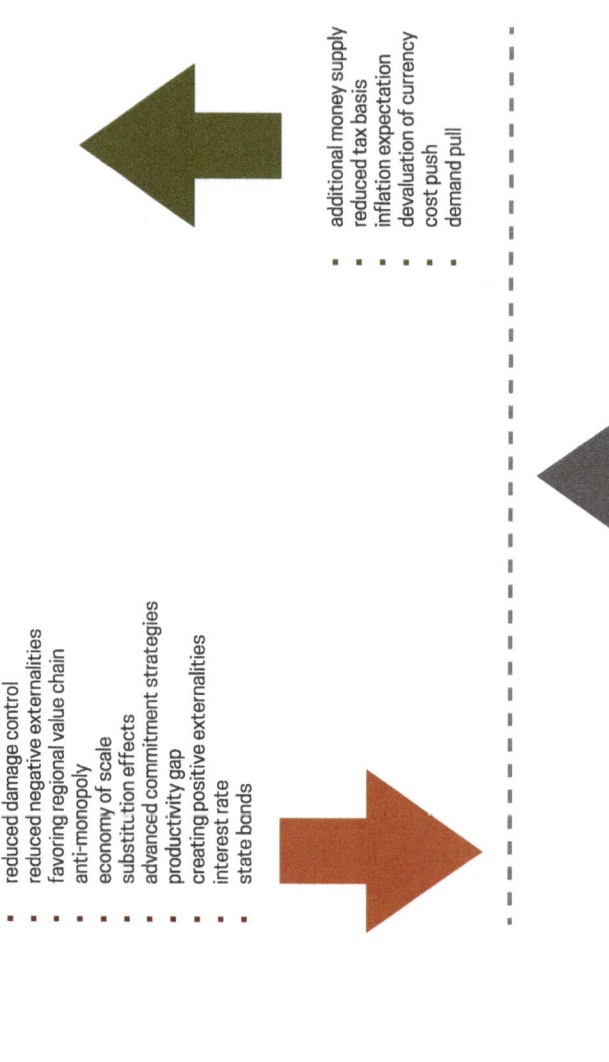

reduced damage control
reduced negative externalities
favoring regional value chain
anti-monopoly
economy of scale
substitution effects
advanced commitment strategies
productivity gap
creating positive externalities
interest rate
state bonds

additional money supply
reduced tax basis
inflation expectation
devaluation of currency
cost push
demand pull

Graph 6.2 The CPI revised—push and pull factors

Some examples verify this. Economic theory demonstrates that monopolies in general lead to higher price levels and lower-quality output. They are therefore less efficient. This is true of any monopoly, including a monetary monopoly. Establishing a dual-currency system will thus create regulated competition that lowers prices and increases quality, increasing the efficiency of the overall system.

Regional value chain: one third of the price of a cappuccino reflects capital costs[19]; the longer the value chain, the higher the risk fees and the potential costs for logistics and transportation because of increased uncertainty. By contrast, the more local or regional a value chain is, the less risky it becomes and the cheaper a good can be produced. If we all drank local coffee, the price would be cheaper.

Energy carrier: Over 90% of all goods and services are linked to fossil energy either directly and indirectly. The less dependent we become on fossil energy, the lower the costs we generate.

Box 6.1 The Standard Economic Model Revised in the Age of the Anthropocene

This time is different: A more rigorous argument with regard to the standard economic model. Under free market conditions, the standard economic model predicts that the global factor prices for goods, services and capital are converging, creating a higher welfare for the world as a whole (Pareto optimum). Meaning the wages between countries are converging first, whereas the differences between wages within each country may still remain high, but will eventually converge, too. This is especially true in the relatively peaceful times, with low and manageable negative spillovers, that we experienced in the Northern Hemisphere from 1945–2015. We can currently observe such income convergences between the EU and USA on one side and China and India on the other, and we can observe these wage differentials within each of these countries. Injecting additional liquidity, simply speaking printing money, in such a business as usual scenario will devaluate the future consumption/purchasing power of the capital owner and therefore will reduce welfare for all of us in the long run.

However, the situation today is somewhat different to a business as usual scenario in at least three aspects, which can sterilize and even overcompensate the devaluation of the consumption or purchasing power of capital owners in the future: (a) The preparedness of additional liquidity injected *today* reflects an investment in an age of increasing asymmetric external shocks (pandemics, forced migrations, natural disasters etc.), which is characteristic for the age of the Anthropocene. We now have to operate within planetary boundaries and under conditions of full interconnectedness. Such negative rebounds could be reversed intentionally through internalizing the negative externalities (total cost analysis), or they happen in an unintended and uncontrolled manner through asymmetric shocks. Either way, asymmetric shocks are increasing in frequency and magnitude. They hit a society without there being any chance to prepare for

(continued)

Box 6.1   (continued)

them, and are uneven and disruptive. If not addressed, they cause additional costs that can outweigh the devaluation of consumption of capital owners in the future. Investing in SDGs and global commons therefore become the largest preventive and anti-inflationary program the world has ever seen. (b) If the additional liquidity is invested *today* in projects (SDGs) that have a high welfare effect (Return on Investment) and promise a higher productivity in the future (like investing in pre-schooling, health care or mitigating the negative impact of global warming), the capital owner *today* can expect a higher return and revenue on his *future* capital investment. In this case, the additional liquidity injected *today* does not compete with the capital owner's consumption *today*, as he or she hoards the money anyway (liquidity trap). This affects debtors and creditors in a positive way. Creditors have a higher chance to get their money back, as productivity will increase in the *future* and debtors have a higher chance to solve their problems and increase welfare overall. (c) The additional liquidity invested in projects (SDGs) reduces costs *today and tomorrow*, costs which already are part of the overall factor costs and wages of *today*, stabilizing the overall price level. This mainly refers to investment in damage control, preventing loss of biodiversity and the costs of global warming. The total factor productivity (TFP) still leaves us with the unknown dark matter or "residuum" of two thirds of any growth path. As we do not know what the components of the entire TFP are, we had better initiate qualified growth and benefit from it now and in the future. Therefore, this time is different, as asymmetric shocks, negative rebounds, planetary boundaries and interconnectedness taken together are changing the playing field and the incentives to do business. Injecting money in the abovementioned manner is not a gift of God, but a contribution of the monetary domain to provide a more enriching environment in order to enable the financing of our common future. This is why an additional green QE *today* can create additional welfare *today and in the future*. Finally, we can maximize this approach by parallelizing the money system towards a dual system, creating unlimited positive second-round effects for the consumers and multiple positive carry-trade effects for investors (Pareto superior).

In fact, the design of the digital currency we favor has the additional advantage that it can be fully adjusted with an interest rate to balance our supply and demand through issuing state bonds. Multiple components prevent inflationary pressure on the price system, some of which are listed in the following Table 6.1.

Beyond Paucity—Plenty and Proportion: Certain economies currently operate with two currencies in parallel, for example a national currency and the US dollar. Traditionally, the main reason for the use of two currency systems has been hyperinflation. In these contexts, however, both currencies are designed and operate in the same way: issued by central banks, they are interest-bearing, offer liquidity for the commercial banking system, and have scarcity as a criterion. Because they both

Table 6.1 Why a parallel currency system is essentially not inflationary

Anti-inflationary factors	Explanation
Reducing negative externalities	A parallel system is designed to reduce social and ecological externalities, which in consequence reduces the costs and potential future costs partly priced in
Economy of scale	The sheer scale required will make it possible to benefit from an additional economy of scale (e.g. toilet bowls for 3 billion people, 250,000 kindergartens), which can reduce the costs of investment and living
Closing the productivity gap	Most businesses do not operate at an optimum, but have a productivity gap to fill before price levels rise
Regional value chain	The smart contract of the blockchain technology favors regional and sectoral business and trading, which reduces the transport costs of the global value chain and the associated fee for additional capital and risks
The anti-fragile factor	The costs of a monetary monopoly (instability, banking and sovereign debt crises, currency crises) are reduced due to a dual system, which operates anti-cyclically and renders the overall system more stable to shocks and therefore less expensive
Substitution	The steering effect of the parallel system has a substitution effect on the conventional value chain, replacing commodities, goods and services, making them less beneficial and attractive and in consequence cheaper
Productivity	As fraud, illicit transactions and corruption decrease, transaction costs are reduced and efficiency increases over time
Advanced commitment strategy (ACS)	Describes a private-public partnership tool that guarantees a fixed sales volume to corporations in advance, which stabilizes the market price and allows for better future planning. A pre-emptive, pre-loading strategy of the real sector can ensure an adjusted demand and supply
Anti-monopoly strategy	A monetary monopoly produces higher prices and lower quality. Dual systems instead lead to a competitive situation, which will lower prices and increase quality, hence increasing efficiency and allocation
State bonds and interest rate	Both can withdraw excess money from the circulation to avoid inflationary pressure

have the same design and are used alongside one another, they remain within the realm of monetary monoculture.[20]

While scarcity and plenty, referring to competition and inflation respectively, describe options within the conventional system, a third option exists. The mechanism described here differs by virtue of its focus on proportionality, meaning that it is appropriate and accurate in proportion. So rather than competing for liquidity or having too much of it, we generate adequate liquidity according to the problems identified. For example, if a region identifies the need to build ten universities, 100 hospitals, 1000 schools, 10,000 kindergartens and 100,000 public toilets, the money to finance these projects would not be withdrawn at the end of the value chain and then redistributed, as is the conventional approach. Instead, the corresponding amount of necessary liquidity would be created through this new monetary mechanism. We would then benefit from the multiple positive feedback loops, the significant ROI of common goods, the boost in efficiency generated by use of DLT, the additional employment in this sector, as well as the additional tax revenue in the

Graph 6.3 The triangle of money supply: where paucity generates competition, plenty causes inflation and proportion initiates wealth

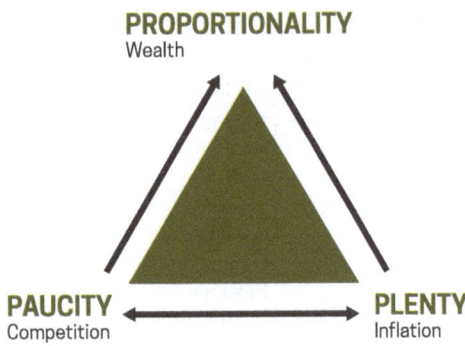

PROPORTIONALITY
Wealth

PAUCITY ←————————→ **PLENTY**
Competition   Inflation

public sector. Central banks traditionally have had a pretty sophisticated understanding of proportion, especially concerning price stability. If the mandate of monetary regulators were to be extended to include SDG-related projects under this new type of parallel currency, this sense of proportion would need to be readjusted accordingly (Graph 6.3).

In this sense, the two currency systems are intertwined; they lead to multiple positive feedback loops and operate in a complementary manner to one another. This difference is key and represents a major shift in mindset from a linear to a complementary one. It is this complementary mindset that will provide the best answers as we search for a new balance in finance and the future. The TAO of Finance is about being complementary, not linear. With this change in mindset, something astonishing happens: insurmountable problems suddenly turn into goals and challenges that humans are capable of achieving and overcoming.

6.6   The Difference Between a War and a Peace Economy

There is a saying that we must win the peace so as not to lose the war.21 If this is the case, civil non-military projects should be treated on a similar scale to military ones. As long as we spend trillions of USD globally on military and military-like security measures, a similar amount of money should be invested in socio-ecological, humanitarian and civil projects to achieve balance. Such investments operate as preventive measures and in parallel to military activities. However, even though the expenses for civil, non-military conflict management measure only a small fraction of the military ones,[22] the benefits of this rationale are still far from being achieved. If we had 5 million kindergartens, 500,000 schools, 50,000 hospitals and 5000 more universities on this planet, we not only would generate more education and greater health and wealth, we also would achieve greater peace. Taking this argument one step further, we could claim that the question of war and peace in the twenty-first century will be answered not on the frontline between different religious groups, between capitalism and communism, between open societies versus autocracies, but at the frontier of whether or not we are able to identify an institutional setting or system that engages 7.5 billion people on the planet regardless of their cultural beliefs, their geographic and socio-economic position, and the legal system they belong to. The social mechanism of a dual-currency system, as described here in this text, forms one component of such a peace strategy.

Entire societies change when war is present, including their economy. A war economy has three major characteristics. First, free market allocation is abandoned, giving rise to a planned economy where input-output benchmarking determines the value chain. Second, war economies need to ensure their resource supply, which in the past primarily consisted of fossil energy, but now can consist of any relevant resource (rare minerals, fossil energy, information), particularly when the resource is monopolized. Thirdly, a war economy exerts inflationary pressure, especially in import-dependent countries where there is a so-called demand-pressure inflation on domestic goods and services. When there is war, politicians tend to print money to boost their war industry, forcing the CPI to increase. Because there is no proportional increase in the goods of daily life, more people compete for these goods, leading to inflation. So war economies, or war-prepared economies, entail over-regulated or oligopolistic markets, ongoing inflationary pressure on the CPI, and high military expenses to ensure access to required resources.

Conversely, a peace-prepared economy entails a free, liberal market economy, decentralized or non-monopolized resources (renewables) and lower military expenses.[23] This is because the expectation of needing to enter or prepare for a belligerent scenario is lower, and therefore need not be factored in to such a large extent. Energy sources form one aspect of a peace economy. As fossil fuels such as oil, gas and coal are geographically limited, there will always be conflict over access to these resources and the currency they are billed in. In this sense, the fossil energy sector is monopolized. The energy sources in a peace economy are unlimited because they consist of renewables (water, wind and sun) that by nature are more decentralized and regionalized. Competition thus occurs less on the level of resources and more on the level of the technology required to access them. This difference has a fundamental impact on war or peace.[24]

Violence is extremely costly for our world community, locking us in to unsustainable behaviors and pulling our global community in the wrong direction. Military expenses represent the single largest part of the cost of violence, standing at 5.5 trillion USD, while internal security measures, including police, prison and judicial measures, rank second at 3.8 trillion USD. Homicide and interpersonal violence represents the third largest component, with significant indirect economic impacts. Taken together, the direct and indirect costs of war, defense and security measures globally amount to over 14.7 trillion USD, or almost 2000 USD per person.[25] This money could have been spent on something else more peaceful. Armed conflicts negatively affect the overall economy. Economic growth can be up to three times higher under peaceful conditions, as we see when comparing the most peaceful countries with the countries with the greatest burden of violence and war. For example, the costs of forced migration and refugees in 2017 amounted to over 350 billion USD globally. This leads to the crowding out of positive peace investments such as education, health, WASH or renewable energy initiatives. The global loss in GDP due to loss of opportunity under war and violence is up to 6%, representing a "prosperity gap" of trillions of USD that would be available under conditions of peaceful development.

However, positive peace is also associated with costs, which include violence containment and preventive measures such as ODA and UN peacekeeping efforts. Expenditure to contain violence is economically efficient if it can prevent violence cost-effectively. There is a fine line between costs to contain and prevent violence versus costs to manage violence and its ensuing consequences. Prevention costs account for two thirds of the overall costs arising from violence. Whereas Syria spends up to two thirds of its GDP on costs related to violence, Switzerland only spends 1% of its GDP on these costs, including direct and indirect costs and prevention. Empirically, a high level of human capital, low levels of corruption, a well-functioning government and an equitable distribution of resources are the four most important factors preventing violence between human beings. Any mechanism providing evidence that it can reduce the curse of violence is worth considering. The TAO of Finance is part of such a mechanism.

Box 6.2   The Common Denominator of the Belt and Road Initiative and the Petrodollar Regime

What Is the Common Denominator of the Belt and Road Initiative and the Petrodollar Regime?

The Silk Road or Belt and Road Initiative is about trading and infrastructure, and petrodollars are about energy.[26] Both appear to be completely different national projects by China and the USA respectively, but they follow a similar monetary rule: they both generate additional liquidity in a national currency by printing, lending and conditioning this money. This additional money is invested in an extra-domestic market separate from domestic policy, such as the Silk Road or the Middle East, and generates additional purchasing power in these regions.[27] This enables additional jobs and wealth to be created in these regions and benefits the national sovereign interests of the Chinese and the Americans respectively. The Silk Road project will cost between 4–8 trillion USD and involve over 150 countries by 2050, nominated in Renminbi or US dollars.[28] The additional liquidity comes in the form of conditioned grants or loans to other countries, which is almost entirely state controlled. The Petrodollar Regime led by the US costs up to 81 billion USD a year; its aim is to protect the oil supply and ensure over 160 billion USD in net oil imports annually. It provides countries in the Middle East with liquidity for infrastructure and security measures in order to stabilize the region[29] and reinvest that money in the Western hemisphere.[30] However, neither the liquidity for the Petrodollar Regime nor the liquidity for the Silk Road project

(continued)

> **Box 6.2   (continued)**
>
> comes from taxpayers. It is the result of a money and credit creation process in which national banks generate liquidity through loans that either buy fossil energy (petrodollars) or infrastructural projects, such as airports (Silk Road Yuan) or respective currency reserves. This is true of 95% of all money in circulation globally. It is based not on conventional savings that allow investments, but on a credit creation process, mainly through the commercial banking sector. In our case, the money is created partly by public- and state-owned banks and partly by the commercial banking system. Silk Road Yuan and petrodollars represent a kind of "extra Yuan" and "extra dollars" creating additional wealth. If we take this policy one step further, we can adapt it to our topic of financing the future: we have a parallel market that is currently underfunded (SDGs). Additional earmarked liquidity in these markets would create additional wealth and multiple positive effects for all of us. If we look at this process from a different angle, we can see that there are 173 million unemployed people and over 1 billion underemployed people globally, or that we will be lacking 69 million teachers by 2030. So instead of financing fossil energy or investing in a trade route, here we are investing in the future of our planet, as mapped out by the SDGs.

Parallelization of the financial sector is key. This perspective provides a balance between the extraction and redistribution of wealth on the one hand, and the protection and regeneration of wealth on the other, both steering our society towards a more balanced future.

6.7   A History of Tomorrow: Ending Poverty and Hunger

This is the story of Amina Mwele, whose name in the Bantu language means "hope" and "the capacity to change the world". Amina is a 41-year-old single mother with five children who lives in the suburban slum of a big metropolis in a sub-Saharan country. Her husband died during a civil war two years ago, after which Amina and her 5 children fell into poverty. She and her children are undernourished and suffer from chronic diarrhea. She sometimes receives food and other assistance from international NGOs, but this redistributive charity mechanism remains an unreliable source of income.

Economists calculate that a global growth rate of 15% would be required to eradicate poverty at a 2.50 USD/day level, assuming the current redistribution mechanism remains the same. Despite decreasing global poverty and hunger rates over the last three decades, poverty and hunger in sub-Saharan Africa remains the same as in 1990, affecting 400 million people.[31]

About 18 months ago, the Mwele family's situation dramatically changed. Amina received a mobile phone and a solar panel for the roof of her hut, funded and distributed by the UN. She was registered as part of a Financing the Future program via biometric iris identification. As part of this program, she is identified by an iris scanner when she enters the market every morning, and when this happens 2.50 USD are immediately uploaded to her cellphone. She now can afford to purchase the food her family needs. Rather than the conventional currency used in her country, the funds come in the form of "green" coins and bills, which allow her to purchase specific goods such as vegetables, schoolbooks, and clothes, but not other goods such as alcohol, cigarettes, drugs or guns. This green currency is only available in electronic form.

The shop owners who accept this currency can use it to pay part of their employees' wages as well as taxes in proportion to the amount of green currency they accept in the shop. Regional tax offices use this additional revenue exclusively to finance common goods. This means that they can invest in kindergartens, schools and health care infrastructure and/or pay governmental employees, hire more nurses and teachers using this electronic currency. Those who receive their salary partly in green currency can use it in turn to go shopping at the market. This technically is a closed loop, where the additional wealth created through this electronic green format steers the region towards a more sustainable future.

Meanwhile, Amina's solar panel produces and stores enough power during the day to run an electronic stove and provide light in the evenings. In fact, because the sun shines 10 hours every day, Amina now sells the surplus power she is generating to a regional smart grid. This additional green currency revenue allows her to pay schooling fees for her children and boost the local economy.[32]

National and international corporations now increasingly invest in the country, because use of the electronic format in conjunction with a smart social contract has led to a decrease in fraud, corruption and illicit transactions. Because the governmental system has increased its effectiveness, a first democratic election is in sight. Through a special agreement between the public and the private sector, a so-called Advance Commitment Strategy (ACS), businesses now have a safe environment in which to sell their products and services. Price levels have stabilized further due to economies of scale. Reduced indirect costs for outdoor and indoor pollution, cleaner water, better education and a reduced crime rate are other positive effects. The overall economy has become more robust due to reduced corruption, stable aggregate domestic demand, reduced income spread, and reduced costs for environmental burdening.

This all started 18 months ago. The officials called it a nation-wide inclusive growth strategy. It consists of pre-market measures targeting investment in education and access to health care, followed by market strategies addressing wages, gender issues, jobless growth, AI and precarity. Additionally, this strategy includes post-market programs such as taxes and income supplements. This initiative was only made possible because the country's Central Bank, Ministry of Finance, local authorities and Chamber of Commerce, guided by a UN proposal, collaborated and worked together to make it happen. They created new liquidity in the form of a parallel electronic-based currency using distributive ledger technology and earmarked to fund common goods. Because this parallel system runs through different monetary channels, it does not replace the existing national currency. Instead, it complements it using an intelligent design, and thus provides the liquidity and purchasing power necessary for traditionally underfunded social and ecological programs.

On a systemic level, a change in the mindset of the local authorities has occurred. They now feel that politics come first. Politics first means that when sufficient liquidity is available to fund social projects, politics regains control and self-efficacy. Because this monetary channel describes a closed loop, the circular nature of this and other systems is now clear.

On an individual level, Amina's consciousness has also changed. While at the beginning she often asked herself why two systems were necessary and focused on the burdensomeness of it, she soon realized that—akin to putting all her eggs in one basket—having only one system involves instability and risk. She uses two baskets to carry things because they balance each other out—and now she sees that this is also true of the monetary system and many other things. Additionally, because she can channel the extra power from her solar panels back into the public grid, she also realizes that her life is interconnected with that of everyone else, and that her actions can have a positive or negative impact on others in her community.

Amina Mwele still has a long way to go with her 5 kids, but she is no longer in absolute poverty. Her children are no longer hungry and the family has better future perspectives. The children attend school regularly now and Amina even has enough liquidity to think of attending school herself. In fact, she is proud that they are now on the right path.

6.8   Conclusion: Financing the Future Is Not Like Financing the Past

"Art" in the Greek language is τέχνη or téchnē. The term describes the human activity of mastering or achieving something new, or the ability to do so, based on knowledge and wisdom, constant discipline and creativity, talent and exercise, perception, thinking and aesthetic endeavor.[33] Art is a cultural achievement, not a natural course of events. If an individual produces art or téchnē, or if a society operates in a téchnē mode, that individual or that society becomes flexible, failure-friendly and open to ongoing revision. The ultimate will to achieve something becomes the predominant modus operandi. It is a kind of piecemeal engineering, where we create an enabling environment that allows us to make mistakes and backtrack if necessary in a constructive and purposeful way. In this sense, the art of transformation is not an inductive procedure only, where we start bottom-up with a single experience and end up with a final grand theory, but a procedure where we honor what we have already achieved and improve whatever is necessary in order to create something new. It is this balance between the past and the future that characterizes art and transformation at the same time.

This art of change is not sporadic or random, nor does it happen by chance. Such a change is never a mere reflex or a response to an external stimulus, nor is it a mechanical or algorithmic procedure. When we decide to embark upon a path of change, we do not repeat history, but start to create something new. We start to change our behavior, our perception and our gravity of consciousness. And every real change starts with a good idea, where we apply a general regulative concept to a special single event or case, which never remains fully determined by this idea. This idea represents a kind of rule-based vision or narrative. It is not traumatic, disruptive or chaotic. It tells us a story about options, changes and possibilities, not curses or problems. However, this story in itself is not strong enough to ensure the change required. Whereas a minority of the world population can adopt such an inner picture or narrative and live accordingly, the rest of us require an institutional intermediary: technology (such as digitization), the conformity of group experiences, laws, incentives, rules and sanctions. The appropriate monetary system can take on this intermediary role, and we as humans have the power to build such a new world. This is what the TAO of Finance is all about.

There are two fundamental forms of activity in times of uncertainty. The first deals with the given system. We spend most of our time and energy regulating and repairing, stabilizing, defending, criticizing or fighting the given system. We may be successful, but there also is a chance that we will fail. The second form of activity is different. It deals with something new, something that has never happened before in history. We become involved in creating this novelty that seeks to improve what we have at present. It is like a crack in the wall that gives us a glimpse of future possibilities we have not yet grasped. Whereas the first form of activity is best described by terms such as consolidation, harmonization and regulation, the second is best described using terms such as comprehensiveness, complexity and transformation. And this finally leads us to a more integral view of our concerns. A perspective in which the design of the monetary system plays a crucial role, and in which nothing is left behind: neither the planet, nor people, nor profit, nor purpose, nor pleasure.

Throughout this book we have tried to provide multiple arguments showing that we are psychologically trapped in the idea that there can only be one monetary system, providing a single, specific form of liquidity for all purposes, and assume that allocative distribution through a monetary monoculture is most efficient and effective. The costs of "business as usual", "wait and see" and "doing nothing" strategies, meaning the costs of not implementing a mechanism such as that described here or a very similar one, are increasing exponentially as time goes on and will outweigh any other foreseeable scenario by far. In this situation, thinking the unthinkable and thinking and acting outside of the box represents the most advantageous strategy. Any successful risk analysis requires us to overcome the executive myopia and linear thinking predominant in corporate and public leadership, beyond the "least drama" and the "lowest common denominator" scenarios. Precisely this is what the TAO of Finance does.

A silent storm: A day will come when we wake up and simply start paying our bills and taxes, conducting our business, trading and shopping through two optional channels: a conventional and a parallel complementary one. And on this day we will slowly but surely begin to change the world. This mechanism, once properly in place, will silently affect almost everything: it will start to reconcile urban and rural life, globalization and regionalization, migration and settlement, labor and unemployment, income and wealth disparities. It will slowly but surely reduce the shadow economy, illicit transactions and human trafficking. This mechanism will contribute to improving the state of the planet (biodiversity, water, global warming) and it will stabilize our civil societies, democracies and free market systems. Such a dual monetary system has the potential to reduce asymmetric wars and ethnic tensions. It has the power to act anti-cyclically, to create jobs and to reduce social and ecological externalities. In short, it will set in motion a silent storm, dealing with the most pressing challenges the world is facing. This mechanism does not solve all problems, but all problems will be affected by this mechanism. It has the potential to be the single most effective and fastest mechanism we know of, beyond what is being discussed in the media, science and politics, to address the fundamental problems of the twenty-first century. The future we are discussing here is not a mere prolongation of the present that is a little bit greener or fairer, but a future that is different to what we are experiencing now.

Each generation makes its own choices: We are both the first and the last genera-tion in human history capable of ending poverty and hunger, stopping resource depletion, halting the loss of biodiversity and reducing global warming. The tools, technology, scientific knowledge, and evidence are all at our disposal to do so. We are also the first and last generation capable of destroying all of this for decades, if not centuries. One particular challenge is that it is easier to formulate ecological, social and human rights standards than it is to demonstrate how to finance them. This is why the current financing of global commons is happening neither at the pace nor at the magnitude able to end conflict, poverty, hunger, inequality and other socio-economic hardships. Everything could be different if we wanted it to be. Despite all the different definitions of sustainability, there is one aspect they all have in common. Sustainability is about future capabilities, not curses, about possibilities and changes, not restrictions. And this other world is not only possible but profit-able. Knowledge, know-how, opportunity, acting with foresight, and prevention are more appropriate criteria to describe a narrative of the future. Judged by these crite-ria, our generation is the worst in human history. Imagine the opportunities modern medicine, education, technology, civil society could offer if everyone on the planet had access to them. Just imagine. What we are lacking is not more analysis, but answers; not more information and knowledge, but the right practice and adaptabil-ity that enables and ensures that 7.5 billion humans do the right thing 24/7. With this mechanism at hand, we turn from time-tellers into clock-makers (Jim Collins) and can start to build another world. We don't know whether we will adapt, but we surely know that we now know how to adapt.

Inefficient academic rituals: From a Taoist perspective, the well-known ritual of debate between neoliberal and Keynesian arguments (between austerity and stimu-lus) is relatively unproductive, intellectually exhausting and economically ineffi-cient. Identifying the smallest common denominator will lead to a suboptimal solution. It resembles a "feel-good" exercise or a symbolic gesture with next to no practical use that does not change the game. Instead of repeating the debate over and over, it would be more fruitful to identify the unquestioned commonalities that both parties rely on, of which the monetary monopoly and linear, sequential thinking are undoubtedly two.

In a nutshell: The mechanism described here is not a distributive mechanism in which the (inter)national trading and payment system is taxed or subsidized and the revenue subsequently transferred to social and ecological projects. We identified this procedure as linear thinking, sensitive to expansive growth and inefficient as a stand-alone solution. The mechanism described here is pre-distributive. It offers an optional, parallel and complementary channel or algorithm for solving future prob-lems and simultaneously stabilizing the existing system before market mechanisms or state interventions have taken place. We have identified this as parallel and cycli-cal thinking, where coping with complexity and uncertainty is dominant. It is a mechanism that acknowledges and appreciates the advantages of the two main eco-nomic schools: market-dominated versus state-dominated or, in other words, auster-ity versus stimulus. It acknowledges free market allocation, risk assessment, competitiveness and regulatory efforts, such as accountability or transparency in a neoliberal sense. It also acknowledges the interventional aspect of any state-dominated economy in a Keynesian sense by providing a selective tool to discriminate towards commons, encouraging bounded investments through an electronic-based, earmarked additional liquidity process that is fast and targeted. Through this parallel and optional process, which can be scaled up and down according to regional requirements, a global sum of roughly 5 trillion USD annually can be injected into our common future. The scale of the solutions needs to match the scale of the problems ahead. The solution is not to extract around 300–500 billion USD a year from the given market system to provide a living for 80% of the population on this planet; a sum around ten times larger is required. The procedure we suggest would reduce the negative impact of shadow banking and the black-market economy. It would formalize and integrate one of the largest economies of the planet, System D, enhancing the stability and resilience of the international trading and payment system. It would reverse pricing away from disaster management, the entropic sector and negative externalities towards a greener, fairer and more sustainable future. Through a proxy mechanism, it would steer labor away from the unregulated and risky shadow and black markets towards more stable and forward-looking jobs. And finally, as a complementary system operating in parallel and anti-cyclically to the given one, it would make monetary policy and regulation more sound, transparent and resilient. In a sense, the multiple crises and challenges ahead are not a fait accompli, but rather symptoms and signs. If we want to identify the root causes, we have to look at the financial system, as we have done in this book. We can turn things around if we start the required paradigm shift with ourselves first. The TAO of Finance has the potential to create more wealth for all and is confirmed by different, unrelated disciplines; it is the way to balance, harmonize and integrate unreconciled opposites and ambiguities; and it is the everyday practice where micro and macro, where each single individual and each collective society is mirrored in the same light.

   To conclude: the real tragedy of the commons is not the free-rider problem, moral hazard or their non-excludability, but the fact that we are managing them through a trading and payment system that does not discriminate towards and acknowledge the very nature of commons. It is not the fault of the commons that they are chronically under-financed within the current monetary system; this is the result of an inadequate alignment of the economic system with the nature of commons. This means that we have to design a system that fits the nature of commons and not the other way around to optimize their benefits for humanity. Commons do not fit into our conceptual framework; therefore we neglect and overuse them, damaging our community. The dual mechanism creating a parallel new economy proposed in this book will allow us to implement much of what is already known: more cyclical and cascade economies, more shared economies and local value chains, including behavioral and lifestyle changes. This is all implemented much more easily than in the conventional approach, for along this green parallel path, there are no lock-in effects with trillions of dollars of subsidies, and here a new technology is implemented to ensure the shift required, namely distributive ledger technology with a smart social contract: fast, efficient, resilient, cheap, fair und targeted. It is this dual mechanism that can provide the match between unmet needs and under-utilized resources, it can offer a complement to the given currency system and therefore can balance out society towards greater wholeness and integrity.

The proposal of a green, optional, parallel mechanism, as part of a "six-pack" as described in the present text, is able to respond to our current dilemma, allowing the full potential inherent in commons to unfold for the benefit of humanity. An optional parallel currency system, providing different forms of liquidity, running through different monetary channels, operating via different new technologies, but all still interlinked with the traditional financial sector creating cyclical feedback loops, provides a complementary monetary system. The common well-known candidates for achieving a more sustainable future, such as social corporate responsibility (SCR), green investments, consumer behaviors, taxation and new technology also will play a relevant and significant role. Monetary regulators are not the only game in town, but they probably are the single most important players that need to be involved to achieve greater sustainability.

Societal change always starts with the minds and hearts of individuals and small groups who are prepared to think, feel and act differently. In contrast to former times, this change has accelerated and gained momentum in recent decades and years. Whereas most changes in history took place unconsciously, we are now in a situation to refer to scientific information and data and apply that knowledge and wisdom in order to take charge of this process intentionally and consciously, steering our society towards higher values, increased wealth and greater sustainability. Consciously we are able to convert the best ideas into power and promote "leadership in thoughts that lead to actions" (WAAS). Whereas any scientific knowledge remains divided, the reality will always remain an unseparated, integral whole. The financial mechanism described in this text acknowledges the empirical findings of different disciplines, applying new technologies and approving new monetary governance. It should be part of a future social equation that maximizes individual freedom, embedded in a social construct that catalyzes the change required. The TAO of Finance should be a component of such a future whole.[34]

The world we live in is profoundly shaped and limited by the dominant monetary system. This system is not neutral with regard to decision-making: it is basically a hidden device conditioning our future. In its current monopolistic version, it operates antagonistically towards any form of sustainability. However, it is not a given! What is required is firstly a shift in consciousness that balances out system 1 and system 2 and/or the left and the right cerebral hemispheres, and secondly systemic thinking instead of silo thinking, as described in this text. The mechanism proposed here has the potential to change the world. This necessary paradigm shift requires an academic and public debate that not happened thus far. However, it is hoped that the present text will set this debate in motion. This is the way we are going to finance our future.

> More patrifocal societies favor practices around having, taking, extracting and doing something. Matrifocal societies by contrast favor caring, maintaining, regenerating and being some one. We require both, and this is exactly what the tao of finance provides.

The advantages of implementing this or a similar mechanism are manifold. It can be implemented in a fast and targeted manner and is relatively cheap. It would have an anti-cyclical, anti-inflationary and resilient impact on our trading and payment system. It builds upon findings in systems theory, thus avoiding the tedious discussion between the different schools of economics. Further, it draws upon findings in the life sciences (neurobiology and clinical and social psychology) in order to provide a match for real human behavior (beyond the homo economicus). Finally, it addresses the magnitude, volume and significance of the global challenges ahead. In short: The TAO of Finance is based on a new kind of thinking on how to design a monetary ecosystem to make the world a better place. Acknowledging the multiple lock-ins and constraints we are facing, which have been explained in this text, we are not proposing an ideal-typical solution for the financial system (which inevitably will remain a theoretical proposition). We are rather advocating for the best single practical next step in the development of our monetary system that will maximize our ability to finance our common future over the next 15 years.

Graph 6.4 The TAO of Finance—the future wealth of nations or a mechanism that can change the world

If readers have had the patience to follow our argument up to this point, they will realize that the TAO of Finance does not neglect the achievements of the conventional financial system. In fact, we need both the old and the new systems, a kind of a mixed blended finance, according to the purpose that each of these systems needs to achieve. If we want to fly to Mars or invent a new AI algorithm, we may still need conventional tools in order to accumulate sufficient private venture capital and entrepreneurial spirit. But if we decide that we want to clean up the air, protect biodiversity, overcome hunger and achieve universal access to health care, we will need to shift to a complementary and alternative pathway. We can learn to honor and appreciate the given system and still criticize, extend, transcend and integrate it into a larger whole. This is the TAO of Finance.

Over the last centuries, humanity has tried to balance scarcity and abundance, difference and equality, wisdom and folly. The TAO of Finance provides one component of an answer to this endeavor (Graph 6.4).

Notes

1. According to Transparency International (2018), the average corruption index globally is 43 out of 100. This means that corruption is endemic and systemic, especially in the public sector. We require a mechanism that does not enhance, but reduces corruption. The mechanism described in this text has this effect.
2. A widely used taxonomy to differentiate between different forms of illicit financial transactions is: (1) criminal market (human trafficking, drugs); (2) theft-type market (resources of any kind); (3) corruption; (4) illicit tax transactions (misinvoicing).
3. There is an empirical link between public spending and wealth over time. The higher the share of tax in government expenditure (in contrast to FDI, ODA), the higher and stronger the developments over time and the higher the commitment to public health care and education.
4. We are witnessing a corporate tax race to the bottom: globally, the corporate tax rate is around 20–30%. However, whereas OECD countries have retained their general tax base, developing countries have lost it. From an administrative perspective, it would require 650,000 tax officers for Africa to meet OECD standards (OECD 2019).
5. There is an ongoing net outflow from the South to the North. Historically this outflow was due to external debt payments, but now this has become superimposed with increasing illicit financial flows (IFF).
6. External debt payment in proportion to governmental revenue is a more comprehensive figure than a country's absolute debt burden. After 2014, external debt payments increased by 60% globally, and total debt stands one third higher than before the 2008 crisis (Jubilee Debt Campaign 2018).
7. See Cobham and Janský (2018). Further data support the magnitude of the problem: there is increasing private wealth (10% of global GDP) in tax havens, causing tax losses of 200 billion a year; terror financing amounts to 2.5 trillion USD annually; and 10% of total global trading takes place through illicit financial transactions. This results in a global tax gap of 5 trillion USD annually. 20% of this tax gap is due to transnational corporations and 80% due to individual businesses and SMEs, mainly trading informally and in cash. Illegal transactions amount to 20–25% of GDP globally, corruption costs the world community 2.6 trillion USD annually, and money laundering amounts to 1.6 trillion USD annually. Global revenue losses due to tax base erosion and profit shifting (BEPS) have risen to 100–240 billion USD annually. These figures demonstrate the magnitude of the amounts lost to the public sector. It appears next to impossible to regulate such volumes within the given monetary system. A parallel system would correct these illicit financial transactions indirectly. See Alstadsæter et al. (2018); OECD (2014, 2015); Pietschman and Walker (2011).

8. See Grubb et al. (2019); United Nations Conference of Environment and Development (UNCED) (1992).
9. Neuwirth (2011).
10. Measured in inflation-adjusted USD as of today globally. See Soto (2000).
11. *The Economist*, Sept 12–18, 2020, pp. 31–33.
12. The unacknowledged taxpayer contribution to public R&D assisting private revenues is well documented by economist M. Mazzucato in *The Entrepreneurial State* (2013). The same is true of taxpayer investment in urban infrastructure including airports, sanitation, universities, hospitals, kindergartens, administration, security and defense; all substantially lower any state debt-to-GDP ratio, allowing private business to flourish.
13. To note: the connection between the size of a bank's balance sheet and the quantity of collateral is empirically weak. A large proportion of bank lending is uncollateralized (40% of all US commercial and industrial lending is uncollateralized) (FRED 2017).
14. For experts to note: central banks can create additional liquidity through a so-called open market policy, where they buy up state bonds, which in turn provides additional liquidity for the state. In that case, the relative risk of that state's debt portfolio is reduced and the risk premium in form of the interest rate is lower because it is a non-defaultable loan. In consequence, this will provide such a state with an additional fiscal space for additional investments or taxation (see Kumhof and Tanner 2005).
15. We need to differentiate between a real market failure and the lack of a market. Markets created through a regulatory and political process are highly formalized, with transparent liabilities and property entitlements. If there is no such market to ensure state bonds in developing countries, we cannot characterize this as a market failure. Real market failures occur when there is a monopoly with a lack of competition, where negative externalities are socialized instead of internalized, where there is a significant information asymmetry between the supplier and the client with regard to the quality of the good or service, or where public goods are overused or neglected. In all these cases, it is important that politics and civil society control, regulate and determine the activities of the market.
16. Hyperinflation has been relatively rare. Since 1945 about 56 cases, mainly due to war or revolution, have been documented (Hanke and Krus 2013). From a financial perspective, weak public finance (one single source of tax revenue, public corruption and unclassified welfare) was an important accelerator of hyperinflation. The mechanism described here prevents all that: it increases the sources of tax revenue, reduces public fraud and corruption, and reduces disaster management costs.
17. Banks are considered to be intermediaries offering a specific service for the public and private sectors and adding value to their productivity. However, the financial sector is highly concentrated. For example, in the UK 5 private banks cover 85% of all deposits (Gond et al. 2014). The larger the bank, the larger the loan, the larger the bonus, and the smaller the liability and accountability of the process. In order to increase accountability, the banking sector ought to be more decentralized, the way it is in Germany with over 1500 Raiffeisenbanken, Volksbanken and Sparkassen. There has never been any need to bail out a decentralized and regionalized banking sector. The banking system is not primarily an intermediary; banks do not deposit money on the one hand and lend money on the other. The commercial banks create money. Just to clarify the situation: a deposit in a bank is a loan to the bank. 97% of the overall aggregate money supply is created through the commercial banking system. In this more realistic view, a credit is a fictitious loan. As long as banks invest in productive goods and services, it is a form of a productive lending. However, over two thirds of lending go to the FIRE sector. Here, the credit finances an asset ownership transaction, but does not produce goods or services. The purchasing power increases the API, which in consequence increases inequality. Only consumer credits might increase the CPI. Therefore the decisive question is: where does the money go? We might better say: money is what money does. This is one of the reasons why the regulatory efforts of BASEL III (and its follow-ups) will not work, because this regulation basically considers banks as intermediaries only. What is required here is a form of regulation that steers the banking sector and bans unproductive FIRE investment. The bank still can

speculate but should do this with funds or money from the capital market. To note: the City of London legally is not part of the UK and not part of the EU, the citizens have no right to vote and the Queen has no legal right to intervene. Strictly speaking, the City of London is an unregulated offshore place and the UK officially has no financial sector. Which simply means: "The emperor has no clothes." See literally Werner (2014).

18. Hyperinflation is often created by external speculative exchange rates with other currencies through carry traders and other private currency investors. This in consequence causes the domestic central banks to print even more money. The mechanism of a parallel currency regime, targeted to a green future with a soft peg to the conventional currency, backed up by defined collateral commons and operating through digital distributive ledger technology, is much less prone to such external speculation.

19. Bruce-Lockhart and Terazono (2019).

20. According to the CIA world factbook (2014), the following countries and regions use more than one currency to stabilize their economy: China, which uses Yuan for international trade and renminbi for domestic activities, starting officially in 2004; Bhutan, which uses ngultrum (BTN) and the Indian rupee (INR); Cyprus, which in the Greek Cypriot area uses the Cypriot pound (CYP) and in the Turkish Cypriot area uses the Turkish lira (TRL); Guatemala, which uses the quetzal (GTQ) and the US dollar (USD); Guernsey, which uses the British pound (GBP) and the Guernsey pound; Jersey, which uses the British pound (GBP) and the Jersey pound; Lesotho, which uses loti (LSL) and the South African rand (ZAR); the Isle of Man, which uses the British pound (GBP) and the Manx pound; Namibia, which uses the Namibian dollar (NAD) and the South African rand (ZAR); Panama, which uses the balboa (PAB) and the US dollar (USD); Tuvalu, which uses the Australian dollar (AUD) and the Tuvaluan dollar. The argument here is simply that about 10% of nation states use two currencies more or less effectively to stabilize their economy. This is a hybrid form of financing. We could do this better when introducing the official dual currency system described in this text. It would allow us to benefit from the advantages and avoid the disadvantages of the current dual systems.

21. Research on the nature of peace economies as opposed to war economies goes back to Keynes (1920) and Boulding (1978).

22. We are constantly falling into the same trap. From a game theory and psychological perspective, we are confronted with an *asymmetric power dynamic*, where the weaker partner remains necessary in finding a more stable solution overall (like the USA and Russia during the Cold War period). Such a scenario requires a different rationale to a *symmetric power game*, where competitive strategies might dominate. By contrast, in an asymmetric power game cooperation is more successful than competition. Here, inclusive measures outweigh exclusionary ones and positive reinforcement is preferable to scenarios of punishment.

23. In *Reinventing Fire*, Amory Lovins demonstrates that a shift from fossil energy to renewables can make our economy more efficient, peaceful, robust, resilient and productive (Lovins 2013). Extremely high hidden costs underlie the fossil industry, including oil price volatility, costs for the gasoline itself, military expenses to ensure the import of oil, blackouts and further indirect costs associated with additional health care costs etc. Lovins calculated that for the US economy alone, the benefits of this shift would be up to 5 trillion USD in savings and a boost of GDP of up to 158% over the next decades.

24. The prevention and containment of violence on the one hand and the costs associated with violence on the other are two partly opposed aspects. Both reinforce each other in a potentially negative feedback loop in which humans are always the losers. Within a peace economy, the multiplier, accelerator or enhancer operates in the opposite direction any time peaceful, cooperative behavior is exerted, reinforcing itself. The new financial instruments mentioned in this text can operate like a second peace dividend. Humanity received its first peace dividend in the 1990s at the end of the Cold War—an opportunity we squandered. Now we have a second chance. Incorporating the mechanism described here, generating a "peace-prone economy", we will have lower military expenses, less centralized energy sources and a less planned economy. The SDGs form our road map and the financial mechanisms described are the tools required to achieve them. See Institute for Economics and Peace (2018).

25. This includes security services and prevention costs (military, internal security, UN peace-keeping, ODA, security agencies and private agencies), armed conflicts, and the direct and indirect cost of interpersonal violence and its associated negative multipliers. See Stockholm International Peace Research Institute (SIPRI 2019).

26. The Silk Road is an ancient trade route connecting the East and the West (Elisseeff 2000). More recently, literature has spoken of a "new silk road" linking China to the rest of Asia and Africa (Broadman 2006; Simpfendorfer 2009). Petrodollars refer to the USD earned by a country "through exportation of petroleum" (Vassiliou 2009).

27. We are talking about over 5000 loans and grants (including FDI debts, trade credits and directs loans) in over 150 countries. Over 50% of these lendings are hidden, which substantially distorts price allocation and debt analyses. See Horn et al. (2019);

28. Desjardins (2018), Luft (2016), Khanna (2019).

29. Securing America's Future Energy (2018), ITC (2019).

30. The petrodollar system is built on a huge recycling strategy, where the international billing of any crude oil is contracted through OPEC in USD, which then in consequence is reinvested in OECD countries (military devices, corporate shares, buildings or state bonds). This closed loop guarantees that the USD will remain the leading global currency. This privileged leading position of the United States is expressed mainly in two figures: two thirds of all central bank currency reserves are in USD, and about 90% of trade contracted on the global exchange market involves USD (IMF 2019; Bank for International Settlements 2019). This has led to a high seigniorage for the American people. The US government would act in its own national interest to proactively fade out the petrodollar system and gradually install the green dollar mechanism instead. While the petrodollar system has close links to the industrial military complex, the green dollar system would boost the market for renewable energy in tandem with huge civil infrastructural and job programs worldwide.

31. From 1.9 billion to less than 740 million, with around 1 billion of those lifted out of poverty from East Asia and the Pacific. See Roser and Ortiz-Ospina (2017). In 1820 90% of the population was poor, while 200 years later 10% are poor in relative terms (Bourguignon and Morrisson 2002; UN 2018; World Bank 2018a). In absolute terms the amount of poverty has not changed significantly. If you are poor, you do not care whether 10% or 90% are not poor, as you yourself remain poor. When we subtract China from the equation, the absolute number of people who are poor has stayed roughly the same!

32. Monetary economics differ according to the aimed-for goals. For example, overcoming poverty and hunger often simply requires enough liquidity as a medium of exchange to link the goods and services in the disparate region with one another. For example, see the POI from Kenya by Will Ruddick and his team, who showed that in an underserved suburban slum, there is also a lack of national currency. A community-based currency (soft-pegged to the Kenyan shilling), operating as medium of exchange among the citizens, blockchain associated, with a negative interest rate and using cellphones without internet, can overcome these constraints (see for example Ruddick and Mariani 2013). More information on the work of Ruddick and his organization is available on the website www.grassrootseconomics.org

33. Parry (2003).

34. Catalyzing strategies for socially transformative leadership (WAAS, forthcoming 2020).

Correction to: Financing Our Future

Correction to:

S. Brunnhuber, *Financing Our Future*,
https://doi.org/10.1007/978-3-030-64826-8_7

This book was inadvertently published without updating the following corrections:

Abbreviations:
p. = page
Corrections:
p. vii: Keep the epigraph before 'Dedication' in p.v
p. ix, xi, xiii, xv, xvii, xix: remove epigraphs
p. xxiii: 'The TAO of Finance Team' – Change to heading level-1.
p. xli: Replace 'Introduction' with 'What This Book Is All About: Finance—Future—Balance and the Rest'.
p. xxv: Correct 'The Academy' title.
p. xxv: Move 'Impressum' to left lower corner in same page
p. 33, 52, 68, 76, 84, 88, 123, 164, 177, and 185: Set pull quotes in Box without heading.

The updated versions of the chapters can be found at
https://doi.org/10.1007/978-3-030-64826-8
https://doi.org/10.1007/978-3-030-64826-8_2
https://doi.org/10.1007/978-3-030-64826-8_3
https://doi.org/10.1007/978-3-030-64826-8_4
https://doi.org/10.1007/978-3-030-64826-8_5
https://doi.org/10.1007/978-3-030-64826-8_6

p. 125: Correct the second black arrow in Graph 5.2.

p. 139: Remove the lettering in Graph 5.6.

p. 144: Correct big and small green arrows in Graph 5.8-b.

p. 115, note 16: Remove hyphen after 'sustain' in the link - https://sustain-

p. 158, note 40: Remove hyphen after 'new' in the link - http://new-

p. 161, note 66: Remove hyphen after 'three' in the link - https://three-

About the Author

Stefan Brunnhuber is a trained car mechanic, studied Medicine and Socioeconomics in tandem, PhD in Medicine, PhD in Socioeconomics, student of Sir R. Dahrendorf, over 12 international guest professorships (Medicine, Finance, Sustainability), two board-certified medical specializations, multiple sub-specializations, over 10 years as vice-chairman of the European Institute of Medicine, currently Medical Director and Chief Medical Officer in Germany (Saxony), Senator (elected in 2015) of the European Academy of Science and Arts, Full International Member of the Club of Rome, political and corporate consulting, founding member of Alma Mater Europeae, Board of Trustees of the World Academy of Art and Science, Endowed Professor and Chair for Psychology & Sustainability, Member of the Lancet-Commission (2021) special expertise and experience in the impact of life science on sustainability issues, especially Psychology of the Anthropocene, new financing engineerings, Psychology of Interfaith Dialogue, over 300 publications and talks, several international lecture series, several book awards, co-author of the Report of the Club of Rome EU Chapter Money and Sustainability (2014), co-author of a textbook that has been a bestseller in Germany for the last 25 years, The Art of Transformation (2018), The Open Society—A Plea for Freedom and Order (2019).

S. Brunnhuber, *Financing Our Future*,
https://doi.org/10.1007/978-3-030-64826-8

References

AAAA. (2015, July 27). *Addis Ababa action agenda of the third international conference on financing for development* [Resolution adopted by the General Assembly]. Retrieved from www.un.org/ga/search/view_doc.asp?symbol=A/RES/69/313&Lang=E.

Adami, C., & Hintze, A. (2018). Thermodynamics of evolutionary games. *Physical Review E, 97*(6). Retrieved from https://arxiv.org/abs/1706.03058.

ADB. (2019). *What is co-financing?*. Retrieved from https://www.adb.org/site/cofinancing/what-is-cofinancing.

Adrian, T., & Jones, B. (2018). Shadow banking and market-based finance. *IMF Departmental Paper, 18*(14). Retrieved from https://www.imf.org/en/Publications/Departmental-Papers-Policy-Papers/Issues/2018/08/01/Shadow-Banking-and-Market-Based-Finance-45663.

Aigner, J. (2019, August 30). *The unstoppable surge in negative yields reaches $17 trillion.* Bloomberg. Retrieved from https://www.bloomberg.com/graphics/negative-yield-bonds/.

Ali, R., Barrdear, J., Clews, R., & Southgate, J. (2014). *Innovations in payment technologies and the emergence of digital currencies* [Bank of England quarterly bulletin, Q3]. London: Bank of England.

Alstadsæter, A., Johannesen, N., & Zucman, G. (2018). Who owns the wealth in tax havens? Macro evidence and implications for global inequality. *Journal of Public Economics, 162*, 89–100.

Anderson, V. (2015). *Green money: Reclaiming quantitative easing.* The Greens/EFA. Retrieved from https://mollymep.org.uk/wp-content/uploads/Green-Money_ReclaimingQE_V.Anderson_June-2015.pdf.

Anshel, A., & Kipper, D. A. (1988). The influence of group singing on trust and cooperation. *Journal of Music Therapy, 25*(3), 145–155.

Arabella Advisors. (2016). *Measuring the growth of the global fossil fuel divestment and clean energy investment movement.* Retrieved from https://www.arabellaadvisors.com/wp-content/uploads/2016/12/Global_Divestment_Report_2016.pdf.

Aspinall, N. G., Jones, S. R., McNeill, E. H., Werner, R. A., & Zalk, T. (2018). Sustainability and the financial system review of literature 2015. *British Actuarial Journal, 23*, 1–21.

Atkinson, A. B. (2005). *New sources of development finance.* Oxford: UNU-WIDER Studies in Development Economics.

Atkinson, A. B., Micklewright, J., & Micklewright, M. (1992). *Economic transformation in eastern Europe and the distribution of income.* Cambridge: Cambridge University Press.

Baldwin, R. (2016). *The great convergence: Information technology and the new globalisation.* Cambridge, MA: Harvard University Press.

© The Author(s), under exclusive license to Springer Nature
Switzerland AG 2021
S. Brunnhuber, *Financing Our Future*,
https://doi.org/10.1007/978-3-030-64826-8

Baldwin, R. (2019). *The globotics upheaval: Globalization, robotics, and the future of work.* Oxford: Oxford University Press.

Banerjee, A., & Duflo, E. (2012). *Poor economics: Barefoot hedge-fund managers, DIY doctors and the surprising truth about life on less than $1 a day.* London: Penguin Books.

Banerjee, A. V., & Duflo, E. (2019). *Good economics for hard times: Better answers to our biggest problems.* London: Penguin.

Bank for International Settlements. (2019). *Triennial central bank survey: Foreign exchange turnover in April 2019.* Retrieved from https://www.bis.org/statistics/rpfx19_fx.pdf.

Bank of England. (2016, August). *How much quantitative easing have we done in the UK?* London. Retrieved from https://www.bankofengland.co.uk/monetary-policy/quantitative-easing.

Barder, O., Levine, R., & Kremer, M. (2005). *Making markets for vaccines: Ideas to action* [Report]. Washington, DC: Center for Global Development.

Bardi, U. (2017). *The Seneca effect: Why growth is slow but collapse is rapid.* Cham: Springer.

Barrdear, J., & Kumhof, M. (2016). *The macroeconomics of central bank issued digital currencies* [Working paper number 605]. London: Bank of England.

Barrett, R. (2019). *2019 global consciousness report.* London: Barrett Academy for the Advancement of Human Values. Retrieved from https://assets.website-files.com/5da90782 1e9c2c7ab086dd1d/5dc1f1c66656f70d615cc7eb_2019%20Global%20Consciousness%20 report%20(1).pdf.

Basevi, G., Fratianni, M., Giersch, H., Korteweg, P., O'mahony, D., Parkin, M., …, Thygesen, N. (1975, November 1). The All Saints' Day manifesto for European monetary union. *Economist.*

Basevi, G., Claassen, E. M., Salin, P., & Thygesen, N. (1976). *Towards economic equilibrium and monetary unification in Europe.* Brussels: Commission of the EC.

Bastin, J. F., Finegold, Y., Garcia, C., Mollicone, D., Rezende, M., Routh, D., …, Crowther, T. W. (2019). The global tree restoration potential. *Science, 365*(6448), 76–79.

Bateson, G. (1972). *Steps to an ecology of mind.* New York: Ballantine Books.

Batini, N. (2019). Transforming agri-food sectors to mitigate climate change: The role of green finance. *Vierteljahrshefte zur Wirtschaftsforschung/Quarterly Journal of Economic Research, 88*(3), 7–42.

Batterbury, S. P., & Ndi, F. (2018). Land grabbing in Africa. In J. A. Binns, K. Lynch, & E. Nel (Eds.), *The Routledge handbook of African development* (pp. 573–582). London: Routledge.

Beckert, J. (2016). *Imagined futures.* Cambridge, MA: Harvard University Press.

Beinhocker, E. D. (2006). *The origin of wealth: Evolution, complexity, and the radical remaking of economics.* Boston, MA: Harvard Business School Press.

Bellah, R. N., Madsen, R., Sullivan, W. M., Swidler, A., & Tipton, S. M. (1985). *Habits of the heart: Individualism and commitment in American life.* Berkeley, CA: University of California Press.

Beneš, J., & Kumhof, M. (2012). The Chicago plan revisited.

Bermejo Carbonell, J., & Werner, R. A. (2018). Does foreign direct investment generate economic growth? A new empirical approach applied to Spain. *Economic Geography, 94*(4), 425–456.

Bernanke, B. S. (2000). Japanese monetary policy: A case of self-induced paralysis? *Japan's Financial Crisis and Its Parallels to US Experience Special Report, 13,* 149–166.

Berner, E. K., & Berner, R. A. (2012). *Global environment: Water, air, and geochemical cycles.* Princeton, NJ: Princeton University Press.

Berry, C., & Guinan, J. (2019). *People get ready! Preparing for a Corbyn government.* New York: OR Books.

Binswanger, H. C. (2006). *Die Wachstumsspirale.* Marburg: Metropolis.

Binswanger, H. C. (2009). Wege aus der Wachstumsspirale. In F. Hinterberger, H. Hutterer, I. Omann, & E. Freytag (Eds.), *Welches Wachstum ist nachhaltig? Ein Argumentarium.* Vienna: Mandelbaum.

Bivens, J. (2017). *The potential macroeconomic benefits from increasing infrastructure investment.* Washington, DC: Economic Policy Institute. Retrieved from https://www.epi.org/files/ pdf/130111.pdf.

BlackRock Investment Institute [BII]. (2019). *Dealing with the next downturn.* Retrieved from https://www.blackrock.com/corporate/literature/whitepaper/bii-macro-perspectives-august-2019.pdf.

Bloomberg. (2019, April 2). *One of Africa's most fertile lands is struggling to feed its own people.* Retrieved from https://www.bloomberg.com/features/2019-sudan-nile-land-farming/.

Board of Governors of the Federal Reserve System. (2019). *3-month treasury bill: Secondary market rate* [TB3MS]. Retrieved December 31, 2019, from FRED, Economic Data, https://fred.stlouisfed.org/series/TB3MS.

Bohr, N. (1966). *Atomphysik und menschliche Erkenntnis II. Aufsätze und Vorträge aus den Jahren 1958–1962.* Braunschweig: Vieweg.

Boulding, K. E. (1978). *Stable peace.* Austin, TX: University of Texas Press.

Bourguignon, F., & Morrisson, C. (2002). Inequality among world citizens: 1820–1992. *American Economic Review, 92*(4), 727–744.

Bozesan, M. (2020). *Integral investing. From profit to prosperity.* Heidelberg: Springer.

Braxton, J. M., & Hargens, L. L. (1996). Variation among academic disciplines: Analytical frameworks and research. In J. C. Smart (Ed.), *Higher education: Handbook of theory and research* (Vol. 11, pp. 1–46). New York: Agathon Press.

Breakthrough—National Centre for Climate Restoration Melbourne, Australia.

Breitenfellner, A., Pointner, W., & Schuberth, H. (2019). The potential contribution of central banks to green finance. *Vierteljahrshefte zur Wirtschaftsforschung/Quarterly Journal of Economic Research, 88*(2), 55–71.

Broadman, H. G. (2006). *Africa's silk road: China and India's new economic frontier.* Washington, DC: World Bank.

Brown, G. (2004). The challenges of 2005. *New Economy, 11*(3), 127–131.

Bruce-Lockhart, C., & Terazono, E. (2019, June 4). *From bean to cup: What goes into the cost of your coffee?.* London: Financial Times. Retrieved from https://www.ft.com/content/44bd6a8e-83a5-11e9-9935-ad75bb96c849o.

Brunnhuber, S. (2015). How to finance our sustainable development goals (SDGs): Socioecological quantitative easing (QE) as a parallel currency to make the world a better place. *Cadmus, 2*(5), 112–118.

Brunnhuber, S. (2016). *Die Kunst der Transformation.* Munich: Herder.

Brunnhuber, S. (2018). *The art of transformation: How we learn to change the world.* Dresden: Tredition, CCOMP.

Brunnhuber, S. (2019). *Die Offene Gesellschaft: Ein Plädoyer für Freiheit und Ordnung im 21. Jahrhundert.* Munich: Oekom.

Buchanan, J. M. (1979). *Cost and choice: An inquiry in economic theory.* Chicago, IL: University of Chicago Press.

Buchanan, J. M. (2008). Opportunity cost. In Palgrave Macmillan (Ed.), *The new Palgrave dictionary of economics.* London: Palgrave Macmillan.

Bunge, M. (2003). *Emergence and convergence: Qualitative novelty and the unity of knowledge.* Toronto: University of Toronto Press.

Bureau of Labor Statistics. (2019). CPI inflation calculator. Retrieved from https://www.bls.gov/data/inflation_calculator.htm.

Buteică, A. C., & Huidumac-Petrescu, C. E. (2018). Sovereign wealth funds: Green capital flows for a climate solution. *Hyperion International Journal of Econophysics & New Economy, 11*(1), 175–189.

Byers, W. (2014). *Deep thinking: What mathematics can teach us about the mind.* Singapore: World Scientific Publishing.

Cambridge University Press. (2009). *Cambridge academic content dictionary.* Cambridge: Cambridge University Press.

Cane, J., O'Connor, D., & Michie, S. (2012). Validation of the theoretical domains framework for use in behaviour change and implementation research. *Implementation Science, 7*(1), 37.

Capra, F. (2010). *The Tao of physics: An exploration of the parallels between modern physics and eastern mysticism*. Boston, MA: Shambhala.

Carbon Market Watch. (2017). *Pricing carbon to achieve the Paris goals* [Policy briefing]. Retrieved from https://carbonmarketwatch.org/wp/wp-content/uploads/2017/09/CMW-PRICING-CARBON-TO-ACHIEVE-THE-PARIS-GOALS_Web_spread_FINAL.pdf.

Carney, M. (2015). *Breaking the tragedy of the horizon: Climate change and financial stability*. London: Bank of England.

Carney, M. (2016, September 22). *Resolving the climate paradox* [Arthur Burns Memorial Lecture]. Berlin.

Chen, D. B., van der Beek, J., & Cloud, J. (2017). Climate mitigation policy as a system solution: addressing the risk cost of carbon. *Journal of Sustainable Finance & Investment, 7(3)*, 233–274.

Chen, D. B. (2018). Central banks and blockchains: The case for managing climate risk with a positive carbon price. In *Transforming climate finance and green investment with blockchains* (pp. 201–216). New York: Academic Press.

Chen, D. B., Zappala, G., & Van der Beek, J. (2018). *Central bank policy for managing climate-related risk: Carbon quantitative easing* [Draft]. Retrieved from https://www.academia.edu/38092343/Carbon_Quantitative_Easing_Scalable_Climate_Finance_for_Managing_Systemic_Risk.

CIA. (2004). *The world factbook*. Retrieved from https://www.cia.gov/library/publications/download/download-2004/index.html.

Citigroup. (2015). *Energy Darwinism II. Citi GPS: Global perspectives & solutions*. London: Citigroup.

Claringbould, D., Koch, M., & Owen, P. (2019). Sustainable finance: The European union's approach to increasing sustainable investments and growth–opportunities and challenges. *Vierteljahrshefte zur Wirtschaftsforschung, 88(2)*, 11–27.

Club of Rome (2019). *Climate emergency plan: A collaborative call for climate action*. Retrieved from https://www.clubofrome.org/wp-content/uploads/2018/12/COR_Climate-Emergency-Plan-.pdf.

Cobham, A., & Janský, P. (2018). Global distribution of revenue loss from corporate tax avoidance: Re-estimation and country results. *Journal of International Development, 30(2)*, 206–232.

Cœuré, B. (2018, November). Monetary policy and climate change. In *Speech at "scaling up green finance: The role of central banks" conference hosted by Deutsche Bundesbank*. Berlin (Vol. 8).

Community Currencies in Action [CCIA]. (2015). *People powered money: Designing, developing & delivering community currencies*. London: New Economics Foundation. Retrieved from https://monneta.org/wp-content/uploads/2017/01/CCIA-book-People-Powered-Money.pdf.

Copenhagen Consensus. (2019a). *Post-2015 consensus*. Retrieved from https://www.copenhagenconsensus.com/post-2015-consensus.

Copenhagen Consensus. (2019b) *The economist*. Retrieved from https://www.copenhagenconsensus.com/post-2015-consensus/economist.

Coy, P., Dmitrieva, K., & Boesler, M. (2019, March 21). *Warren Buffett hates it. AOC is for it. A beginner's guide to modern monetary theory*. Bloomberg Businessweek. Retrieved from https://www.bloomberg.com/news/features/2019-03-21/modern-monetary-theory-beginner-s-guide.

Credit Suisse Research Institute. (2018). *Global wealth databook 2018*. Zurich: Credit Suisse.

Creel, H. G. (1982). *What is Taoism? And other studies in Chinese cultural history*. Chicago, IL: University of Chicago Press.

Cross, L., Wilson, A. D., & Golonka, S. (2016). How moving together brings us together: When coordinated rhythmic movement affects cooperation. *Frontiers in Psychology, 7*, 1983.

Crowder, D. W., & Reganold, J. P. (2015). Financial competitiveness of organic agriculture on a global scale. *Proceedings of the National Academy of Sciences, 112(24)*, 7611–7616.

Crutzen, J. (2002). Geology of mankind. *Nature, 415*, 23.

Crutzen, P. J., & Stoermer, E. F. (2000). The Anthropocene. *Global Change Newsletter, 41*, 17–18. Dag Hammarsskjörld Foundation. Retrieved September 6, 2019, from https://www.daghammarskjold.se/wp-content/uploads/2019/08/financial-instr-report-2019-interactive-1.pdf.

Crutzen, P. J., Davis, M., Mastrandrea, M. D., Schneider, S. H., & Sloterdijk, P. (2011). *Das Raumschiff Erde hat keinen Notausgang*. Berlin: Suhrkamp.

Dadush, U., Demertzis, M., & Wolff, G. B. (2017). *Europe's role in North Africa: Development, investment and migration* [No. 2017/10]. Bruegel: Bruegel Policy Contribution.

Dag Hammarskjöld Foundation. (2019). Financing the UN development system time for hard choices. Retrieved September, 2019, from https://www.daghammarskjold.se/wp-content/uploads/2019/08/financial-instr-report-2019-interactive-1.pdf.

Dalio, R. (2018). *A template for understanding big debt crisis*. Westport: Bridgewater, Greenleaf Book Group.

Damgaard, J., Elkjaer, T., & Joahannesen, N. (2019). The rise of phantom investments. *Finance & Development, 56*(3), 11–13. Retrieved from https://www.imf.org/external/pubs/ft/fandd/2019/09/the-rise-of-phantom-FDI-in-tax-havens-damgaard.htm.

Damodaran, A. (2019, January 5). *Annual returns on stock, T. bonds and T. bills: 1928—Current*. Federal Reserve Database. Retrieved from http://pages.stern.nyu.edu/~adamodar/New_Home_Page/datafile/histretSP.html.

Darwin, C. (1859). *On the origin of species by means of natural selection: Or the preservation of favoured races in the struggle for life* (1st ed.). London: John Murray. ISBN 1-4353-9386-4.

Davies, G. (2010). *History of money*. Cardiff, Wales: University of Wales Press.

De Fries, R. S., Edenhofer, O., Halliday, A. N., Heal, G. M., Lenton, T., Puma, M., …, Stainforth, D. (2019). *The missing economic risks in assessments of climate change impacts*. London: Grantham Research Institute on Climate Change and the Environment. Retrieved from http://www.lse.ac.uk/GranthamInstitute/wp-content/uploads/2019/09/The-missing-economic-risks-in-assessments-of-climate-change-impacts-2.pdf.

De Giacomo, P., & Fiorini, R. A. (2017). *Creativity mind*. Seattle, WA: Amazon Digital Services LLC.

De Grauwe, P. (2019). Green money without inflation. *Vierteljahrshefte zur Wirtschaftsforschung/ Quarterly Journal of Economic Research, 88*(2), 51–54.

De Haldevang, M. (2017, November 28). *Why we can't trust basic economic figures*. Quartz. Retrieved from https://qz.com/1133984/the-global-offshore-system-means-we-cant-trust-foreign-direct-investment-figures-and-other-basic-data/.

De Soto, H. (2000). *The mystery of capital: Why capitalism triumphs in the West and fails everywhere else*. London: Civitas Books.

Desjardins, J. (2017, October 26). *All of the world's money and markets in one visualization*. Money Project. Retrieved from http://money.visualcapitalist.com/worlds-money-markets-one-visualization-2017/.

Desjardins, J. (2018, March 18). *Mapped: China's most ambitious megaproject. The new silk road*. Business Insider. Retrieved from https://www.businessinsider.com/chinas-most-ambitious-megaproject-the-new-silk-road-mapped-2018-3?r=US&IR=T.

Dewey, J. (1910). *How we think*. Carbondale, IL: Southern Illinois University Press.

Dill, A. (2019). World social capital monitor (n.d.). Retrieved, 2019, from https://sustainabledevelopment.un.org/content/documents/commitments/6686_11706_commitment_World Social Capital Monitor 2019.pdf.

Dill, A. (2020). Trust your place (n.d.). Retrieved, 2020, from https://trustyourplace.com/.

Dixon, F. (2003, December). Total corporate responsibility: Achieving sustainability and real prosperity. *Ethical Corporation Magazine*. Retrieved from http://globalsystemchange.com/total-corporate-responsibility-achieving-sustainability-and-real-prosperity/.

Dixon, F. (2006, April 18). *Sustainability and system change: Wal-Mart's pioneering strategy*. CSRwire.com. Retrieved from http://globalsystemchange.com/sustainability-and-system-change-wal-marts-pioneering-strategy/.

Dixon, F. (2017, July). *Global system change: A whole system approach to achieving sustainability and real prosperity*. Retrieved from https://globalsystemchange.com/global-system-change-a-whole-system-approach-to-achieving-sustainability-and-real-prosperity/.

Dixon, F. (2019). System change investing and the sustainable development goals. *Cadmus, 3*(6), 98–117.

Dollar, D., Kleineberg, T., & Kraay, A. (2013). *Growth still is good for the poor* [Policy Research Working Paper 6568]. Washington, DC: World Bank. Retrieved from https://openknowledge. worldbank.org/bitstream/handle/10986/16001/WPS6568.pdf?sequence=1.

Domar, E. (1946). Capital expansion, rate of growth and employment. *Econometrica, 14*, 137–147.

Douglas, C. H. (1924). *Social credit*. London: Cecile Palmer.

Draghi, M. (2012, July 26). *Speech at UKTI's global investment conference*. London.

ECB. (2015, January 22). *ECB announces expanded asset purchase programme* [Press release]. Frankfurt. Retrieved from https://www.ecb.europa.eu/press/pr/date/2015/html/pr150122_1. en.html.

Economist. (2018, April 28). Within reach: Universal healthcare, worldwide [Print edition]. *Economist.*

Economist Intelligence Unit. (2015). *The economist*. Retrieved from https://espas. secure.europarl.europa.eu/orbis/sites/default/files/generated/document/en/LongtermMacroeconomicForecasts_KeyTrends.pdf.

Edenhofer, O. (2015). King Coal and the queen of subsidies. *Science, 349*(6254), 1286–1287. https://doi.org/10.1126/science.aad0674.

Ehrlich, P. R. (1968). *1968: The population bomb*. New York: Ballantine Books.

Eichengreen, B. (2014). Secular stagnation: A review of the issues. In C. Teulings & R. Baldwin (Eds.), *Secular stagnation: Facts, causes, and cures* (pp. 41–46). London: CEPR Press.

Elango, S., García, J. L., Heckman, J. J., & Hojman, A. (2015). Early childhood education. In *Economics of means: Tested transfer programs in the United States* (Vol. 2, pp. 235–297). Chicago, IL: University of Chicago Press.

El-Erian, M. (2016). *The only game in town: Central banks, instability, and avoiding the next collapse*. London: Random House.

Elias, N. (1997). *The civilizing process*. London: Blackwell.

Elisseeff, V. (Ed.). (2000). *The silk roads: Highways of culture and commerce*. New York: Berghahn Books. ISBN 978-92-3-103652-1.

Ellen McArthur Foundation. (2015). *Growth within: A circular economy vision for a competitive Europe*. London. Retrieved from https://www.ellenmacarthurfoundation.org/assets/downloads/ publications/EllenMacArthurFoundation_Growth-Within_July15.pdf.

Emerson, J. (2018). *The purpose of capital: Elements of impact, financial flows, and natural being*. San Francisco, CA: Blended Value Group Press.

Engerer, H. (2019). Sovereign Wealth Funds–Finanzierungsquelle für nachhaltige Entwicklung? *Vierteljahrshefte zur Wirtschaftsforschung/Quarterly Journal of Economic Research, 88*(3), 97–111.

Escobar, A. (2011). Sustainability: Design for the pluriverse. *Development, 54*(2), 137–140.

Escobar, A. (2015). Transiciones: A space for research and design for transitions to the pluriverse. *Design Philosophy Papers, 13*(1), 13–23.

ESRB. (2018, January). *Sovereign bond-backed securities: A feasibility study* (Vol. 1). Frankfurt am Main. Retrieved from https://www.esrb.europa.eu/pub/task_force_safe_assets/shared/pdf/ esrb.report290118_sbbs_volume_I_mainfindings.en.pdf.

Esser, I., Ferrarini, T., Nelson, K., Palme, J., & Sjöberg, O. (2013). *Unemployment benefits in EU member states*. Brussels: European Commission. Retrieved from http://www.diva-portal.org/ smash/get/diva2:682677/FULLTEXT01.pdf.

Eurodad. (2018). *History rePPPeated: How public private partnership are failing*. Retrieved from https://www.cenfa.org/wp-content/uploads/2018/10/Eurodad-Report-Oct-2018.pdf.

European Commission. (2016). Commission delegated regulation (EU) 2016/1450 of 23 May 2016 supplementing directive 2014/59/EU of the European Parliament and of the Council with regard to regulatory technical standards specifying the criteria relating to the methodology for setting the minimum requirement for own funds and eligible liabilities. *Official Journal of the European Union, 237*(1). Retrieved from https://eur-lex.europa.eu/legal-content/EN/TXT/?ur i=CELEX:32016R1450.

European Commission. (2018). *Action plan: Financing sustainable growth* [COM/2018/097]. Brussels: European Commission. Retrieved from https://eur-lex.europa.eu/legal-content/EN/TXT/?uri=CELEX:52018DC0097.

Eurostat. (2018). *Agricultural land prices and rents.* [Newsrelease 48/2018]. Retrieved from https://ec.europa.eu/eurostat/documents/2995521/8756523/5-21032018-AP-EN.pdf/b1d0ffd3-f75b-40cc-b53f-f22f68d541df.

EY. (2016). *Untapped potential: Engaging all Connecticut youth* [Parthenon EY Report.] Retrieved from http://cdn.ey.com/parthenon/pdf/perspectives/Parthenon-EY_Untapped-Potential_Dalio-Report_final_092016_web.pdf.

Falk, A., Becker, A., Dohmen, T., Enke, B., Huffman, D., & Sunde, U. (2018). Global evidence on economic preferences. *The Quarterly Journal of Economics, 133*(4), 1645–1692.

FAO. (2017). *The future of food and agriculture: Trends and challenges.* Rome. Retrieved from http://www.fao.org/3/a-i6583e.pdf.

Flachenecker, F., & Rentschler, J. (Eds.). (2018). *Investing in resource efficiency: The economics and politics of financing the resource transition.* Cham: Springer.

Flyvbjerg, B. (2008). Public planning of mega-projects: Overestimation of demand and underestimation of costs. In H. Priemus, B. Flyvbjerg, & B. van Wee (Eds.), *Decision-making on mega-projects.* Northhampton: Edward Elgar Publishing. https://doi.org/10.4337/9781848440173.00014. ISBN 9781848440173.

Food and land use coalition. (n.d.). Retrieved September, 2019, from https://www.foodandlandusecoalition.org/wp-content/uploads/2019/09/FOLU-GrowingBetter-GlobalReport-ExecutiveSummary.pdf.

Ford, J. L. (2016). *The divine quest, east and west: A comparative study of ultimate realities.* Albany, NY: SUNY Press.

Foster, J. B., & McChesney, R. W. (2012). *The endless crisis: How monopoly-finance capital produces stagnation and upheaval from the USA to China.* New York: Monthly Review Press.

Fowler, J. H., & Christakis, N. A. (2010). Cooperative behavior cascades in human social networks. *Proceedings of the National Academy of Sciences, 107*(12), 5334–5338. Retrieved from https://doi.org/10.1073/pnas.0913149107 and https://www.pnas.org/content/107/12/5334.long.

FRED, Economic Data. (2017). *Percent of value loans secured by collateral for all commercial and industry loans: All commercial banks.* St. Louis, MO. Retrieved from https://fred.stlouisfed.org/series/ESANQ.

Freedman, C., Kumhof, M., Laxton, D., Muir, D., & Mursula, S. (2010). Global effects of fiscal stimulus during the crisis. *Journal of Monetary Economics, 57*(5), 506–526.

Freeman, C., & Soete, L. (2009). Developing science, technology and innovation indicators: What we can learn from the past. *Research Policy, 38*(4), 583–589.

Friedman, T. L. (2008). *Hot, flat, and crowded: Why we need a green revolution, and how it can renew America.* New York: Farrar Straus and Giroux.

Friedman, G. (2016, February 27). *Response to the romers.* Retrieved from http://dollarsandsense.org/Friedman-Response-to-the-Romers.pdf.

Frydman, R., & Goldberg, M. D. (2011). *Beyond mechanical markets: Asset price swings, risk, and the role of the state.* Princeton, NJ: Princeton University Press.

Frydman, R., Duncan, I., & Goldberg, M. D. (2007). *Imperfect knowledge economics: Exchange rates and risk.* Princeton, NJ: Princeton University Press.

Gaffney, O., Crona, B., Dauriach, A., & Galaz, V. (2018). *Sleeping financial giants: Opportunities in financial leadership for climate stability.* Global Economic Dynamics and the Biosphere programme, Future Earth, & Stockholm Resilience Centre. Retrieved from https://sleepinggiants.earth/wp-content/uploads/2018/09/Sleeping-financial-giants-report-24-September-2018.pdf.

Galbraith, J. K. (2014). *The end of normal: The great crisis and the future of growth.* New York: Simon and Schuster.

Galilei, G. (1610, August 19). Letter of August 19, 1610. In E. Albéri (Ed., 1842–1856), *Le opere die Galileo Galilei. Prima edizione completa condetta sugli autentici manoscritti Palatini* (Vol. 6, pp. 116–118). Florence: Sociéta editrice Fiorentina.

Gallagher, K. P., & Kozul-Wright, R. (2019, April). *A new multilateralism for shared prosperity: Geneva principles for a global green new deal.* Boston, MA: Global Development Policy Center Boston University, UNCTAD. Retrieved from http://sarkoups.free.fr/unctad419.pdf.

Gapminder. (2018, March 9). *Four income levels.* Retrieved September 20 2019 from https://www.gapminder.org/topics/four-income-levels/.

Gapminder. (2020). Retrieved January, 30, 2020, from https://www.gapminder.org.

Giegold, S., Philipp, U., & Schick, G. (2016). *Finanzwende: Den nächsten Crash verhindern.* Berlin: Verlag Klaus Wagenbach.

Giridharadas, A. (2018). *Winners take all: The elite charade of changing the world.* New York: Knopf Doubleday.

Gladwell, M. (2000). *The tipping point: Howe little things can make a big difference.* New York: Little Brown & Company.

Global Witness. (2019, July). *Enemies of the state? How governments and businesses silence land and environmental defenders.* Retrieved from https://www.globalwitness.org/en-gb/campaigns/environmental-activists/enemies-state/.

Goerner, S. J., Lietaer, B., & Ulanowicz, R. E. (2009). Quantifying economic sustainability: Implications for free-enterprise theory, policy and practice. *Ecological Economics, 69*(1), 76–81.

Gond, J. P., Spicer, A., Patel, K., Fleming, P., Mosonyi, S., Benoit, C., & Parker, S. (2014). *A report on the culture of British retail banking.* London: New City Agenda. Retrieved from http://newcityagenda.co.uk/wp-content/uploads/2014/11/Online-version.pdf.

Goodhart, C. A. (1984). Problems of monetary management: The UK experience. In *Monetary theory and practice* (pp. 91–121). London: Macmillan.

Goodhart, C. A. (2008). The boundary problem in financial regulation. *National Institute Economic Review, 206*(1), 48–55.

Gordon, R. (2016). *The rise and fall of American growth: The U.S. standard of living since the civil war.* Princeton, NJ: Princeton University Press.

Gore, A. (1992). *Earth in the balance: Ecology and the human spirit.* Boston, MA: Houghton Mifflin Company.

Graeber, D. (2011). *Debt: The first 5000 years.* Brooklyn, NY: Melville House.

Griffin, K. (1979). *The political economy of agrarian change: An essay on the Green Revolution* (2nd ed.). London: Macmillan.

Griffin, P. (2017). *The carbon majors database* [CDP carbon majors report 2017]. CDP, Climate Accountability Institute. Retrieved from https://b8f65cb373b1b7b15feb-c70d8ead6ced550b4d987d7c03fcdd1d.ssl.cf3.rackcdn.com/cms/reports/documents/000/002/327/original/Carbon-Majors-Report-2017.pdf?1499691240.

Grubb, M., Koch, M., Thomson, K., Sullivan, F., & Munson, A. (2019). *The 'earth summit' agreements: A guide and assessment. An analysis of the Rio'92 UN conference on environment and development* (Vol. 9). Oxon, NY: Routledge.

Haldane, A. G., & May, R. M. (2011). Systemic risk in banking ecosystems. *Nature, 469*, 351–355.

Hall, P. A. (1993). Policy paradigms. Social learning, and the state: The case of economic policy-making in Britain. *Comparative Politics, 25*(3), 275–296.

Hall, R. (2011). Land grabbing in southern Africa: The many faces of the investor rush. *Review of African Political Economy, 38*(128), 193–214.

Hanke, S. H., & Krus, N. (2013). World hyperinflations. In R. Parker & R. Whaples (Eds.), *The handbook of major events in economic history.* London: Routledge Publishing.

Hansen, A. (1939). Economic progress and declining population growth. *American Economic Review, 29*(1), 1–15.

Harari, Y. N. (2014). *Sapiens: A brief history of humankind.* Toronto: Random House.

Harari, Y. N. (2016). *Homo Deus: A brief history of tomorrow.* New York: Random House.

Hardin, G. (1968). The tragedy of the commons. *Science, 162*(3859), 1243–1248.

Hare, B., & Woods, V. (2020). *Survival of the friendliest: Understanding our origins and rediscovering our common humanity.* New York: Random House.

Harrod, R. F. (1939). An Essay in dynamic theory. *The Economic Journal, 49*(193), 14–33.

Hayek, F. A. (1976). *Denationalization of money: The argument refined*. London: Institute of Economic Affairs.

Heal, G., & Schlenker, W. (2019). *Coase, hotelling and Pigou: The incidence of a carbon tax and CO2 emissions* (No. w26086). National Bureau of Economic Research.

Heckman, J. J. (2012). Invest in early childhood development: Reduce deficits, strengthen the economy. *The Heckman Equation, 7*, 1–2.

Heckman, J. J., Moon, S. H., Pinto, R., Savelyev, P. A., & Yavitz, A. (2010). The rate of return to the high scope Perry preschool program. *Journal of Public Economics, 94*(1-2), 114–128.

Heine, D., Semmler, W., Mazzucato, M., Braga, J. P., Flaherty, M., Gevorkyan, A., …, Radpour, S. (2019). *Financing low-carbon transitions through carbon pricing and green bonds*. Washington, DC: The World Bank.

Heinonen, S., Karjalainen, J., Ruotsalainen, J., & Steinmüller, K. (2017). Surprise as the new normal–implications for energy security. *European Journal of Futures Research, 5*(1), 1–13. https://doi.org/10.1007/s40309-017-0117-5.

Helfrich, S., & Heinrich-Böll-Stiftung (Eds.). (2012). *Commons: Für eine neue Politik jenseits von Markt und Staat*. Bielefeld: Transcript.

Henderson, H., & Sethi, S. (2006). *Ethical markets: Growing the green economy*. White River Junction, VT: Chelsea Green Publishing.

Henderson, H., Long, L., & Nash, T. J. (2019). *Transitioning to science-based investing* [Green transition scoreboard report]. St. Augustine, FL: Ethical Markets Media.

Hertwig, R., & Grüne-Yanoff, T. (2017). Nudging and boosting: Steering or empowering good decisions. *Perspectives on Psychological Science, 12*(6), 973–986.

Hirsch, F. (1977). *Social limits to growth*. London: Routledge and Kegan Paul.

Hoekstra, A. Y., & Chapagain, A. K. (2006). Water footprints of nations: Water use by people as a function of their consumption pattern. In *Integrated assessment of water resources and global change* (pp. 35–48). Dordrecht: Springer.

Hoekstra, A. Y., & Hung, P. Q. (2005). Globalisation of water resources: International virtual water flows in relation to crop trade. *Global Environmental Change, 15*(1), 45–56.

Hogan, M. J. (1989). *The Marshall plan: America, Britain and the reconstruction of western Europe, 1947–1952*. Cambridge: Cambridge University Press.

Holt-Giménez, E., Shattuck, A., Altieri, M., Herren, H., & Gliessman, S. (2012). We already grow enough food for 10 billion people… And still can't end hunger. *Journal of Sustainable Agriculture, 36*, 595–598.

Horn, S., Reinhart, C. M., & Trebesch, C. (2019). China's overseas lending (No. w26050). National Bureau of Economic Research.

Huber, J. (2020a). *Dominant money. Part I: Dominant money and tidal changes in the money supply*. Retrieved from https://sovereignmoney.site/dominant-money-i-taxonomy-and-monetary-tide-changes#ref.

Huber, J. (2020b). *Dominant money. Part II: The rise of sovereign digital currency*. Retrieved from https://sovereignmoney.site/dominant-money-ii-the-rise-of-sovereign-digital-currency.

Huber, J. (2020c). *Monetary financing of helicopter money*. Retrieved April, 30, 2020 from https://sovereignmoney.site/monetary-financing-of-helicopter-money.

Human Rights Foundation. *Political regime map*. Retrieved October 3, 2019., from https://hrf.org/research_posts/political-regime-map/.

IEA. (2017). *Energy access outlook 2017: From poverty to prosperity*. Paris. Retrieved from https://www.iea.org/publications/freepublications/publication/WEO2017SpecialReport_EnergyAccessOutlook.pdf.

ILO. (2019). *World employment social outlook: Trends 2019*. [Executive summary]. Geneva. Retrieved from http://www.ilo.org/wcmsp5/groups/public/%2D%2D-dgreports/%2D%2D-dcomm/%2D%2D-publ/documents/publication/wcms_670554.pdf.

ILO, Department of Statistics. (2019, July). The global labour income share and distribution. Geneva: ILO. Retrieved from https://www.ilo.org/ilostat-files/Documents/LIS%20Key%20 Findings.pdf.

IMF. (2016). *Fiscal monitor. Debt: Use it wisely.* Washington, DC. Retrieved from https://www. imf.org/en/Publications/FM/Issues/2016/12/31/Debt-Use-it-Wisely.

IMF. (2017, October). *Seeking sustainable growth: Short-term recovery, long-term challenges.* Washington, DC.

IMF, Data. (2019). *Currency composition of official foreign exchange reserves (COFER)* [World (U.S. dollars, billions), Q1 2019]. Retrieved from http://data.imf.org/?sk=E6A5F467-C14B-4 AA8-9F6D-5A09EC4E62A4.

Institute for Economics and Peace. (2018, October). *The economic value of peace 2018: Measuring the global economic impact of violence and conflict.* Sydney. Retrieved from http:// visionofhumanity.org/app/uploads/2018/11/Economic-Value-of-Peace-2018.pdf.

Investment & Pensions Europe. (2019). The top 400 asset managers. Retrieved from https://www. ipe.com/Uploads/j/e/b/Top-400-Asset-Managers-2019.pdf.

Ireland, J. D. (2018). *The Udāna and the Itivuttaka: Inspired utterances of the Buddha and the Buddha's sayings* (pp. 78–79). Onalaska, WA: Pariyatti Publishing.

ISO. (2018). *ISO 31000: Risk management guideline* (2nd ed.). Geneva.

ITC. (2019). *Trade map: Imports.* [2709: Petroleum oils and oils obtained from bituminous minerals, crude]. Retrieved from https://www.trademap.org/Index.aspx.

Jackson, A. (2013). *Sovereign money: Paving the way to a sustainable recovery.* London: Positive Money. Retrieved from http://positivemoney.org/wp-content/uploads/2013/11/Sovereign-Money-Final-Web.pdf.

Jacobs, G. (2010). *The book: The spiritual individual in quest of the living organization. Codex for the infinite game.* Seattle, WA: Amazon Digital Services LLC.

Jacobs, G. (2016). Foundations of economic theory: Markets, money, social power and human welfare. *Cadmus, 2*(6), 20.

Jacobs, G., & Slaus, I. (2012). The Power of Money, *Cadmus 1*(5), 68–73.

Jasny, B. R. (2018). Tipping points in social convention. *Science, 360*(6393), 1082. https://doi. org/10.1126/science.360.6393.1082-d.

Jevons, W. S. (1866). *The coal question: An inquiry concerning the progress of the nation, and the probable exhaustion of our coal-mines.* London: Macmillan.

Jubilee Debt Campaign. (2018, March 18). *Developing country debt payments increase by 60% in three years.* Retrieved from https://jubileedebt.org.uk/press-release/ developing-country-debt-payments-increase-by-60-in-three-years.

Kahneman, D. (2011). *Thinking, fast and slow.* New York: Farrar Straus and Giroux.

Kahneman, D., & Tversky, A. (1982). Intuitive prediction: Biases and corrective procedures. In D. Kahneman, P. Slovic, & A. Tversky (Eds.), *Judgment under uncertainty: Heuristics and biases.* London: Cambridge University Press.

Kander, A., Jiborn, M., Moran, D. D., & Wiedmann, T. O. (2015). National greenhouse-gas accounting for effective climate policy on international trade. *Nature Climate Change, 5,* 431–435.

Kant, I. (1784). Beantwortung der Frage—Was ist Aufklärung? [An answer to the question: What is enlightenment?]. *Berlinische Monatsschrift, 4,* 481–494.

Kaplan, S. N., & Schoar, A. (2005). Private equity performance: Returns, persistence, and capital flows. *The Journal of Finance, 60*(4), 1791–1823.

Kar, D., & Schjelderup, G. (2015). *Financial flows and tax havens. Combining to limit the lives of billions of people.* Washington, DC: Global Financial Integrity. Retrieved from https:// secureservercdn.net/45.40.149.159/34n.8bd.myftpupload.com/wp-content/uploads/2016/12/ Financial_Flows-final.pdf.

Kar, D., & Spanjers, J. (2015, December). *Illicit financial flows from developing countries: 2004–2013.* Washington, DC: Global Financial Integrity. Retrieved from https:// financialtransparency.org/wp-content/uploads/2016/03/IFF-Update_2015-Final-1.pdf.

Karlqvist, A. (1999). Going beyond disciplines. *Policy Sciences, 32*(4), 379–383.

Kaya, Y., & Yokobori, K. (1997). *Environment, energy, and economy: Strategies for sustainability.* Tokyo: United Nations University Press.

Keeley, B. (2007). *Human capital: How what you know shapes your life.* Paris: OECD Publishing.

Kennedy, M., & Lietaer, B. A. (2004). *Regionalwährungen: Neue Wege zu nachhaltigem Wohlstand.* München: Riemann Verlag.

Kennedy, M., Lietaer, B. A., & Rogers, J. (2012). *People money: The promise of regional currencies.* Devon: Triarchy Press Limited.

Keynes, J. M. (1920). *The economic consequences of the peace.* New York: Harcourt, Brace and Howe.

Keynes, J. M. (1980). Shaping the post war world employment and commodities. In *Collected writings of J.M. Keynes: Activities 1940–1946* (Vol. 27). London: Macmillan.

Khanna, P. (2019). *The future is Asian.* New York: Simon and Schuster.

Ki-Moon, B. (2015). *The road to dignity by 2030: Ending poverty, transforming all lives and protecting the planet synthesis* [Report of the Secretary-General on the post-2015 sustainable development agenda, A/69/700]. Geneva: UN. Retrieved from https://www.un.org/development/desa/publications/wp-content/uploads/sites/10/2015/01/Synthesis ReportENG.pdf.

Kirkland, R. (2004). *Taoism: The enduring tradition.* London and New York: Routledge.

Kissinger, H. (2015). *World order.* New York: Penguin Books.

Klein, N. (2015). *This changes everything: Capitalism vs. the climate.* New York: Simon and Schuster.

Klein, N. (2019). *On fire: The (burning) case for a green new deal.* New York: Simon & Schuster.

Knapp, G. F. (1924). *The state theory of money.* London: Macmillan.

Knapp, S., & Van der Heijden, M. G. (2018). A global meta-analysis of yield stability in organic and conservation agriculture. *Nature Communications, 9*(1), 3632.

Knight, F. (1933). *Memorandum on banking reform* [President's Personal File 431]. Washington, DC: Franklin D. Roosevelt Presidential Library.

Koenig, P. (2003). *30 lies about money.* iUniverse.

Kompas, T. (2020, February 14). *What are the full economic costs to Australia from climate change?* Melbourne Sustainable society Institute. Retrieved from https://sustainable.unimelb.edu.au/news/what-are-the-full-economic-costs-to-australia-from-climate-change.

Koo, R. C. (2015). *The escape from balance sheet recession and the QE trap.* Singapore: Wiley & Sons.

Korzeniewicz, R. P., & Moran, T. P. (2009). *Unveiling inequality: A world-historical perspective.* New York: Russell Sage Foundation.

Kregel, J. A. (2004). *External financing for development and international financial instability.* Geneva: UN.

Kregel, J. A. (2019, March). *Democratizing money.* Levy Economics Institute Public Policy Brief, 147.

Krugman, P. (2012). *End This Depression Now.* New York: Norton.

Krugman, P. (2014). Four observations on secular stagnation. In C. Teulings & R. Baldwin (Eds.), *Secular stagnation: Facts, causes, and cures* (pp. 61–68). London: CEPR Press.

Kuhn, T. S. (1962). *The structure of scientific revolutions.* Chicago, IL: University of Chicago Press.

Kumhof, M. M., & Tanner, M. E. (2005). *Government debt: A key role in financial intermediation* [Working paper number 05/57]. Washington, DC: IMF.

Kuznets, S. (1955). Economic growth and income inequality. *The American Economic Review, 45*(1), 1–28.

Laeven, L., & Valencia, F. (2013). Systemic banking crises database. *IMF Economic Review, 61*(2), 225–270.

Lagarde, C. (2018, November 14) *Winds of change: The case for new digital currency* [Speech at fintech festival]. Singapore. Retrieved from https://www.imf.org/en/News/Articles/2018/11/13/sp111418-winds-of-change-the-case-for-new-digital-currency.

Lagarde, C., & Gaspar, V. (2019). *Getting real on meeting Paris climate change commitments.* IMF Blog.

Lakoff, G. (2004). *Don't think of an elephant! Know your values and frame the debate: The essential guide for progressives.* White River Junction, VT: Chelsea Green Publishing.

Lakoff, G., & Johnson, M. (1980). *Metaphors we live by.* Chicago, IL: University of Chicago Press.

Lammar, R. (2013). *Das ist unsere Welt: Der Mensch im 21. Jahrhundert.* Norderstedt: Books on Demand GmbH.

Lancet. (1978). Water with sugar and salt. *Lancet, 312,* 300–301.

Larsen, L. B. (2018). *A fair share of tax: A fiscal anthropology of contemporary Sweden.* Cham: Springer.

Laszlo, E. (1996). *The systems view of the world: A holistic vision for our time.* New York: Braziller.

Law, J. (Ed.). (2014). *A dictionary of finance and banking.* Oxford: Oxford University Press.

Lazonick, W. (2014, September). Profits without prosperity: Stock buybacks manipulate the market and leave most Americans worse off. *Harvard Business Review.* Retrieved from http://gesd.free.fr/lazonick14.pdf.

LeDoux, J. E. (1996). *The emotional brain: The mysterious underpinnings of emotional life.* New York: Simon and Schuster.

LeDoux, J. E. (2000). Emotion circuits in the brain. *Annual Review of Neuroscience, 23*(1), 155–184.

Lempert, D., & Nguyen, H. (2011). The global prisoners' dilemma of unsustainability: Why sustainable development cannot be achieved without resource security and eliminating the legacies of colonialism. *Sustainability: Science, Practice and Policy, 7*(1), 16–30.

Lessenich, S. (2019). *Living well at others' expense: The hidden costs of western prosperity.* Medford, MA: Polity Press.

Lewis, M. C. (2014, April 24). *Stranded assets, fossilised revenues* [ESG sustainability research report]. Kepler Cheuvreux.

Lidell, H. G., & Scott, R. (1869). *A Greek-English dictionary.* Oxford: Macmillan.

Liermann, V., & Stegmann, C. (Eds.). (2019). *The impact of digital transformation and FinTech on the finance professional.* Cham: Springer, Palgrave Macmillan.

Lietaer, B., & Brunnhuber, S. (2005). Economics as an evolutionary system: Psychological development and economic behavior. *Evolutionary and Institutional Economics Review, 2*(1). Retrieved from http://www.econ.kyoto-u.ac.jp/~evoeco/eng/eier.html.

Lietaer, B. A., & Dunne, J. (2013). *Rethinking money: How new currencies turn scarcity into prosperity.* San Francisco, LA: Berrett-Koehler Publishers.

Lietaer, B., Arnsberger, C., Goerner, S., & Brunnhuber, S. (2012). *Money and sustainability: The missing link. A report from the Club of Rome-EU chapter.* Axminster: Triarchy Press.

Lietaer, B., Preuss, H., Hudon, M., De Spiegeleer, K., Legat, D., & Sherburne, C. (2019). *Towards a sustainable world: 3 paradigm shifts to achieve.* Vienna: Delta Institute - Dieter Legat E.U.

Light, D. W. (2005). Making practical markets for vaccines. *PLoS Medicine, 2*(10), e271.

Liu, X., Klemeš, J. J., Varbanov, P. S., Čuček, L., & Qian, Y. (2017). Virtual carbon and water flows embodied in international trade: A review on consumption-based analysis. *Journal of Cleaner Production, 146,* 20–28.

Lomborg, B. (2017, April 19). *The low cost of ending poverty.* Project Syndicate. Retrieved from https://www.project-syndicate.org/commentary/low-cost-of-ending-global-poverty-by-bjorn-lomborg-2017-04?mc_cid=ab47031854&mc_eid=6c0209759f&barrier=accesspaylog.

Lomborg, B. (2020). *False alarm—How climate change panic costs us trillions, hurts the poor, and fails to fix the planet.* New York: Basic books.

Lovins, A. (2013). *Reinventing fire: Bold business solutions for the new energy era.* White River Junction, VT: Chelsea Green Publishing.

Luft, G. (2016). *It takes a road: China's one belt one road initiative. An American response to the new silk road.* Madrid: Institute for the Analysis of Global Security [IAGS].

MacIntyre, A. (1984). *After virtue: A study in moral theory* (2nd ed.). Notre Dame, IN: University of Notre Dame Press.

Macy, J. (1991). *Mutual causality in Buddhism and general systems theory: The dharma of natural systems*. Albany, NY: Suny Press.

Maddison, A. (2001). *The world economy: A millennial perspective*. Paris: OECD.

Mai, H., & Schneider, F. (2016). Size and development of the shadow economies of 157 worldwide countries: Updated and new measures from 1999 to 2013. *Journal of Global Economics, 4*(3), 1–15.

Mancini-Griffoli, T., Peria, M., Agur, M. I., Ari, M. A., Kiff, M. J., Popescu, M. A., & Rochon, M. C. (2018). *Casting light on central bank digital currencies* [IMF Staff Discussion Note SDN/18/08]. Washington, DC: IMF.

Mandelbrot, B. B. (1977). *Fractals: Form, chance, and dimension*. San Francisco, CA: WH Freeman.

Mandelbrot, B. B. (1983). *The fractal geometry of nature*. New York: WH Freeman.

Mariana, M. (2013). The entrepreneurial state: Debunking public vs. private sector myths.

Masters, R., Anwar, E., Collins, B., Cookson, R., & Capewell, S. (2017). Return on investment of public health interventions: A systematic review. *Journal of Epidemiol Community Health, 71*(8), 827–834.

Mazzucato, M. (2013). *The entrepreneurial state: debunking public vs. private sector myths*. London: Anthem Press.

Mazzucato, M. (2018). *The value of everything: Making and taking in the global economy*. New York: Hachette Book Group.

McAfee, A. (2019). *More from less: The surprising story of how we learned to prosper using fewer resources—And what happens next*. New York: Scribner.

McCaffery, E. J. (1994). The uneasy case for wealth transfer taxation. *The Yale Law Journal, 104*(2), 283–365.

McCormack, G., Keay, A., & Brown, S. (2017). *European insolvency law: Reform and harmonization*. Northhampton: Edward Elgar Publishing.

McDonough, W., & Braungart, M. (2002). *Cradle to cradle: Remaking the way we make things*. New York: North Point Press.

McGath, T. (2018, April 9). M-Pesa: How Kenyan revolutionised mobile payments. *N26 Magazine*. Retrieved from https://mag.n26.com/m-pesa-howkenya-revolutionized-mobile-payments-56786bc09ef,

McGilchrist, I. (2009). *The master and his emissary: The divided brain and the making of the Western world*. New Haven, CT: Yale University Press.

McGlade, C., & Ekins, P. (2015). The geographical distribution of fossil fuels unused when limiting global warming to 2°C. *Nature, 517*, 187–190. https://doi.org/10.1038/nature14016.

McIntosh, S. P. (2015). *The redesign of the global financial architecture: The return of state authority*. London: Routledge.

McKibben, B. (2012). Global warming's terrifying new math. *Rolling Stone, 19*(7).

McKibbin, W. J., Morris, A. C., Panton, A., & Wilcoxen, P. (2017). Climate change and monetary policy: Dealing with disruption.

McLeay, M., Amar, R., & Thomas, R. (2014). *Money creation in the modern economy. Bank of England's monetary analysis directorate* [Quarterly Bulletin Q1]. London: Bank of England.

Mead, G. H. (1934). *Mind, Self, and Society*. Chicago: University of Chicago Press.

Mead, M. (1964). *Continuities in cultural evolution*. New Haven, CT: Yale University Press.

Meadows, D. H. (2002). Dancing with systems. *Systems Thinker, 13*, 2–6.

Meadows, D. H. (2008). *Thinking in systems: A primer*. White River Junction, VT: Chelsea Green Publishing.

Meadows, D. H., Meadows, D. L., Randers, J., & Behrens, W. W. (1972). *The limits to growth: A report for the club of Rome's project on the predicament of mankind*. New York: Universe Books.

Meyer, J., Reinhart, C. M., & Trebesch, C. (2019). *Sovereign bonds since Waterloo* (No. w25543). National Bureau of Economic Research.

Meyer-Abich, K. M. (1965). *Korrespondenz, Individualität und Komplementarität*. Wiesbaden: Steiner.

Miles, L., Nind, L., & Macrae, C. N. (2010). Moving through time. *Psychological Science, 21*(2), 222.

Miller, E. K., & Cohen, J. D. (2001). An integrative theory of prefrontal cortex function. *Annual Review of Neuroscience, 24*(1), 167–202.

Miller, W. R., & Rollnick, S. (2012). *Motivational interviewing: Helping people change*. New York: Guilford Press.

Minsky, H. P. (1965). The role of employment policy. In M. S. Gordon (Ed.), *Poverty in America*. San Francisco, CA: Chandler Publishing.

Mitchell, R. B. (2017). *International environmental agreements database project* [Version 2017.1]. Eugene, OR: University of Oregon. Retrieved from https://iea.uoregon.edu/sites/iea1.uoregon.edu/files/MEAs-1857-2016.jpg.

Mitchell, W., Wray, L. R., & Watts, M. (2019). *Macroeconomics*. London: Macmillan.

Mosler, W. (2010). *Seven deadly innocent frauds of economic policy*. Christiansted, US Virgin Islands: Valance Co.

Mudaliar, A., & Dithrich, H. (2019). *Sizing the impact investing market*. Global Impact Investing Network. Retrieved from https://thegiin.org/assets/Sizing%20the%20Impact%20Investing%20Market_webfile.pdf.

Murphy, R., & Hines, C. (2010). *Green quantitative easing: Paying for the economy we need*. Norfolk, VA: Finance for Future. Retrieved from http://openaccess.city.ac.uk/id/eprint/16569/1/GreenQuEasing.pdf.

Nash, J. (1950). Equilibrium points in n-person games. *Proceedings of the National Academy of Sciences, 36*(1), 48–49.

Nassehi, A. (2019). *Muster: Theorie der digitalen Gesellschaft*. Munich: CH Beck.

Nefiodow, L., & Nefiodow, S. (2017). *The sixth kondratieff: A new long wave in the global economy*. Scotts Valley, CA: CreateSpace Independent Publishing Platform.

Network for Greening the Financial System [NGFS]. (2019). *A call for action: Climate change as a source of financial risk* [First comprehensive report]. Paris: Banque de France. Retrieved from https://www.banque-france.fr/sites/default/files/media/2019/04/17/ngfs_first_comprehensive_report_-_17042019_0.pdf.

Neuwirth, R. (2011). *Stealth of nations: The global rise of the informal economy*. New York: Pantheon. ISBN 978-0-375-42489-2.

Niedenthal, P. M., Barsalou, L. W., Winkielman, P., Krauth-Gruber, S., & Ric, F. (2005). Embodiment in attitudes, social perception, and emotion. *Personality and Social Psychology Review, 9*(3), 184–211.

Norbert, E. (1994). *The civilizing process: The history of manners and state formation and civilization* (reprint). Oxford: Blackwell Publishers.

Nordhaus, W. (2018a). Projections and uncertainties about climate change in an era of minimal climate policies. *American Economic Journal: Economic Policy, 10*(3), 333–360.

Nordhaus, W. (2018b). *Climate change: The ultimate challenge for economics* [Nobel lecture in economic sciences]. Retrieved from https://www.nobelprize.org/uploads/2018/10/nordhaus-slides.pdf.

Nordhaus, W. (2019). Climate change: The ultimate challenge for economics. *American Economic Review, 109*(6), 1991–2014.

O'Neill, J. (2018). Factfulness: Ten reasons we're wrong about the world-and why things are better than you think. *Nature, 556*(7699), 25–26.

Obama, B. (2017). The irreversible momentum of clean energy. *Science, 355*(6321), 126–129. Retrieved from http://science.sciencemag.org/content/sci/early/2017/01/06/science.aam6284.full.pdf.

Obstfeld, M., & Taylor, A. M. (1998). The great depression as a watershed: International capital mobility over the long run. In *The defining moment: The great depression and the American economy in the twentieth century* (pp. 353–402). Chicago, IL: University of Chicago Press.

Ockham, W. (1495). *Quaestiones et decisiones in quattuor libros Sententiarum Petri Lombardi.* Editioni Lugdenensi, i, dist. 27, qu. 2, K.

Ocklenburg, S., & Gunturkun, O. (2017). *The lateralized brain: The neuroscience and evolution of hemispheric asymmetries.* London: Academic Press, Elsevier.

OECD. (2007). *Human capital: How what you know shapes your life.* Paris. Retrieved from https://www.oecd.org/insights/humancapitalhowwhatyouknowshapesyourlife.htm.

OECD. (2014). *The rationale for fighting corruption* [Background brief]. Paris. Retrieved from http://www.oecd.org/cleangovbiz/49693613.pdf.

OECD. (2015). *Measuring and monitoring BEPS, action 11* [2015 Report, OECD/G20 Base Erosion and Profit Shifting Project]. Paris.

OECD. (2017). *Net ODA* [Total, % of gross national income, 2000–2017]. Retrieved from https://data.oecd.org/oda/net-oda.htm.

OECD. (2018). *States of fragility 2018.* Retrieved from http://www.oecd.org/dac/conflict-fragility-resilience/docs/OECD%20Highlights%20documents_web.pdf.

OECD. (2019). *Corporate tax statistics.* Paris: OECD Publishing. Retrieved from https://www.oecd.org/tax/tax-policy/corporate-tax-statistics-database-first-edition.pdf.

Oladele, O. I., Bam, R. K., Buri, M. M., & Wakatsuki, T. (2010). Missing prerequisites for green revolution in Africa: Lessons and the challenges of Sawah rice eco-technology development and dissemination in Nigeria and Ghana. *Journal of Food, Agriculture & Environment, 8*(2), 1014–1018.

One Planet Sovereign Wealth Funds. (n.d.). Retrieved March 30, 2020, from https://oneplanetswfs.org.

Oppenheimer, D. M., & Trail, T. E. (2010). Why leaning to the left makes you lean to the left: Effect of spatial orientation on political attitudes. *Social Cognition, 28*(5), 651–661.

Orlov, S., Rovenskaya, E., Puaschunder, J. M., & Semmler, W. (2017, December 12). Green bonds, transition to a low-carbon economy, and intergenerational fairness: Evidence from an extended DICE model. *Transition to a Low-Carbon Economy, and Intergenerational Fairness: Evidence from an Extended DICE Model.*

Orlov, S., Rovenskaya, E., Puaschunder, J., & Semmler, W. (2018). *Green Bonds, Transition to a Low-Carbon Economy, and Intergenerational Fairness: Evidence from an Extended DICE Model.* IIASA Working Paper, Laxenburg, Austria.

Ostrom, E. (1990). *Governing the commons: The evolution of institutions for collective action.* Cambridge: Cambridge University Press. https://doi.org/10.1017/CBO9780511807763.

Oswald, M. E., & Grosjean, S. (2004). Confirmation bias. In R. F. Pohl (Ed.), *Cognitive illusions: A handbook on fallacies and biases in thinking, judgement and memory* (pp. 79–96). Hove: Psychology Press. ISBN 978-1-84169-351-4, OCLC 55124398.

Otte, M. (2019). *Weltsystemcrash: Krisen, Unruhen und die Geburt einer neuen Weltordnung.* München: Finanzbuch Verlag.

Otto, I. M., Kim, K. M., Dubrovsky, N., & Lucht, W. (2019). Shift the focus from the super-poor to the super-rich. *Nature Climate Change, 9*(2), 82–84.

Otto, I. M., Donges, J. F., Cremades, R., Bhowmik, A., Hewitt, R. J., Lucht, W., …, Lenferna, A. (2020, January). Social tipping dynamics for stabilizing Earth's climate by 2050. *Proceedings of the National Academy of Sciences.*

Our World in Data. (2020). Retrieved January 30, 2020, from https://ourworldindata.org.

Oxelheim, L. (1990). *International financial integration.* Berlin: Springer-Verlag.

Oxfam. (2011, 22 September). *Land and power: The growing scandal surrounding the new wave of investments in land.* Retrieved from https://www.oxfam.de/system/files/20110922_land-power-rights-acquisitions.pdf.

Oxfam. (2015, December 2). *Extreme carbon inequality: Why the Paris climate deal must put the poorest, lowest emitting and most vulnerable people first.* Oxfam Media Briefing. Retrieved from https://www-cdn.oxfam.org/s3fs-public/file_attachments/mb-extreme-carbon-inequality-021215-en.pdf.

Paarlberg, R. (2009). *Starved for science: How biotechnology is being kept out of Africa*. Boston, MA: Harvard University Press.

Parry, R. (2003). Episteme und techne. In *Stanford encyclopedia of philosophy*. Retrieved from https://plato.stanford.edu/entries/episteme-techne/.

Parry, I. W., Heine, M. D., Lis, E., & Li, S. (2014). *Getting energy prices right: From principle to practice*. Washington, DC: International Monetary Fund.

Pavlov, I. P. (1927). *Conditioned reflexes*. Oxford: Oxford University Press.

Perkins, D. (2014). *Future wise: Educating our children for a changing world*. Hoboken, NJ: John Wiley & Sons.

Pietschmann, T., & Walker, J. (2011). *Estimating illicit financial flows resulting from drug trafficking and other transnational organized crimes*. UNODC. Retrieved from https://www.drugsandalcohol.ie/16151/1/Illicit_financial_flows_2011_web.pdf.

Pigou, A. C. (1920). *The economics of welfare*. London: Macmillan.

Piketty, T., & Saez, E. (2013). Optimal labor income taxation. In A. J. Auerbach, R. Chetty, M. Feldstein, & E. Saez (Eds.), *Handbook of public economics* (Vol. 5). Amsterdam, NL: Elsevier.

Pink, D. H. (2005). *A whole new mind*. New York: Riverhead Books.

Pink, D. H. (2009). *Drive: The surprising news about what motivates us*. New York: Riverhead Books.

Pinker, S. (2018). *Enlightenment now: The case for reason, science, humanism, and progress*. New York, NY: Viking.

Pogge, T. (2005). World poverty and human rights. *Ethics & International Affairs, 19*(1), 1–7.

[Pope] Francis. (2015). *Laudato Si': On care for our common home*. Vatican City: Vatican Press.

Popper, K. R. (2003). *Die Offene Gesellschaft und Ihre Feinde. Band II: Falsche Propheten. Hegel, Marx und die Folgen*. Tübingen: Mohr Siebeck.

Positive Money. (2014). *How to fuel the economy without increasing debt, through sovereign money*. Retrieved September 30, 2019, from https://positivemoney.org/videos/presentations-by-positive-money/fuel-economy-without-increasing-debt-sovereign-money/.

Preston, S. H. (1975). The changing relation between mortality and level of economic development. *Population Studies, 29*(2), 231–248.

Project Drawdown. (2019). *Summary of solutions by overall rank*. Retrieved June 20, 2019, from https://www.drawdown.org/solutions-summary-by-rank.

Radermacher, F. J. (2018). *Der Milliarden-Joker–Scientific Edition: Wie Deutschland und Europa den globalen Klimaschutz revolutionieren können*. Hamburg: Murmann Publishers GmbH.

Ram, M., Bogdanov, D., Aghahosseini, A., Oyewo, S., Gulagi, A., Child, M., …, Breyer, C. (2017). *Global energy system based on 100% renewable energy-power sector*. Lappeenranta and Berlin: Lappeenranta University of Technology and Energy Watch Group.

Randers, J., Rockström, J., Stoknes, P. E., Golüke, U., Collste, D., & Cornell, S. (2018). *Transformation is feasible: How to achieve the sustainable development goals within planetary boundaries*. [A report to the Club of Rome]. Retrieved from https://www.stockholmresilience.org/download/18.51d83659166367a9a16353/1539675518425/Report_Achieving%20the%20Sustainable%20Development%20Goals_WEB.pdf.

Rathi, A. (2017, December 2). *The world's astonishing dependence on fossil fuels hasn't changed in 40 years*. Quartz. Retrieved from https://qz.com/1144207/the-worlds-astonishing-dependence-on-fossil-fuels-hasnt-changed-in-40-years/.

Raworth, K. (2012). A safe and just space for humanity: Can we live within the doughnut? *Oxfam Policy and Practice: Climate Change and Resilience, 8*(1), 1–26.

Reckwitz, A. (2019). *The society of singularities: On the transformation of modernity*. Cambridge: Polity Press.

Reinhart, C. M., & Rogoff, K. S. (2009). *This time is different: Eight centuries of financial folly*. Princeton, NJ: Princeton University Press.

Rennung, M., & Göritz, A. S. (2016). Prosocial consequences of interpersonal synchrony: A meta-analysis. *Zeitschrift für Psychologie, 224*, 168–189.

Rich, N. (2018, August 1). Losing earth: The decade we almost stopped climate change. *New York Times Magazine*. Retrieved from https://www.nytimes.com/interactive/2018/08/01/magazine/climate-change-losing-earth.html.

Ricupero, R. (2004). *Beyond conventional wisdom in development policy. An intellectual history of UNCTAD (1964–2004)*. Geneva: UN.

Rifkin, J. (2019). *The green new deal*. New York: St. Martin's Press.

Ro, S. (2015, February 12). *Here's what the $294 trillion market of global financial assets looks like*. Business Insider. Retrieved from https://www.businessinsider.com/global-financial-assets-2015-2?r=US&IR=T.

Robinson, J. A., & Acemoglu, D. (2012). *Why nations fail: The origins of power, prosperity and poverty*. London: Profile.

Rockström, J., & Klum, M. (2016). *Big world. Small planet. Wie wir die Zukunft unseres Planeten gestalten*. Berlin: Ullstein.

Rodrik, D. (2000). How far will international economic integration go? *Journal of economic perspectives, 14*(1), 177–186.

Rodrik, D. (2012). *The globalization paradox*. Oxford: Oxford University Press.

Rogoff, K. (2016, April 22). *Debt supercycle, not secular stagnation*. VoxEU. Retrieved from http://www.voxeu.org/article/debt-supercycle-not-secular-stagnation.

Roosevelt, F. D. (1938). Inaugural address, March 4, 1933. In S. Rosenman (Ed.), *The public papers of Franklin D. Roosevelt, volume two: The year of crisis, 1933* (pp. 11–16). New York: Random House.

Roser, M., & Ortiz-Ospina, E. (2017, March 27) *Extreme poverty*. Our World in Data. Retrieved from https://ourworldindata.org/extreme-poverty.

Roser, M., & Ortiz-Ospina, E. (2018, September 20). *Literacy*. Our World in Data. Retrieved from https://ourworldindata.org/literacy.

Rosling, H., Rosling Rönnlund, A., & Rosling, O. (2018). *Factfulness: Wie wir lernen, die Welt so zu sehen, wie sie wirklich ist*. Berlin: Ullstein Buchverlage.

Rosset, P., Collins, J., & Lappé, F. M. (2000). Lessons from the green revolution. *Third World Resurgence*, 11–14.

Rössner, P. R. (2012). *Deflation, devaluation, rebellion: Geld im Zeitalter der Reformation*. Stuttgart: Franz Steiner.

Rössner, P. R. (2018). Monetary theory and Cameralist economic management, c. 1500–1900 AD. *Journal of the History of Economic Thought, 40*(1), 99–134.

Ruddick, W. O., & Mariani, L. (2013, May). *Complementary currencies strengthening the social and solidarity economy: Case studies from Kenya*. [UNRISD International Symposium on Potential and Limits of the Social and Solidarity Economy Special Session on Alternative Finance and Complementary Currencies]. Geneva: UN.

Rulli, M. C., Saviori, A., & D'Odorico, P. (2013). Global land and water grabbing. *Proceedings of the National Academy of Sciences, 110*(3), 892–897.

Ryan-Collins, J., Greenham, T., Werner, R., & Jackson, A. (2012). *Where does money come from: A guide to the UK monetary and banking system*. London: New Economics Foundation.

Ryan-Collins, J., Werner, R., Greenham, T., & Bernardo, G. (2013). *Strategic quantitative easing: Stimulating investment to rebalance the economy*. London: New Economics Foundation. Retrieved from http://www.neweconomics.org/publications/entry/strategic-quantitative-easing.

Sachs, J. D. (2006). *The end of poverty: Economic possibilities for our time*. New York: Penguin.

Sachs, J. D. (2014). Climate change and intergenerational well-being. In *The Oxford handbook of the macroeconomics of global warming* (pp. 248–259).

Sachs, J. (2015). Climate Change and Intergenerational Well-Being. In L. Bernard & W. Semmler (Eds.). *The Oxford Handbook of the Macroeconomics of Global Warming*. Oxford: Oxford University Press.

Sachs, J., McCord, G., Maennling, N., Smith, T., Fajans-Turner, V., & Loni, S. S. (2019, September). *SDG costing & financing for low-income developing countries*. New York: UN Sustainable Development Solutions Network [SDSN]. Retrieved from https://irp-cdn.

multiscreensite.com/be6d1d56/files/uploaded/FINAL_SDG%20Costing%20%26%20 Finance%20for%20LIDCS%2028%20Oct.pdf.

Saez, E. & Zucman, G. (2019). *The Triumph of Injustice: How the Rich Dodge Taxes and How to Make Them Pay*. New York: Norton.

Saez, E., & Zucman, G. (2019a). Progressive Wealth Taxation. *Brookings Papers on Economic Activity 2019*(2), 437–533.

Safaricom. (2019). *M-Pesa Rates*. Retrieved August 30, 2019, from https://www.safaricom.co.ke/ personal/m-pesa/getting-started/m-pesa-rates.

Saha, D., Hong, S. H., Shao, A., Modi, A., & Zemlytska, I. (2018). *2017 private participation in infrastructure (PPI): Annual report*. Washington, DC: World Bank. Retrieved from http://ppi. worldbank.org/~/media/GIAWB/PPI/Documents/Global-Notes/PPI_2017_AnnualReport.pdf.

Sandel, M. J. (1982). *Liberalism and the limits of justice*. Cambridge: Cambridge University Press.

Santarius, T. (2015). *Der Rebound-Effekt. Ökonomische, psychische und soziale Herausforderungen für die Entkopplung von Wirtschaftswachstum und Energieverbrauch*. Weimar: Metropolis.

Saxe, J. G. (1936). The blind men and the elephant. In H. Felleman (Ed.), *The best loved poems of American people* (pp. 521–522). New York: Doubleday.

Schelling, T. C. (1971). Dynamic models of segregation. *Journal of Mathematical Sociology, 1*(2), 143–186.

Schenk, D. H. (1999). Saving the income tax with a wealth tax. *Tax Law Review, 53*, 423.

Schmelzing, P. (2019). *Eight centuries of global real rates, RG, and the 'suprasecular' decline, 1311–2018* [working paper number 845]. London: Bank of England.

Schneider, M. (2007). The nature, history and significance of the concept of positional goods. *History of Economics Review, 45*(1), 60–81.

Schröder, M. (2018). *Warum es uns noch nie so gut ging und wir trotzdem ständig von Krisen reden*. Wals: Benevento.

Schroeder, F. (2006). *Innovative sources of finance after the Paris conference: The concept is gaining currency but major challenges remain*. [FES Briefing Paper.] New York: FES. Retrieved from https://library.fes.de/pdf-files/iez/global/50423.pdf.

Schultz, W. (2015). Neuronal reward and decision signals: From theories to data. *Physiological Reviews, 95*(3), 853–951. https://doi.org/10.1152/physrev.00023.2014.

Schumacher, E. F. (1973). *Small Is beautiful: Economics as if people mattered*. New York: Harper & Row.

Schumpeter, J. (1912). *Theorie der wirtschaftlichen Entwicklung*. Leipzig: Duncker & Humblot.

Scott, H. K., & Cogburn, M. (2017). *Behavior modification*. Treasure Island, FL: StatPearls Publishing.

Securing America's Future Energy. (2018, September 21). *The military cost of defending the global oil supply*. Washington, DC. Retrieved from http://secureenergy.org/wp-content/ uploads/2018/09/Military-Cost-of-Defending-the-Global-Oil-Supply.-Sep.-18.-2018.pdf.

Shah, A. (2013, June 30). *World military spending*. Global Issues. Retrieved July 10, 2019, from http://www.globalissues.org/article/75/world-military-spending.

Shorrocks, A., Davies, J., & Lluberas, R. (2018). *Global wealth report 2018*. Zurich: Credit Suisse Research Institute, Credit Suisse.

Simon, J. L. (1983). *The ultimate resource*. Princeton, NJ: Princeton University Press.

Simpfendorfer, B. (2009). *The new silk road: How a rising Arab world is turning away from the west and rediscovering China*. London and New York: Palgrave Macmillan.

Singer, P. (1972). Famine, affluence, and morality. *Philosophy & Public Affairs, 1*(3), 229–243.

Sinn, H. W. (2012). *The green paradox: A supply-side approach to global warming*. Cambridge, MA: MIT press.

Sinn, H. W. (2016). *Der Schwarze Juni. Brexit, Flüchtlingswelle, Euro-Desaster: Wie die Neugründung Europas gelingt*. Munich: Herder. ISBN 978-3-451-37745-7.

Sinn, H. W., & Wollmershäuser, T. (2012). Target loans, current account balances and capital flows: The ECB's rescue facility. *International Tax and Public Finance, 19*(4), 468–508.

SIPRI. (2019). *SIPRI yearbook 2019: Armaments, disarmament and international security*. Stockholm. Retrieved from https://www.sipri.org/sites/default/files/2019-06/yb19_summary_ eng.pdf.

Skinner, B. F. (1990). *The behavior of organisms: An experimental analysis*. Cambridge, MA: BF Skinner Foundation.

Slaus, I., Giarini, O., & Jacobs, G. (2013). Human centered development perspective. *Cadmus, 1*(6), 18–23.

Sloterdijk, P. (2016). *Was geschah im 20. Jahrhundert? Unterwegs zu einer Kritik der extremistischen Vernunft*. Berlin: Suhrkamp Verlag.

Snidal, D. (1985). Coordination versus prisoners' dilemma: Implications for international cooperation and regimes. *American Political Science Review, 79*(4), 923–942.

Solid. *Welcome to solid*. Retrieved January 30, 2020., from https://solid.inrupt.com/.

Sorel, E., & Padoan, P. C. (2008). *The Marshall plan: Lessons learned for the 21st century*. Paris: OECD.

Soroos, M. S. (1994). Global change, environmental security, and the prisoner's dilemma. *Journal of Peace Research, 31*(3), 317–332.

Soros, G. (2015). *The alchemy of finance*. Hoboken, NJ: John Wiley & Sons.

Sorrell, S., & Dimitropoulos, J. (2008). The rebound effect: Microeconomic definitions, limitations and extensions. *Ecological Economics, 65*(3), 636–649.

Sperry, R. W. (1975). Left-brain, right-brain. *Saturday Review, 2*(23), 30–32.

Spitzer, M. (2018). *Einsamkeit: Die unerkannte Krankheit. Schmerzhaft, ansteckend, tödlich*. Munich: Droemer eBook.

Spratt, D., Armistead, A., & Dunlop, I. (2020). *Fatal calculations: How economics has underestimated climate damage and encouraged inaction*. National Centre for Climate Restoration Melbourne. Retrieved from https://climateactionaustralia.wordpress.com/2020/04/16/how-economics-has-underestimated-climate-damage-and-encouraged-inaction-climateemergency-fatal-calculations/.

Stahel, W. R. (2019). *The circular economy: A user's guide*. London: Routledge.

Steffen, W., Broadgate, W., Deutsch, L., Gaffney, O., & Ludwig, C. (2015). The trajectory of the Anthropocene: The great acceleration. *The Anthropocene Review, 2*(1), 81–98.

Steffen, W., Rockström, J., Richardson, K., Lenton, T. M., Folke, C., Liverman, D., et al. (2018). Trajectories of the earth system in the Anthropocene. *Proceedings of the National Academy of Sciences, 115*(33), 8252–8259.

Stern, N. (2006). *The economics of climate change: The Stern review*. Cambridge: Cambridge University Press.

Stern, N. (2007). *The economics of climate change: The Stern review*. Cambridge: Cambridge University Press.

Stern, N. (2016). Economics: Current climate models are grossly misleading. *Nature, 530*(7591), 407–409.

Sternberg, R., & Jordan, J. (Eds.). (2005). *A handbook of wisdom: Psychological perspectives*. Cambridge: Cambridge University Press.

Stiglitz, J. E. (2017a, March 6). *The overselling of globalization* [Paul Volcker prize lecture]. Washington, DC: National Association of Business Economists.

Stiglitz, J. E. (2017b). *Globalization and its discontinents revisited*. New York: W.W. Norton.

Storm, S., & Schroeder, E. (2018). *Economic growth and carbon emissions: The road to 'hothouse earth' is paved with good intentions*. Institute for New Economic Thinking Working Paper Series, 84.

Summers, L. H. (2015). Demand-side secular stagnation. *American Economic Review: Papers and Proceedings, 105*(5), 60–65.

Sumner, S. (2010, September 11). *The other money illusion*. Retrieved from https://www.themoneyillusion.com/the-other-money-illusion/.

Taleb, N. N. (2007). *The black swan: The impact of the highly improbable*. New York: Random House.

Taleb, N. N. (2012). *Antifragile: Things that gain from disorder* (Vol. 3). New York: Random House.

Taylor, C. (1989). *Sources of the self*. Cambridge, MA: Harvard University Press.

Taylor, C. (1998). Fallback to a common currency: What to do if EMU stumbles? In J. Arrowsmith (Ed.), *Thinking the unthinkable about EMU: Coping with turbulence between 1998 and 2002* (pp. 104–117). London: National Institute of Economic and Social Research London.

Tetlock, P. E., & Gardner, D. (2015). *Superforecasting: The art and science of prediction.* New York: Crown Publishers.

The Economist. (2020). Who owns that? *Enforceable property rights are still far too rare in poor countries* (pp. 31–33). Retrieved September 12, 2020, from https://www.economist.com/leaders/2020/09/12/who-owns-what.

Threefold Network. (2020). Retrieved January 30, 2020, from https://www.threefold.io/.

Tiftik, E., & Mahmood, K. (2019). *Global debt monitor: Devil in the details.* IIF. Retrieved from https://www.iif.com/Portals/0/Files/Global%20Debt%20Monitor_January_vf.pdf.

Tinbergen, J. (1962). *Shaping the world economy.* New York: Twentieth Century Fund.

Tobin, J. (1978). A proposal for international monetary reform. *Eastern Economic Journal, 4*(3/4), 153–159.

Transparency International. (2018). *Corruption Perceptions Index 2017.* Retrieved from https://www.transparency.org/news/feature/corruption_perceptions_index_2017.

Turner, A. (2013, February 6). *Debt, money, and Mephistopheles: How do we get out of this mess?* [lecture delivered at Cass business school]. London. Retrieved from https://www.ineteconomics.org/uploads/downloads/DEBT-MONEY-AND-MEPHISTOPHELES-HOW-DO-WE-GET-OUT-OF-THIS-MESS.pdf.

Turner, A. (2015). *The case for monetary finance: An essentially political issue* [Paper presented at the 16th Jacques Polak Annual Research Conference]. Washington, DC: IMF. Retrieved from https://www.imf.org/external/np/res/seminars/2015/arc/pdf/adair.pdf.

Ulanowicz, R. E., Goerner, S. J., Lietaer, B., & Gomez, R. (2009). Quantifying sustainability: Resilience, efficiency and the return of information theory. *Ecological Complexity, 6*(1), 27–36.

UN. (2015). *Transforming our world: The 2030 agenda for sustainable development.* New York. Retrieved from https://sustainabledevelopment.un.org/content/documents/21252030%20Agenda%20for%20Sustainable%20Development%20web.pdf.

UN. (2018). *The sustainable development goals report 2018.* New York. Retrieved from https://unstats.un.org/sdgs/files/report/2018/TheSustainableDevelopmentGoalsReport2018-EN.pdf.

UN. (2019). *World population prospects 2019: Special aggregates.* Retrieved from https://population.un.org/wpp/Download/SpecialAggregates/EconomicTrading/.

UNCED. (1992). *Agenda 21.* Rio de Janeiro. Retrieved from https://sustainabledevelopment.un.org/content/documents/Agenda21.pdf.

UNCTAD. (2014). *World investment report 2014. Investing in the SDGs: An action plan.* New York and Geneva. Retrieved from https://unctad.org/en/PublicationsLibrary/wir2014_en.pdf.

UNCTAD. (2019). *Debt and development finance. About: History.* Retrieved September 30, 2019, from https://debt-and-finance.unctad.org/Pages/History.aspx.

UNDP. (2019). *Global multidimensional poverty index 2019: Illuminating inequalities.* New York. Retrieved from http://hdr.undp.org/sites/default/files/mpi_2019_publication.pdf.

UNEP. (2013). *The emissions gap report 2013.* Nairobi. Retrieved from http://web.unep.org/sites/default/files/EGR2013/EmissionsGapReport_2013_high-res.pdf.

Utke, A. R. (1998). Introduction: The (re) unification of knowledge: Why? How? Where? When? *Counterpoints, 39*, 1–33.

Van der Knaap, P., & De Vries, T. (2018). *World cash report 2018.* Utrecht: G4S Global Cash Solutions. Retrieved from. https://cashessentials.org/app/uploads/2018/07/2018-world-cash-report.pdf.

Van Lerven, F. (2016). *A guide to public money creation: Outlining the alternatives to quantitative easing.* [Positive Money report]. Retrieved from https://positivemoney.org/2016/04/our-new-guide-to-public-money-creation/.

Vassiliou, M. S. (2009). *Historical dictionary of the petroleum industry.* Plymouth: Scarecrow Press.

Vaubel, R. (1990). Currency competition and European monetary integration. *The Economic Journal, 100*(402), 936–946.

Veblen, T. (1899). *The theory of leisure class.* New York: Macmillan.

Véron, N., & Wolff, G. B. (2016). Capital markets union: A vision for the long term. *Journal of Financial Regulation, 2*(1), 130–153.

Vicary, S., Sperling, M., Von Zimmermann, J., Richardson, D. C., & Orgs, G. (2017). Joint action aesthetics. *Public Library of Science One, 12*(7), e0180101.

von Uexkull, J., Jacobs, G., Šlaus, I., Hoffman, R., & Marien, M. CADMUS.

Von Weizsäcker, E. U., & Wijkman, A. (2017). *Come on!: Capitalism, short-termism, population and the destruction of the planet.* New York: Springer.

Walach, H. (2010). Complementary? Alternative? Integrative? *Forschende Komplementärmedizin, 17*(4), 215–216.

Walach, H. (2019). *The Galileo commission report: Beyond a materialistic world view. Towards and Expanded Science.* Scientific and Medical Network. Retrieved from https://www.galileocommission.org/wp-content/uploads/2019/04/Science-Beyond-A-Materialist-World-View_compressed.pdf.

Wason, P. C. (1968). Reasoning about a rule. *Quarterly Journal of Experimental Psychology, 20*(3), 273–281. https://doi.org/10.1080/14640746808400161, ISSN 1747-0226.

Water Corporation. (2018). *Statement of corporate intent 2018–19.* Osborne Park: Water Corporation. Retrieved from https://www.watercorporation.com.au/-/media/files/residential/about-us/our-performance/annual-report/statement-of-corporate-intent-2018-19.pdf.

Wehling, E. (2016). *Politisches Framing: Wie eine Nation sich ihr Denken einredet und daraus Politik macht.* Cologne: Herbert von Halem Verlag.

Weisberg, H. I. (2014). *Willful ignorance.* Hoboken, NJ: John Wiley & Sons.

Werner, R. (2003). *Princes of the yen: Japan's central bankers and the transformation of the economy.* New York: Taylor & Francis Inc.

Werner, R. A. (2014). Can banks individually create money out of nothing? The theories and the empirical evidence. *International Review of Financial Analysis, 36*, 1–19.

WHO, & Unicef. (2017). Progress on drinking water, sanitation and hygiene: 2017 update and SDG baselines. Geneva, Switzerland. Retrieved from https://apps.who.int/iris/bitstream/handle/10665/258617/9789241512893-eng.pdf;jsessionid=832C087A189FFA4D249EBD26F172DBF1?sequence=1

Wilber, K. (2000). *Integral psychology: Consciousness, spirit, psychology, therapy.* Boston, MA: Shambhala.

Willett, W., Rockström, J., Loken, B., Springmann, M., Lang, T., Vermeulen, S., …, Jonell, M. (2019). Food in the Anthropocene: The EAT–Lancet Commission on healthy diets from sustainable food systems. *The Lancet, 393*(10170), 447–492.

Williamson, J. (1993). Democracy and the 'Washington consensus'. *World Development, 21*(8), 1329–1336.

Winthrop, R., & McGivney, E. (2015). *Why wait 100 years? Bridging the gap in global education.* Washington, DC: DeBrookings Institution. Retrieved from https://www.brookings.edu/wp-content/uploads/2015/06/global_20161128_100-year-gap.pdf.

Wolff, E. N. (2017). *Household wealth trends in the United States, 1962 to 2016: Has middle class wealth recovered?* [Working paper number 24085]. Cambridge, MA: National Bureau of Economic Research.

Woodward, D. (2015). Incrementum ad absurdum: Global growth, inequality and poverty eradication in a carbon-constrained world. *World Economic Review, 4*, 43–62.

Working Group on New International Contributions to Finance Development. (2004). *Report to the French president Jacques Chirac.* Retrieved from https://www.globalpolicy.org/images/pdfs/12landau.pdf.

World Academy of Art and Science [WAAS]. (2020). *Catalytic strategies for transformative leadership: Leadership principles, strategies, & examples* (in press). Retrieved from http://www.worldacademy.org/files/global_leadership/socially_transformative_leadership.pdf.

World Bank. (2016). *Development goals in an era of demographic change* [Global monitoring report 2015/2016]. Washington, DC. https://doi.org/10.1596/978-1-4648-0669-8.

World Bank. (2017). *Guidance on PPP contractual provisions: 2017 edition.* Washington, DC. Retrieved from https://ppp.worldbank.org/public-private-partnership/sites/ppp.worldbank.org/files/documents/Guidance_%20PPP_Contractual_Provisions_EN_2017.pdf.

World Bank. (2018a). *Poverty and shared prosperity 2018: Piecing together the poverty puzzle*. Washington, DC. Retrieved from https://openknowledge.worldbank.org/bitstream/handle/10986/30418/9781464813306.pdf.

World Bank. (2018b). *The world bank annual report 2018*. Washington, DC.

World Bank. (2019). *Global economic prospects, June 2019: Heightened tensions, subdued investment*. Washington, DC: World Bank. https://doi.org/10.1596/978-1-4648-1398-6.

World Bank, Indicators. (2018a). *Population, total*. Retrieved from https://data.worldbank.org/indicator/SP.POP.TOTL.

World Bank, Indicators. (2018b). *GDP (current, US$)*. Retrieved from https://data.worldbank.org/indicator/NY.GDP.MKTP.CD.

World Data Lab. (n.d.). Retrieved April 30, 2020, from https://worlddata.io/?utm_source=google&utm_medium=cpc&utm_campaign=Worlddatalab&campaignid=6444202480&adgroupid=80923113321&adid=378525020332&gclid=Cj0KCQjwy6T1BRDXARIsAIqCTXpOBPxrHeu-f9SSNN5dhWGJ5vnRy2TpOHP7yN5UMHtKFtupcUmkY1waAlcEEALw_wcB.

World Economic Forum. (2018). *Global gender gap report 2018*. Geneva. Retrieved from http://reports.weforum.org/global-gender-gap-report-2018/.

World Food Programme. (2017, March 7). *What is 'blockchain' and how is it connected to fighting hunger?* Retrieved from https://insight.wfp.org/what-is-blockchain-and-how-is-it-connected-to-fighting-hunger-7f1b42da9fe.

Worldbank, Indicators. (2015). *Fossil fuel energy consumption (% of total)*. Retrieved from https://data.worldbank.org/indicator/EG.USE.COMM.FO.ZS.

Wray, L. R. (1998). *Understanding modern money: The key to full employment and price stability*. Northhampton: Edward Elgar.

Wray, L. R. (2015). *Modern money theory: A primer on macroeconomics for sovereign monetary systems* (2nd ed.). New York: Palgrave Macmillan.

Wu, K., & Dunning, D. (2018). Unknown unknowns: The problem of hypocognition. *Scientific American Mind, 29*(6), 42–45.

Wuebbles, D. J., Fahey, D. W., Hibbard, K. A., Dokken, D. J., Stewart, B. C., & Maycock, T. K. (Eds.). (2017). *Climate science special report: Fourth national climate assessment* (p. 470). Washington, DC: U.S. Global Change Research Program.

Yuan, G., Drost, N. A., & McIvor, R. A. (2013). Respiratory rate and breathing pattern. *McMaster University Medical Journal, 10*(1), 23–25.

Zuboff, S. (2019). *The age of surveillance capitalism: The fight for a human future at the new frontier of power: Barack Obama's books of 2019*. London: Profile Books.

Index[1]

---

[1] Note: Page numbers followed by 'n' refer to notes.